FLAME OF LOVE

A THEOLOGY OF THE HOLY SPIRIT

CLARK H. PINNOCK

InterVarsity Press
Downers Grove, Illinois

InterVarsity Press
P.O. Box 1400, Downers Grove, IL 60515
World Wide Web.www.ivpress.com
E-mail: mail@ivpress.com

InterVarsity Press® is the book-publishing division of InterVarsity Christian Fellowship/USA®, a student movement active on campus at hundreds of universities, colleges and schools of nursing in the United States of America, and a member movement of the International Fellowship of Evangelical Students. For information about local and regional activities, write Public Relations Dept., InterVarsity Christian Fellowship/USA, 6400 Schroeder Rd., P.O. Box 7895, Madison, WI 53707-7895.

Scripture quotations, unless otherwise noted, are from the New Revised Standard Version of the Bible, *copyright 1989 by the Division of Christian Education of the National Council of the Churches of Christ in the USA. Used by permission. All rights reserved.*

Cover illustration: Roberta Polfus

ISBN 0-8308-1590-2

Printed in the United States of America ♾

Library of Congress Cataloging-in-Publication Data

Pinnock, Clark H., 1937-
   Flame of love: a theology of the Holy spirit/by Clark Pinnock.
     p.   cm.
   Includes bibliographical references.
   ISBN 0-8308-1590-2 (pbk.: alk. paper)
   1. Holy Spirit.   I. Title.
 BT121.2.P55 1996
  231'.3—dc20   *96-19407*
                                                                   CIP

---

21   20   19   18   17   16   15   14   13   12   11   10 9 8 7 6 5

16   15   14   13   12   11   10   09   08   07   06   05   04

*"Holy Spirit, renew your wonders in our day
as by a new Pentecost."*
—POPE JOHN XXIII

*I dedicate this book to
Richard Foster, Charles Nienkirchen, Jim Houston
and my beloved wife Dorothy,
who along with others challenge me to
catch the fire and dwell in the presence of God.*

Introduction

The Spirit is elusive but profound and worthy of adoration. If Father points to ultimate reality and Son supplies the clue to the divine mystery, Spirit epitomizes the nearness of the power and presence of God. St. John of the Cross (b. 1542) aptly calls the Spirit a living flame of love and celebrates the nimble, responsive, playful, personal gift of God.

As we begin, let us say: Welcome, Holy Spirit, come and set us free! Let each one catch the living flame and be ravished by your love! Let our souls glow with your fire. Help us overcome our forgetfulness of Spirit.[1]

On January 23, 1959, Pope John XXIII, announcing plans for the Second Vatican Council, prayed that the windows of the church be opened to God's breath, which he hoped would sweep away deadness and unleash refreshing renewal. Nearly thirty years later, in 1986, Pope John Paul II issued an encyclical called *On the Holy Spirit in the Life of the Church and the World,* in which he urged Christians to be attentive to the Spirit as they prepare to enter the third Christian millennium. He wrote: "The church's mind and heart turn to the Holy Spirit as this twentieth century draws to a close and the third millennium since the coming of Jesus Christ into the world approaches and as we look towards the great jubilee with which the church will celebrate the event." Here we join our voices with his voice and turn our hearts and minds to the third mysterious Person.

At the end of his life, the Swiss theologian Karl Barth felt the need of a more satisfactory theology of the Spirit (sometimes called "theology of the third article" because of the Spirit's position in the creed). Barth's own theology would have been stronger, and it might even have permitted him to have issued a kinder judgment on liberal theologians and their appreciation of the role of experience. In Jürgen Moltmann's book *The Spirit of Life* it is obvious that he is distancing himself from Barth's polemic against religious experience and striving to recover a more experiential basis for the doctrine of Spirit.[3] Though this doctrine is less neglected now, work remains to be done on the subject—there are truths to recover and possibilities to explore. Far from being an incidental or isolated topic in theology, Spirit is a major theme, supplying a standpoint, in fact, for surveying the whole vista of Christian truth.[4]

How could so rich a subject have suffered neglect? On other topics there is enough in the tradition to make one feel overwhelmed, but not here. On this one the offerings are relatively sparse. Neglect may be less of a problem in Orthodoxy than in Western traditions, but in both Catholic and Protestant theology the place of the Spirit has surely been diminished.[5] Reflection on the Spirit has lagged behind thinking on other topics. Even in the creeds common to East and West, references to the Spirit are brief and occasional, at times sounding even perfunctory. In liturgy one will find many lines praising Father and Son, followed by a phrase "with the Holy Spirit" as a kind of afterthought.

Our language is often revealing—the Spirit is a third person in a third place. At times the Spirit can even sound like an appendage to the doctrine of God and a shadowy, ghostly, poor relation of the Trinity. In the church year the celebration of Pentecost hardly compares to the observance of Christmas and Easter. Even worse, it may be completely forgotten, eclipsed by Mother's Day or some other cultural holiday. It is time for us to heed the East's complaint that Western Christianity has confined the Spirit to the margins of the church and subordinated it to the mission of the Son.

To some extent the lack may reflect not neglect but a paucity of biblical instruction. The role of Spirit in creation, for example, is crucial theologically but not often or much discussed in the Scriptures. Nevertheless, it is important to draw out the truth, even if lightly attested. The Bible may be like the fish that, when asked to describe its environment, neglected to say much about water.

Spirit in Western traditions tends to be confined to the institutional church and to be seen as the power of salvation, not of creation also. We have placed emphasis on the sermon and the clergy at the expense of the Spirit. We have prized our versions of decency and order so highly that outpourings of the Spirit pose a threat. Many appear afraid of the Spirit, lest their worlds be shaken and they be swept up into God's sabbath play. So often we set up barriers to the Spirit and stifle the voices that speak to us of openness and celebration. "Forgetfulness" may be too kind a way to refer to the problem. We cannot even rule out the possibility of suppression at times.

Forgetfulness is not easily overcome, but perhaps if some reflections are set forth, a discussion will ensue, leading to reform. This book's chapters reveal the themes: the identity of the Spirit within the Trinity (chapter one), the power of the Spirit in continuing creation (chapter two), the joint mission of Son and Spirit in atonement (chapter three), God's presence in the sacramental, charismatic and diaconal dimensions of church life (chapter four), salvation as a Spirit-empowered path to union with God (chapter five), the universal prevenience of Spirit which graces everyone everywhere (chapter six) and the Spirit's guidance of the church in the development of doctrine and mission (chapter seven).

The Spirit challenges theology at numerous points—this may partly explain our neglect. But let the challenges stimulate growth in us as hearers of the Word of God. Let us ask what light is shed on our central Christian doctrines when they are considered from the standpoint of the Spirit.[6]

This book is a theology of the Spirit and attends to the grand picture, not to every topic of passing interest. Such an exploration of necessity touches other central themes in theology, because it acts like a magnet that causes a convergence of other doctrines.

Though this is not a testimony book, I hope the reader will sense how in love with God I am and how much practical usefulness there is in improved theology. Poor theology can hurt us, for we will miss certain stirrings of the Spirit where we are not expecting them and are not open to them owing to an inadequate doctrinal map. If, on the other hand, places and situations are identified where we ought to be expecting the Spirit to be at work, our eyes may be opened to new possibilities. A person who does not expect the Spirit to be at work in the natural order, for example, will not be attentive to such activities in nature and will be impoverished as a result. Similarly, a person unaware of the full range of spiritual gifts that are available will not be open to receive them or may not value certain gifts. This book, then, though not testimonial, can help people overcome a confinement of spirit by identifying certain places and ways of the Spirit's working where they have not been looking for it.

Religious experience needs good theology the way a traveler needs a reliable map. A traveler with lots of enthusiasm but no map for the journey is a dangerous person to travel with. Together you can get hopelessly lost.[7]

Mind and Heart

In theology, mind and heart—study and prayer—are both important. With the mind we analyze data, while in the heart we wait for illumination on it. We place the truths discovered in God's Word into the sanctuary of the soul for pondering. The mind attends to analysis; the heart dreams and listens to God. One blessing of the coming of the Spirit at Pentecost was to give us the ability to dream and see visions (Acts 2:17-18). The Spirit makes us open to new horizons and new possibilities. We are empowered with hope to transcend situations and limitations. Therefore it is important to experience the Spirit and reflect on our experience.

In the new covenant, people have God's law written on their hearts and need no one to teach them because of the knowledge of God they have instinctively (Jer 31:33-34). In the words of Isaiah, "When you turn to the right or when you turn to the left, your ears shall hear a word behind you, saying, 'This is the way; walk in it' " (30:21).

In writing and reading, let us combine analysis and contemplation. Let us imitate Mary, mother of our Lord, who treasured what she heard and pondered it in her heart (Lk 2:19, 51). The heart does not supply us with new information but leads us to a deeper acquaintance with the divine mysteries and a finer sensitivity to their timeliness. We need to listen to the Spirit if we hope to grasp the significance of what we believe. Let theologians observe times of silence in God's presence as the elders and the angels do in heaven, pondering everything they hear (Rev 8:1).[8]

On one level the Scriptures do inform the mind and offer comprehensible teaching in the interests of a better understanding. The Spirit is elusive but comprehensible too. The Scriptures give us most definite clues for understanding, and it is our responsibility to grasp what can be known by the mind. Therefore we will be dipping into the testimony of Scripture and into insights from the ecumenical church, catholic in both space and time, and will engage many challenging and worthwhile discussions. The subject may be mysterious, but it is not obscure or beyond accounting.[9]

On the other hand, we cannot master the subject rationally. The Spirit cannot be imprisoned in concepts. Spirit is known by prayer as well as by study. The Bible contains few abstract statements about the Spirit, but many symbols such as water, wind and fire. Such images, while they can be studied, need to be appropriated by the heart. The path of meditation has to be followed alongside a scholarly approach.

To know the Spirit we must become persons of prayer who are willing to yield in complete openness to God. Waiting in silence and patient receptivity will cultivate a heart-knowledge of our Life-giver. Theology must always be more than rational, especially in this case. For we are speaking of a reality that is active in our lives and that cannot be captured altogether in cognitive ways. There are depths of the mystery that cannot be accessed by reason alone. As well as studying the Scriptures on the Spirit, we must be prayerful and open, longing to fall in love with the One who frees and surprises, delights and searches, energizes and purifies us. We have to be sensitive to things that are only spiritually discerned (1 Cor 2:14).

Let us learn to operate on two levels simultaneously. Even as we are thinking, deep within we can be at prayer and be receptive to the divine breath.[10]

Speaking of the Spirit

The heart dimension comes into play immediately. For of all theological topics, Spirit is one of the most elusive. Knowing the Spirit is experiential, and the topic is oriented toward transformation more than information.

So how do we grasp the breath of God? How do we speak of the power that gives understanding or convey in words the uncreated energies of God? How do we define Spirit? It is hard to speak of any of the divine Persons worthily, since they transcend the world and tax the powers of reason. Yet it is easier to speak of Father and Son, if only because of the familiar family imagery employed in these designations. The Spirit, however, presents a unique challenge to speech. How does one render that reality that is wind, fire, breath, life—tangible yet intangible, invisible yet powerful, inexpressible yet intimate, powerful yet gentle, reliable yet unpredictable, personal yet impersonal, transcendent yet immanent?[11]

Certain things are clear. The fundamental idea of Spirit in Hebrew and Greek is breath, air, wind, storm—the intensity depending on the context. It may be a gentle breath (Jn 20:22), a gale-force wind (Ex 15:8), a cooling breeze (Gen 3:8). Most essentially Spirit is transcendent and divine, not mere flesh; it is the energy of life itself and is present in nature and in history. Most wonderfully, the Spirit is God's face turned toward us and God's presence abiding with us, the agency by which God reaches out and draws near, the power that creates and heals.

Though we speak of the Spirit as a third Person, from the standpoint of experience Spirit is first, because it is the Spirit that enables us to experience God's flying by and drawing near. Through the Spirit we feel the warmth of God's love and the fire that kindles our heart. By the Spirit we drink from fountains of living water and receive the grace that is poured out. We may not be able to know God with our limited sensibilities, but we certainly can love God and desire him and his will.[12]

Spirit is the ecstasy of the divine life, the bond of love in the Trinity and the overflowing abundance of God outwardly. Spirit sustains loving relationships within the (immanent) Trinity and also implements the grace of the (economic) Trinity in creation and history. Moltmann offers this captivating definition: "Spirit is the loving, self-communicating, out-fanning and out-pouring presence of the eternal divine life of the triune God." By the Spirit, God draws near to the creature and mediates a knowledge of divinity in a hundred thousand ways.[13]

He, She or It?

Many people are concerned with gender and theology and therefore with the issue of which pronoun to use for Spirit. Spirit is not gender-specific quite the way Father and Son are. The Hebrew term (*rûah*) is (usually but not always) grammatically feminine; yet this may not be regarded as very significant, for personhood is relatively undeveloped in relation to Spirit in the Old Testament. Had Hebrew been the language used by the New Testament, where the Spirit's personhood becomes apparent, it might have been different—the feminine pronoun might have been used. But as it is, *Spirit* in the New Testament (*pneuma*) is grammatically neuter in the Greek, and the pronoun *it* predominates. *Spirit* is also neuter in English, which allows us to use *it* as well. The use of *he* for the Spirit is rare in the Bible, except where John uses it because the title *Paraclete* is masculine (Jn 14:26; 15:26; 16:13-14).

The Scriptures do not settle the question of pronouns but leave the matter open. It would be permissible to use any one—*he, she* or *it*. English speakers have the custom of referring to the Spirit as *he* not because the Bible does so but because of tradition. *Spirit* in Latin is masculine, and that has affected us. Using *he* feels right to us, but we have no necessary biblical grounds for it.[14]

What is the prudent course to take then? Avoiding pronouns altogether would force us to use ponderous expressions of circumlocution. Using *it* is grammatically right, based as it is on the Greek term, but it may detract from the personhood of the Spirit. In the book of Acts, for example, the Spirit is presented as a character or agent in the narrative. The Spirit doesn't sound like an "it." The disciples were led by a Someone, not a Something. Is it good enough to call the Spirit who speaks and can be grieved *it?*[15]

One could fall back on the masculine pronoun, which, though biblically rare, is used by John, is consonant with Latin and is common in the Western tradition. The disadvantage as I see it, however, is that in this case all three Persons of the Trinity are denoted by masculine pronouns. This is no problem in the sense that God is beyond gender, but it does result in the Trinity's being depicted in exclusively male language, which revelation does not require and modern sensibility does not find easy.[16]

What about using the pronoun *she?* It would not be the first time. Aphrahat wrote in his *Demonstration* 6:14, "By baptism we receive the Spirit of Christ, and at that moment when the priests invoke the Spirit, she opens the heavens and descends and hovers over the waters, and those who are baptized put her on." The word *Spirit* in Syriac (as in Hebrew) was grammatically feminine. Perhaps it is time to follow Aphrahat's example. It would introduce feminine pronouns into God-talk in an orthodox way.[17]

Using a feminine pronoun would pick up the grammatical feminine of the Hebrew and honor femalelike functions of the Spirit, such as birthing, nurturing, grieving and sheltering. It would also recognize Spirit as associated with such feminine images as wisdom and the shekinah presence. Spirit fosters receptivity in our hearts vis à vis the Father and is often femininelike in experience—coming as gentle dove, mother eagle and poured-out love. Mystics like St. Teresa and John of the Cross feel free to use imagery such as the soul's nursing on the breasts of God, receiving nourishment from his spiritual milk. It might seems reasonable, then, to use the feminine pronoun for the Spirit: "The Spirit comforts, encourages, yearns and brings to birth. Most of her activities are best expressed in feminine terminology."[18]

But there are valid objections. Aside from the fact that we are not used to hearing the Spirit referred to this way, using the feminine pronoun would not always be best. For example, using *it* often works well, and *he* is the Johannine choice. We would not want to refer to the Spirit only in a feminine way, as if no masculine or neutral nuances were possible. Doing so might cause one to ignore the feminine dimensions of Father and Son. One does not want to pose the femininity of Spirit against the nonfeminitity of Father and Son. We human beings are male and female in the image of the triune God, Father, Son and Spirit. Using *she* could project a feminine persona onto Spirit or be stereotypical with regard to so-called feminine traits.[19] It gets mixed up when Spirit causes the conception of Jesus in Mary and when the church is so often the feminine counterpart to God. Are we to imagine Spirit as playing the peacemaker in a community of males? No, using the feminine pronoun exclusively could create more problems than it solves.

I admit that something in me wants to use the feminine pronoun. It seems to capture the gracefulness of Spirit and is an orthodox way of using feminine language in reference to God. Politically, it also says to feminists in the church that we are concerned about this problem and agree that steps must be taken. The problem is, which steps?

This is clearly an issue that requires further discussion and thought. Our dilemma may be due in part to the elusiveness of Spirit, which will not be pinned down. But symbols are not static, and Spirit can be spoken of in different ways depending on the context.[20] This study, then, will generally use the masculine pronoun for the Spirit, but I hope it will be read in the light of the concerns I have outlined.

Looking Ahead

Mark Noll has noted the absence of an evangelical mind when it comes to science and politics, but he exempts theology from his indictment. He needed not do so. If the doctrine of the Spirit is any indication, evangelical theology too has tended to be shallow and uncreative. In relation to this subject at least, we have overlooked a great deal.[21]

This book is not really a biblical study but moves beyond exegesis to historical and theological reflection. It is important, after examining the text, to step back and assess what has been found. Exegesis alone cannot provide the full perspective required by the church. There has to be a wider sweep of investigation that takes into account other dimensions—historical, theological, philosophical, cultural and mystical.

This is a systematic theology of the Spirit that examines the Christian vision from the vantage point of the Spirit. It is a doctrinal exploration rather than a testimony book or a program for congregational renewal. Theology on any topic is supposed to be a faithful and creative response to the scriptural canon. My desire here is not to repeat what has been said by others but to discover fresh applications and insights from the Lord for our time.[22]

The book is catholic in the sense that it respects the beliefs and practices of the historic churches. Truths about the Spirit are scattered throughout segments of a divided church and ought to be gathered from anywhere and everywhere. We are bound in the Spirit to believers of every continent and every century. Therefore I have dipped into the treasures of Catholic and Orthodox traditions in ways that I had not done before and have found affinities that surprised and delighted me.[23]

The book is evangelical too in the sense that I find value in the witness of the Reformation and in the experience of modern evangelicalism, where I found faith. At the same time the book continues my struggle with aspects of evangelicalism and continues my search for nondeterministic theology. Furthermore, it is charismatic in celebrating Pentecostalism as a mighty twentieth-century outpouring of the Spirit. I think of this as the most important event in modern Christianity.[24]

There is a growing interest in spirituality and religious experience in modern culture, owing no doubt to the extreme dryness of secularism. People cannot go for long without raising questions about meaning and transcendence. Church statistics go up and down, but interest in ultimate questions does not. It stays high.

If Christians are to be effective in mission, they must offer a faith that is vibrant and alive. People want to meet God and will not be satisfied with religion that only preaches and moralizes. Knowing *about* God is not the same as *knowing* God. Christianity was born on the day of Pentecost because a question was asked about a transforming experience: "What does this mean?" (Acts 2:12). Speaking about God is meaningful only if there is an encounter with God back of it. Only by attending to the Spirit are we going to be able to move beyond sterile, rationalistic, powerless religion and recover the intimacy with God our generation longs for.

May the Spirit kindle a fire in us all and put within us a longing for the power of love to be poured out into our hearts. With the prophet we cry out: "O that you would tear open the heavens and come down!" (Is 64:1).[25]

ONE

SPIRIT &
TRINITY

*I*N PRESENTING A VISION of the Spirit, let us begin with the doctrine of God and focus on the liveliness of the Trinity and the identity of the Spirit within a loving relationality. Let us consider the Spirit as One who bonds the loving fellowship that God is and creates access to the Father through the Son (Eph 2:18). The Spirit reaches out to creatures, catches them up and brings them home to the love of God.

Almost everything else I will have occasion to say will spring from this ontology. Spirit is essentially the serendipitous power of creativity, which flings out a world in ecstasy and simulates within it an echo of the inner divine relationships, ever seeking to move God's plans forward. The Spirit is bringing God's plans to completion in the direction of new creation and union with God through the participatory journey of Jesus Christ. Spirit also makes Christ's work of redemption universally accessible and fosters unity amidst diversity in the midst of the segmented body of Christ.

We begin with the identity of the Spirit as a divine Person in a social Trinity and with the sheer liveliness of God. According to the gospel the nature of God is a communion of loving Persons, the overflowing shared life that creates and upholds the universe. Early theologians spoke of the divine nature as a dance, a circling round of threefold life, as a coming and going among the Persons and graciously in relation to creation. We start with the identity of the triune God and with the face of the Spirit within this community as the ecstasy of its life.[1]

Why Begin Here?

This is not an easy topic; one might ask why I would begin with it. I do so because God's triune identity and the Spirit as the bond of love within it underlie so much else that I want to say. It is also a practical truth, for clarity concerning Being (ontology) helps us understand not only who God is but who we are and what kind of world we inhabit. The Christian understanding of God as pure relationality is such a stunning contribution to human understanding about ultimate matters that it must come first.[2]

Theology must break certain habits surrounding this theme. Often, having defended the doctrine of the Trinity against its various denials, theologians become complacent and fail to go further and make the belief intelligible. Theologians stare, as it were, at a priceless treasure, an expression of the relational essence of God, yet do not perceive its immense value in terms of proclamation. To miss it is to overlook a major aspect of the fair beauty of the Lord.[3]

Because the matter has often been left enigmatic, we need to reflect theologically on the meaning of the Trinity. I hope to counter the impression that while the Trinity is an important belief that must be embraced by anyone who would be orthodox, it is not a belief one should expect to understand. There is an aphorism along these lines: "Try to explain the Trinity and you'll lose your mind; try to deny it and you'll lose your soul." This sends a bleak message regarding the intelligibility of faith and invites the criticism that the Trinity is a piece

of outdated mythology. Effective communication requires that doctrine not be left unintelligible if light *can* be shed on it. I think some
light can be shed on it, though the mystery remains great. Revelation
of the triune God is both significant and limited.[4]

Nevertheless, the truth of the doctrine is meaningful and quite
marvelous. From the Trinity we learn that the Creator is not static or
standoffish but a loving relationality and sheer liveliness. It informs us
that creation is grounded in God's love and that grace underlies the
gift of life itself. If God is a loving relationality, grace is primary,
because it is rooted in the loving divine communion. Creation as well
as redemption flows from the Trinity as pure gift. God did not invent
grace when sin entered the world. What happened then was that grace
abounded all the more (Rom 5:20). The goal of redemption as union
with God was not thought up later on but is the outworking of God's
original purpose.[5]

As loving communion, God calls into being a world that has the
potential of realizing loving relationality within itself. God projected
a created order in which he delights and to which the Spirit gives life
(see chapter two). When things went wrong through the misuse of
freedom, God sent forth the Spirit on a mission of restoration through
incarnation, so that injury and brokenness might be healed from within
our nature by God's power (chapter three). Healing continues to
happen through the power of the Spirit, who indwells the body of
Christ, and that power is present and real both sacramentally and
charismatically, so that justice and salvation may be brought to all the
nations (chapter four).

Relationality features also in the understanding of salvation as union
with God. Spirit is moving humanity toward personal communion and
participation in the divine nature, which was God's everlasting
purpose (chapter five). And just as the work of the Creator is the
source of all that exists, so the scope of reconciliation has a universal
tendency. God has the whole human race in view in his desire to save,
and the Spirit everywhere draws sinners from the far country to the
Father's love (chapter six). And, because the church is so important
to God as his dwelling place, anointed servant and beloved bride,
Spirit ceaselessly strives within the community through time and space

to bring us deeper into unity and truth (chapter seven).

God as Spirit

Spirit is a subtle word and is used in different ways in Scripture. The diversity of usage makes it natural for readers to ask whether the term refers only to God's presence or to the third Person of the Holy Trinity. Here I hope first to show that both usages in fact obtain and then turn to the question of the face of the Spirit. How does Spirit fit the triune figuration? What is the Spirit's identity?

As to whether God *is* spirit or *has a* Spirit, it is not an either-or but a both-and. There are texts that say God is spirit *and* that God has Spirit. The term can refer to God in a general way and also to the third Person of the Trinity. This double pattern is reminiscent of the way the term *wisdom* is used in the Bible also, both in a general way to refer to the wisdom of God and in a specific way to refer to the Son, who is God's wisdom in person. Wisdom both symbolizes God's power to order the world (Prov 1:20) and is identified with the Word made flesh (1 Cor 1:30).

Similarly, *spirit* refers both to God's presence in a general sense and to the third Person. As to the general meaning of *Spirit,* Jesus states it plainly: "God is spirit" (Jn 4:24). Obviously the term can be used to define the divine essence. However, this kind of usage is rare. Scripture does not usually speak abstractly. It prefers to put emphasis on God as an agent and avoids giving the impression that God is any kind of impersonal absolute. Hegel liked to call God absolute Spirit, which for him came close to an impersonal force. The Bible prefers to take the risk of anthropomorphic speech. This may be why it rarely says "God is spirit" or similar things, lest the impression be left that God is ethereal and not a dynamic, personal agent.

So what does Jesus mean? He does not mean that God is immaterial. His point is that God is like a powerful wind, not like a frail creature that is easily pushed around. To say God is Spirit is to say God is mighty wind, power of creation, reservoir of inexhaustible life. What Jesus is saying is like what Isaiah had said: "The Egyptians are human, and not God; their horses are flesh, and not spirit" (Is 31:3). When Jesus says that God is spirit, he is saying not that God is ghostly but that God is the power of creation, the incalculable energy that can give life to the dead and call things that do not exist into being (Rom 4:17).

It is easy for us to be misled about the meaning of spirit, since in Western languages and philosophies we think of it standing in antithesis to matter. So when we hear that God is spirit, we think in terms of Platonic ideas of incorporeality. But spirit in the Bible has to do less with immateriality than with power and life—the invisible, mysterious power of a gale-force wind that we cannot begin to track (Jn 3:8). *Spirit* is the Bible's way of speaking of what we would call the transcendent power of creation.[6]

In saying that God is spirit, the mighty power of creation, I am referring to what Wolfhart Pannenberg calls the field of deity. *Spirit* here refers to the power of Godhead and to the divine field in which persons of the Trinity exist in the fellowship of Father, Son and Spirit. In this use of the term all the Persons are spirit, and it refers to the deity common to them. All three persons exist in the field that Jesus calls spirit and constitute eternal forms of that field.[7]

Spirit may sometimes refer then to the presence of God in the world, not to a third Person distinct from Father and Son. Spirit in this sense denotes the power that creates and renews the world. This is the sense of many passages, especially in the Old Testament, where trinitarian reflection has not yet arisen, since the incarnation has not yet taken place. In such texts spirit (wind) is an image like power, fire, light, water—an image about God that bypasses the issue of Trinity. *Spirit* does often refer to God's presence in a quite general sense.

Nontrinitarians are right to say God is spirit and that when we encounter spirit we encounter God himself. *Spirit* can refer to divine immanence, as opposed to a reference to a distinct Person in the Godhead. Liberalism was right to associate spirit with the general presence of God in the world, because it often refers to precisely that and to our experience of communion with God. As spirit, God inspires, motivates and empowers people everywhere.

God Also Has Spirit
It would be a mistake, however, to deny other texts that use *Spirit* in

a trinitarian way.[8] For in addition to evidence that God *is* spirit, there is evidence to support the claim that God *has* Spirit in a trinitarian sense. It is a little confusing for one term to refer to two related realities, but it is so. Perhaps there is a reason for this rooted in the Spirit's chosen identity in the history of salvation. Perhaps Spirit wishes no other name than the generic ascription for God. The others are called "Father" and "Son," but Spirit takes no special name and chooses to remain anonymous. Deferentially he turns away from himself and graciously points to the others.

The idea of the Trinity lies at the core of and indwells the narratives concerning Jesus Christ in the New Testament. The Gospels give insight into the trinitarian structure of the divine nature. This witness forces us to go beyond an understanding of spirit as God's presence to the truth of Spirit also in fellowship with Father and Son. The triadic pattern first becomes visible in the story of Jesus, which we take to be God's self-communication and the source of trinitarian developments in theology. To see God as relational Trinity is not human speculation but an insight arising from the narrative of salvation, which is God's self-revelation.

The economy of salvation history affords insight into the being of God, that God is the Father, revealed by the Son, through the Spirit. The doctrine of the Trinity is the product of reflection on God's activity in history and is the explanation of what happened. Leonard Hodgson remarks, "The doctrine of the trinity is an inference to the nature of God, drawn from what we believe to be the empirical evidence given by God in his revelation of himself in the history of the world."[9]

God does not reveal himself mostly in an abstract way, through propositions. God causes revelation to happen in human history, particularly in the events surrounding Jesus Christ, where we glimpse the threefoldness that characterizes the nature of God. Jesus is conscious of being the Son of God and proclaims the nearness of the kingdom of his Father in the power of the Holy Spirit. The story of Jesus does not yield the dogmatic formula of the Trinity as such, but it yields the foundations of trinitarian thought. The insight arises from observing Jesus' relationship with God.

At his baptism in the Jordan, Jesus was conscious of his sonship as the Father's beloved and experienced the power of the Spirit for mission. At this time Jesus experienced sonship (filiation) in an intimate relationship with the God whom he called "abba." The voice from heaven says, "You are my Son, the Beloved; with you I am well pleased" (Mk 1:11). From experiencing God as his father, Jesus knew he was sent to proclaim God's kingdom as the Father's Son. His prayer life reveals this relationship as he cries, "Abba, Father" (Mk 14:36). This language was remembered by his followers, and Paul even preserves the Aramaic term (Rom 8:15; Gal 4:6).

Jesus says, "All things have been handed over to me by my Father; and no one knows the Son except the Father, and no one knows the Father except the Son and anyone to whom the Son chooses to reveal him" (Mt 11:27). The saying captures the relationship out of which Jesus understood his mission. From this filial consciousness came the more developed Christology of the epistles and of later tradition.

Alongside the experience of filiation, Jesus experienced the baptism of the Spirit and became the unique bearer of the Spirit. At his baptism the heavens were opened and the Spirit descended upon him like a dove. This was basic for his life and ministry. People experienced Jesus as Spirit-filled, as prophet and healer, not as professional clergy. The Spirit was upon him to preach good news to the poor and enabled him to speak with authority, to heal the sick and to cast out demons (Mt 12:28). Jesus was aware of being God's Son in a unique sense and at the same time being the unique bearer of the Spirit.

Later trinitarian doctrine is rooted in this foundational experience. It comes from the life of Jesus as itself a trinitarian event. Jesus knew God as his loving Father, he knew himself as the Father's beloved Son, and he knew the Spirit as God's power at work in him. In this relationship Jesus distinguished himself from the Father but also submitted himself obediently to the Father with respect to the mission he had been given. The Spirit in turn was experienced as distinct from Father but as dedicated to implementing the work of the Father through the Son. Even Jesus' death—*especially* his death—was a trinitarian event in which the Son yielded up his life and the Father suffered with his beloved, while the Spirit both supported Jesus in his self-sacrifice and vindicated him by raising him up.[10]

Building on this narrative, the New Testament supplies key elements for the trinitarian development of doctrine.[11] First, writers identify Jesus as a divine Person, as the eternal Son who is distinct from the Father. The evidence is abundant and can be seen, for example, in the titles ascribed to Jesus, such as *Lord* and even *God*. More evidence appears in the way in which Old Testament texts that refer originally to God are applied to Jesus and in the divine functions Jesus performs, such as creating and judging. Jesus is spoken of as preexistent and the One whom it is appropriate to worship. There are many direct and remarkable claims for him (for example, Phil 2:6; Col 1:19; 2:9; Heb 1:3).

Clearly, then, the New Testament requires us to recognize at least two subjects or Persons in the Godhead. The change in Jewish monotheism has been made. Now the question is, Having posited two Persons, should we posit a third?

The New Testament does in fact posit a third Person distinct from Father and Son. Though it can speak of the Spirit impersonally as the Old Testament does, as God's gift and power, it also presents Spirit in richly personal ways as One who speaks, intercedes, teaches, grieves and the like. In such texts Spirit is being understood as a person, taking initiative and doing things. In short, Spirit is being regarded as a Person like the Father and the Son. Plainly the move is on toward fully trinitarian speech. There are not only one or two but three distinct and associated subjects in the Godhead. The Nicene Creed properly names the Spirit as the Lord and giver of life—titles proper to the divine being—and properly exhorts us to worship the Spirit together with Father and Son.[12]

The Gospel of John completes the picture by presenting God as actually experiencing intradivine personal relationships and differences within the unity. It points to mutual indwelling and to personal interactions among the three. It assumes personal distinctions in the unity of Father, Son and Spirit. We read that God sends the Spirit in the name of Jesus to teach us (Jn 14:26). The three Persons are involved in mutual relations: "When the Advocate comes, whom I will send to you from the Father, . . . he will testify on my behalf" (Jn 15:26). "As you, Father, are in me and I am in you, may they also be in us" (Jn 17:21).

God Is Love

The picture is of a transcendent society or community of three personal entities. Father, Son and Spirit are the members of a divine community, unified by common divinity and singleness of purpose. The Trinity portrays God as a community of love and mutuality. While it is true that the New Testament does not address all the issues regarding substance, person and equality that would surface later, it lays the foundations firmly for trinitarian doctrine. It is aware of a threefoldness in the life of God and supplies rich material from which to construct the doctrine. Though the inner life of God remains mysterious, there is a threeness in it which was disclosed when God saved humanity through incarnation. God is not an isolated individual but a loving, interpersonal communion, to which we owe our very existence.

Believing this is not a leap into the dark. It is historically grounded in the history of Jesus. At the cross the truth of the Trinity was in doubt, but not for long. After three days Jesus was "declared to be Son of God with power according to the Spirit of holiness by resurrection from the dead" (Rom 1:4 mg). God manifested his triune nature by raising Jesus from the dead by the Spirit. By that event, even more than Jesus' baptism, the truth of the Trinity was established. This is not theological subjectivism or a venture of faith without justification. The truth of the Trinity is grounded in the bodily resurrection of the Son through the Spirit.[13]

Belief in the Trinity is even rational to a degree. Unity is a relatively simple notion in mathematics, but not simple elsewhere. For example, it is not simple in "single" organisms, which are highly complex. The higher the entity, the more complex unity seems to be. Think of the unity of a work of art.

Unity is not a simple idea. Unity can admit of great complexity. Why expect divine unity to lack complexity? Trinity is a mystery, but it is not an irrationality. It epitomizes the complexity in unity that we find everywhere in experience.[14]

Earlier we encountered the short statement "God is spirit." Now we turn to another: "God is love" (1 Jn 4:8). This one also describes the nature of God and complements the other. The God who is spirit is also love. God's essence is spirit—God's character is love.

Now on one level this refers to God's benevolent disposition to save sinners. Jesus exalted God as a merciful Father with a loving heart. On another level, however, the phrase "God is love" refers to the inner life of God. God loves sinners in history because, prior to that, God loves the Son and the Spirit, and loves us in relation to them.

John is saying that the love God has for sinners flows from the love that circulates everlastingly within the Trinity. As Jesus says, "As the Father has loved me, so I have loved you" (Jn 15:9). God's love for sinners is not just the love of a single, unitarian Subject. John is making reference to a triune love that flows among the persons of the Godhead. Not only concretions of the divine field of deity, these persons make up a relational Being, a community of love and mutual indwelling.[15]

The trinity was revealed when the Father, seeking to show his love for lost humanity, communicated with us through Word and Spirit. From this divine saving activity we are given insight into the inner life of God and glimpse a reciprocal community of love between Father, Son and Spirit, three Persons relating in distinctive patterns.[16]

God's nature is that of a communion of three Persons who exist in mutual relations with one another. Each is distinct from the others, but each is what it is in relation to the others. God exists in a dynamic of love, an economy of giving and receiving.

Note that this yields a different understanding of "person" than is common in Western culture, where *person* is equated with the individual. For Descartes a person is a thinking individual, and in his view social relationship does not enter the picture. The human is defined as an individual substance of rational nature, not as a person related to other persons essentially. But *person* when seen in the context of the Trinity signifies relationality. The divine Persons exist in relationship with others and are constituted by those relations. They are individuals in a social matrix.

This is also true, by way of analogy, of us. We are persons who depend on one another in order to be ourselves. We are distinct from other persons but realize ourselves in and through them. Persons are individuals in relationship and communion, not in isolation.[17]

The Trinity is a divine reality constituting three Persons in relationship. God is Father in the relation to the Son, and God is Son in relation to the Father. Father and Son are what they are because of the other one. The Father is the father in relation to the generation and sending of the Son. The Son is the son in his obedience to the Father. The Spirit is the spirit as he glorifies the Father in the Son and the Son in the Father.

Gregory of Nanzianzus captured the mystery of triune life using the image of the dance *(perichoresis),* translated by Latin writers as "circumincession." The metaphor suggests moving around, making room, relating to one another without losing identity. The divine unity lies in the relationality of Persons, and the relationality is the nature of the unity. At the heart of this ontology is the mutuality and reciprocity among the Persons. Trinity means that shared life is basic to the nature of God. God is perfect sociality, mutuality, reciprocity and peace. As a circle of loving relationships, God is dynamically alive. There is only one God, but this one God is not solitary but a loving communion that is distinguished by overflowing life.[18]

Classical theism considers God apart from Trinity, as though there were a divine nature to discuss apart from there being three Persons in it. We can indeed consider the divine nature in a general way, but an effect of doing so is that we can lose sight of relationality and its importance to God's identity. Considering the divine nature in isolation from Trinity might even lead to error, because it would encourage us to suppose that we know a fair amount about the divine nature from our own speculations, apart from revelation. Out of confidence in our own metaphysical acumen, we might even question whether there can be real relations within God or between God and the world. Aquinas came to that conclusion, owing to his prejudice against allowing change in God. Assumptions about what it is "proper" for the divine nature to be like can make it difficult for us to take seriously what God's nature is like as revealed in the gospel.

The problem in Greek thinking is that God suffers, as it were, from his own completeness. God is so perfect in that way of thinking that people are inclined to deny any degree of dynamic in God, whereas in the gospel the divine nature is essentially a dynamic communion of love and a transcendence capable of immanence by virtue of it.[19]

Both-And

Spirit both names the essence of God and refers to the third Person of the Trinity. Spirit is the nature common to all the Persons and, at the same time, a distinct Person alongside Father and Son. Spirit is the life common to all and a Person with his own face and the center of distinctive actions.

It might have been easier for us if the Bible had reserved the term for the deity as a whole and employed a different term (like *Paraclete*) when referring to the third Person. This would have kept the two categories separate and simplified the task of interpreters. As it stands, one has to determine which category *spirit* refers to in any given passage.[20]

Trinitarian insight into the life of God derives from revelation in history, not from philosophy. God differentiates himself in the incarnation in a triune way. Accepting Jesus as the revelation of God, we take it that God as he is revealed in the economy of salvation corresponds to God as he is in his inner being. We assume that the economic Trinity is the immanent Trinity. The immanent Trinity (God in himself) is revealed by the economic Trinity (God in history), from which we learn that God is Father, Son and Spirit.[21]

What can we say about the inner life of God? On the one hand, the economic Trinity does not exhaust the immanent Trinity, since the divine mystery overflows revelation and is unattainable by the creature. On the other hand, revelation does establish the Trinity and three Persons in God. We are in the situation of having been given a true, though partial, knowledge of God in the economy of salvation. What has been revealed about the relationship of Father, Son and Spirit reveals something about the divine relationships.

What we see happening in the Gospel narrative between the Persons we understand also to take place in the life of God. Thus the self-giving love that we see in the Gospels has roots in what transpires within God the Trinity. We joyfully name God Father, Son and Spirit, even while remaining well aware that our knowledge in these matters is very limited.[22]

A Struggle to Understand

Theology has not found it easy to take plurality in God seriously. There are several reasons for this. Given the background of Old Testament thinking, it was a significant development of monotheism to posit three Persons in God. From the Greek side, plurality did not fit easily into Hellenistic thinking, because it introduced complexity into God's nature, challenging the assumption of simplicity. The effect of such impediments has made trinitarian thinking often quite disappointing.

There were some good beginnings in early theology, such as in the social trinitarianism of the Cappadocian fathers. Gregory of Nyssa allowed for real personhood in his concept of Father, Son and Spirit. He did not see them as modes of existence only but as subjects of the divine life enjoying personal relations. But it has not been easy to maintain this insight. An exception was Richard of St. Victor, who focused on love as most characteristic of the divine nature and came to the realization that if God is love everlastingly, this implies a circulation of love in the social context of the Trinity and the understanding of God as loving society.[23]

Augustine made a bad move for trinitarian reflection when he proposed a psychological analogy of Trinity which could not handle relationality in God. He thought of God as a single mind and the Persons as aspects of it. The analogy sounds modalistic and even unitarian, though Augustine did not intend it so. His problem was the idea of the simplicity of God derived from philosophical sources. This notion stood in the way of articulating the social Trinity. An assumption about the unity of God stemming from extrabiblical speculation led him into difficulty.

Theology always gets into trouble when its practitioners think they know what God is like apart from what revelation says God is like. In this case Augustine needed to allow his concept of divine simplicity to be corrected by revelation, rather than determining the meaning of revelation. Failing to give primacy to revelation causes one to lose sight of the distinctions between Persons of the Trinity as the gospel reveals them.[24]

Reluctance to espouse the social model of Trinity has dogged theology's path over the centuries. Even Karl Barth, despite the fact that he made the Trinity central in his theology, elevates unity over diversity when he insists on speaking of three modes, not three

Modalism = Heresy)

Persons, in God. He gives the appearance of thinking of God as a single Person existing in three unidentified modes. Such agnosticism regarding the immanent Trinity has led some of his disciples into unitarianism.[25] Similarly, Karl Rahner, the other truly great modern theologian, refuses to go beyond speaking of three "ways of existing" in God. Though it seems ironic, one can only call these two "neomodalist" in their doctrine of God.[26]

Hans Küng, another truly able theologian who wants to be faithful to Scripture and can be brilliant in the timeliness of his applications, is also plainly modalistic. He takes the Persons of the Trinity as aspects of a single subject. He takes *Father* to refer to God above us, *Son* to refer to the representative human through whom God is revealed, and *Spirit* to refer to God's power within us. It appears Küng is saying that Father is God, while *Son* and *Spirit* refer to God's activity in history. That is, *Son* and *Spirit* refer to roles of one divine Person in the events of revelation and redemption.

In Küng's case, apologetic considerations play a role. He wants to make it easier for Jews and Muslims to understand Christianity in the context of monotheism—but he pays a price for it. Ironically, what he does is to deny such fellow monotheists access to the revolutionary insight concerning God's nature represented by the social analogy of the Trinity.[27]

The problem is much worse in liberal theology, where unitarian thinking is most influential and spirit is understood as God's presence, not as a third Person. Geoffrey Lampe, for example, equates spirit with divine immanence and the consequent nature of God, as in process theism. In effect, Spirit is conscripted to meet the requirements of a philosophy in which it is not a Person but a symbol of creative love.[28]

Fortunately the situation is now changing. Theologians are taking the social Trinity more seriously as involving real community in God. Heribert Muhlen follows Richard of St. Victor in this, and many others such as Wolfhart Pannenberg, Jürgen Moltmann, Colin Gunton, Ted Peters, Cornelius Plantinga, Walter Kasper, Joseph Bracken and William Hill are social trinitarians today. That is, they recognize the personal distinctions of Father, Son and Spirit in God. They take the plurality in God to be real and hold that the Persons relate to each other in love and reciprocity.

"Social Trinity" means that there are three Persons who are subjects of the divine experiences. Spirit in one sense is the nature of God possessed by all the subjects, but *Spirit* also refers to the third Person in the divine fellowship. God's life is thus personal in the fullest sense—it is a life of personal communion. God is constituted by three subjects, each of whom is distinct from the others and is the subject of its own experiences in the unity of one divine life. This means among other things that God does not have to be related to a created order in order to be personal and loving. In the eternal being of God there exist the elements necessary for a fully personal life. This means that God, when he creates, creates freely, not out of necessity.[29]

Moltmann writes, "In order to comprehend the New Testament's testimony to the history of Jesus Christ, the Son of God, the church had to develop the trinitarian concept of God. The history of Jesus the Son cannot be grasped except as part of the history of the Father, the Son and the Spirit."[30] In the New Testament we are confronted with three Persons and only then go on to ask about unity.

In order to avoid tritheism, we say that the Trinity is a society of persons united by a common divinity. There is one God, eternal, uncreated, incomprehensible, and there is no other. But God's nature is internally complex and consists of a fellowship of three. It is the essence of God's nature to be relational. This is primordial in God and defines who God is. God is a triadic community, not a single, undifferentiated unity. Though beyond our understanding, God is a communion of Persons, and creation is a natural expression of God's life, because finite creatures find their fulfillment in relation to God. "At the deepest core of reality is a mystery of personal connectedness that constitutes the very livingness of God."[31]

Identifying the Spirit

The Spirit is more than God's presence: the Spirit is a Person in fellowship with, but distinct from, Father and Son. Called the Paraclete in John's Gospel, the Spirit is personal agent, teacher and friend.

Father and Son have a face. We can picture them, thanks to the narrative of salvation. Does the Spirit have a profile too? Human persons have an identity, thanks to the gift of God. Is this also true of the Spirit?[32]

Before addressing this question, let something more be said about the meaning of "person," a category that has changed over the centuries and requires clarification. In the modern context *person* often indicates an autonomous, independent self. This approach to person may lie behind the hesitation to speak of three Persons in God which I noted in both Barth and Rahner. It would not be true to say that God has three Persons in that sense of person. *Person* should rather be defined as that which enters into relationships and does not exist apart from them. The key to its meaning is intersubjectivity along with mutuality and reciprocity.

With this in mind, we might say that each of the Persons of the Trinity is aware of its identity while relating with the others and sharing the divine consciousness. Each Person is conscious of itself as divine and distinct from the other Persons in reciprocal relationships.[33]

How might we think of the identity of the Spirit in this configuration? Spirit is not as clearly defined for us as Father and Son, because the Son became visible and renders the Father visible, while the Spirit remains invisible and not as easily known. It is easier to assign a face to the Son than to Spirit, because of the historical concreteness of incarnation. By comparison, the Spirit is less well defined. Images like dove, water and fire (for example) are evocative but do not reveal the face of a Person; the Spirit remains somewhat anonymous.

Often one gains the impression that the Spirit likes to be viewed as the influence of the risen Lord and not in its own right. We respect that. It is possible that the Spirit wishes to remain mysterious, a wind that cannot be traced, and values the freedom not to be limited by too many images. He may feel it is enough to be the power of creation and new creation. Revelation drops only hints about the Spirit's identity, and what can be said is limited. Nevertheless, the economy of salvation does allow a glimpse into the divine life. The mystery of God transcends definition, and there are limits to its uncovering. Yet given that Father, Son and Spirit are revealed in the economy of salvation, there is still room to think about their relationships and differences.[34]

Spirit and Communion

One theme is apparent in both the Gospels and the letters. The impression is given that the Spirit is the love that bonds the Father and Son, mediating the relationship and evoking its ecstasy. Consider this passage: "At that same hour Jesus rejoiced in the Holy Spirit and said, 'I thank you, Father, Lord of heaven and earth, because you have hidden these things from the wise and the intelligent and have revealed them to infants' " (Lk 10:21). We are often led to associate the joy of communion and loving with the Spirit. Paul speaks of the communion of the Spirit who brings persons together in fellowship (2 Cor 13:13). He names the primary fruit of the Spirit as love, the love that binds everything together in harmony (Gal 5:22; Col 3:14).

The Spirit confirmed the sonship of Jesus and enriched his relationship with the Father. Similarly, the Spirit testifies to our own adoption as God's sons and daughters (Rom 8:16; Gal 4:6-7). What was true for the experience of Jesus is being communicated in our own. The Spirit's goal is love and fellowship, unity and peace (1 Cor 1:10; 3:3; Eph 4:2). Spirit draws us into the fellowship between Father and Son (1 Jn 1:3-4). A dove descended on Jesus at his baptism, and the beloved in the Song of Solomon is called a dove (2:14; 6:9). We cry, "Open to me, my sister, my love, my dove, my perfect one" (5:2).[35]

Joy is associated with activities of the Spirit, along with love. Paul writes, "The kingdom of God is not food and drink but righteousness and peace and joy in the Holy Spirit" (Rom 14:17). The Spirit filled the disciples with joy (Acts 13:52), gives us wine to drink and raises new songs in us (Acts 2:11; Eph 5:18-19), inspires joy along with love (Gal 5:22; 1 Thess 1:6). Spirit is the joy giver who fills our hearts with singing. The Spirit's inspiration makes us to want to dance and celebrate. It is the Spirit who creates glad and generous hearts in people (Acts 2:46). The Spirit caused Mary to rejoice greatly in God her Savior (Lk 1:47). I hear the Spirit saying: let the party begin, let the banquet be set, let us enter into the play of new creation! The Spirit choreographs the dance of God and also directs the steps of creatures entering God's dance.[36]

One may find the identity of the Spirit in the delight of God's social being, especially in the love that flows between the Father and the

Son. Spirit completes the trinitarian circle and opens it up to the world outside God.

I like the term *ecstasy* for the Spirit. It means "standing outside oneself," which suggests that Spirit is the ecstasy that makes the triune life an open circle and a source of pure abundance. Spirit embodies and triggers the overflow of God's pure benevolence, fosters its ecstatic character and opens it up to history.[37]

Tradition since Augustine has noted this and linked the Spirit to the relationship of Father and Son, even naming the Spirit "the bond of love" *(vinculum amoris)*.[38] It is fruitful to see the Spirit in this way, as the bond of the divine relationship and as the principle of the divine unity. The identity of the Spirit is best located in the communion of Father and Son, as the mutual and reciprocal love that flows between them. Spirit can be seen as the love that they share and even to constitute the *condilectus,* the channel, of their loving. Augustine saw the Spirit not only as the gift of love to us but as the divine love itself, making possible a communion of God with creatures. Spirit opens God up to what is nondivine, as the divine ecstasy directed toward the creature.[39]

In a mysterious manner Spirit may be said to unite the Father and Son in love and to proceed as the love between them. Some seek an analogy in the human family, in the relation of parent and child. One might think of Spirit as child of the Father and Son and the fruit of their love. God is a fuller community than just I-Thou. As husband and wife fashion a more perfect community by the birth of a child, so Father and Son perfect their love by sharing it with the Spirit. What could remain the *eros* of only two is transformed into the *agapē* of three, just as marriage transcends the two who first compacted it. In some sense the Spirit, in creating fellowship between two, can be thought of as the "we" of the I-Thou, as the child born out of the love of the other two.

Love unites persons who cherish one another, and in God's case love reaches fullness in the third Person, who is loved by Father and Son. The presence of the third lifts love out of preoccupation with each other into a fuller expression of self-giving. The perfection of love in turn overflows outward in movements of expansiveness and creativity.[40]

Spirit within the social Trinity fosters community and reveals sensitivity in that area. Spirit brings persons together in heaven and on earth, being both the medium of the communion of Jesus with the Father and the medium of our communion with brothers and sisters.

Spirit mediates the Father-Son relation on two different levels. The Son has access to the Father by the Spirit by nature, and we also have access as a gift (Eph 2:18). In the Son, the Father has chosen humanity to be his sons and daughters; in his self-surrender, the Son lavishes grace on us through his representative journey, while the Spirit seals us as those belonging to God, fostering both love and community. Though at work within us in a hidden way and having no proper name of his own, the Spirit forms and fosters community. As the oneness of the love of Father and Son, Spirit is the source of the oneness of believers in the fellowship of love, creating relationships and bringing about a common life. Even our love for God is the Spirit's gift to us.

The third Person, having no special name like "Father" or "Son," is content with God's generic name of "spirit." It is enough to be known as "bond of love." This does not mean the Spirit does not have a more specific profile, but only that we have not been told about it. Spirit is content to be thought of as the medium and fellowship of love. He delights in the loving relationships of the divine dance and exults in the self-emptying love that binds Father and Son. He delights to introduce creatures to union with God, the dance of the Trinity and the sabbath play of new creation.

Spirit is also associated with hope. The Spirit brooded over the waters of creation to bring life and order out of chaos. Spirit makes dry bones live and raises Christ up as firstfruits of those who sleep in death. Spirit belongs to the future and creates hope in people, being the power by which this present world will be transformed into the kingdom of God. Spirit opens up the future by realizing God's goals for history and pressing toward fulfillment. Therefore Paul writes, "May the God of hope fill you with all joy and peace in believing, so that you may abound in hope by the power of the Holy Spirit" (Rom 15:13).

Spirit does not wish to be focused upon but to remain anonymous, a servant of the economy of salvation. Consumed with its future, he hides his own face. The Spirit of love effaces himself in order to bless others. The flame of love is humble and self-effacing in the presence of the beloved. Like a mother in the service of life, the Spirit is disinterested and does not look to personal advantage. He is humble and dwells in the hearts of the poor in spirit.

Mediating love on earth must be very different from mediating it in heaven. Within the Godhead it must be sheer delight, but on this fallen earth it involves difficult remedial activities, such as exposing lack of love and promoting just relationships. The passion for love has to translate into passion for right relationships as well, which in turn leads to weeping and anguish. Therefore the Spirit does not mediate complacent love but chooses to be present in the midst of brokenness and distress.[41]

Not Just a Bond

Our thoughts are frail indeed when it comes to the immanent Trinity. Even this image, "bond of love," falls short of attributing personality to Spirit, leaving the possible impression of a binity—Father and Son plus a bond—rather than a trinity. It could reduce Spirit to the fostering environment of love. Spirit is more than that, however, being a distinct Person who, besides bonding others in love, shares and participates in it. Spirit bonds the Trinity by being the witness to the love of Father and Son, by entering into it and fostering it, and by communicating its warmth to creatures. Though we delight in the image of bond of love, we do not want to fail to do justice to real reciprocity in the Trinity or leave the impression of an impersonal bond that would obscure the personhood of the Spirit. Augustine had difficulty, as I have noted, with distinctions in the being of God, and perhaps this explains his attraction to this image. He had difficulty accepting that the being of God is a truly interpersonal communion.[42]

Plurality in God is real plurality, and relationality belongs to his essence. The dimension of intersubjectivity is basic—Father, Son and Spirit are three subjects in communion. They constitute a community of persons in reciprocity as subjects of one divine life. They joyously share life together. The social Trinity is the only understanding of God that accounts for the narrative of salvation. The Father sends the Son into the world, and his suffering for us in union with the Father in turn releases the Spirit. The story reveals God as a fellowship of Persons who are open to the joy and pain of the world. Trinity bespeaks a livingness in God, both beyond and within our world.

This speaks eloquently to our human experience at many points. Community is central to our earthly life. We were created for it in the image of the Trinity. We know that the dynamic interaction of persons forms corporate realities far greater than individuals. Similarly, God is an interpersonal process, a community of Persons who love one another and enjoy unanimity. God is the ideal community to which humans aspire but do not attain. The three Persons of God, while distinct and each possessing consciousness, form together a shared life that is the perfect ideal. Human community was created in the first place to reflect God's own perfection, and its destiny is to participate in the very life of God.[43]

The history of salvation discloses a unique relationship between Son and Father, showing how the Father loves the Son and how the Son returns love by embracing lost humanity. It also exposes a relationship of both with the Spirit, who proceeds from the Father and descends on the Son, pouring out the power of God's love on him.

It may be that we should seek the face of the Spirit in the face of the community, God's dwelling and the place where love is being perfected (1 Jn 4:12). As the Son reveals the Father's face and the Spirit reveals the Son's face, perhaps the place where Spirit's is seen is the faces of believers (Rev 22:4). As they grow in grace and holiness, it will become increasingly possible to recognize the Spirit in their faces. Perhaps the church is the face of the Spirit, who shines from the faces of all the saints.

Paul asks, "Do you not know that you are God's temple and that God's Spirit dwells in you?" (1 Cor 3:16). We might ask, Do you not know that the Spirit wishes to find his face made visible among those who believe?[44] We may find the Spirit's face also on those outside the church who give a cup of cold water to thirsty ones.

Such talk is metaphorical—do wind and breath have face? We bow to God's unfathomability. Let me add a word of clarification. The

Trinity is not a picture of the inner life of God in a literal way. True, it speaks to us of a communion marked by overflowing love. But it remains mysterious and analogical, not univocal. It may help us to think about God in terms of human interactions such as between parent and child, husband and wife, friend and friend. But the divine reality is always greater than, always surpasses, any analogy. It is, let us remember, a symbolic picture of the shared life that is at the heart of the universe.

God's Fair Beauty

The social Trinity depicts God as beautiful and supremely lovable. God is not a featureless monad, isolated and motionless, but a dynamic event of loving actions and personal relationality. What loveliness and sheer liveliness God is! We praise the Father, who is primordial light and unoriginated being, absolute mystery, without beginning or end. We praise our Lord Jesus Christ, everlasting Son of the Father, who lives in fellowship with the Father, ever responding to his love. We praise the Spirit, the Lord and giver of life, who is breathed out everlastingly—living, ecstatic, flaming. Each person of the Trinity exists eternally with the others, each has its gaze fixed on the others, each casts a glance away from itself in love to the others, the eye of each lover ever fixed on the beloved other.

Atheism is partly the result of bad theology, an unpaid bill resulting from failures in depicting God. How often have people been given the impression of God as a being exalting himself at our expense! One might be afraid of such a God, but no one would be attracted to love him. So often lacking has been the vision of the triune God as an event of open, dynamic, loving relations. It is not surprising that many have rejected God when there has been so little to attract them to him. Perhaps they would not reject as readily the God disclosed in Jesus Christ, who is an event of loving relationality and relates readily to the temporal world.[45]

The God of revelation is not distant from the world and untouched by its suffering. God cares for the world; it matters much to him. Prayer is a wonderful indicator of how God relates to the world. In asking us to pray and request things to happen, God invites us to join in shaping the future. Prayer reveals God as flexible in his planning and open in regard to what will happen. It indicates that the relationship between God and humanity is truly personal and that both are, in their own way, agents who make a difference to outcomes in a nondeterministic world.[46]

Theology ought to be beautiful, because its subject is so beautiful. Augustine exclaimed, "Too late did I love thee, O Fairness, so ancient yet so new" (*Confessions* 10.27). Barth comments, "Sulky faces, morose thoughts and boring ways of thinking are intolerable in this science."[47] Theology can be beautiful as it focuses on the beauty of God and the treasures of this relational ontology.

Hindrances to faith in God seldom have to do with a lack of proofs. Most people believe God exists because of the sense of divinity in them. Hindrances to faith have more to do with the quality of our theism. Theology has to do not with whether God is, but with *who* God is. Theology gains credibility when we have a doctrine of God that one can fall in love with.

Faith in the social Trinity affects how we understand the attributes of God. Trinitarian doctrine leads one to look at the divine perfections afresh. God's self-revelation discloses not only his inner nature but also God's attributes. Often in the past philosophy has influenced the doctrine of God, so that theology has started with a general under-standing of God rather than the truth of revelation.[48] For example, divine power may be misconstrued as total control because such a notion is thought "fitting" for God. Or righteousness may be conceived of as exactness because that is thought most fitting, despite what revelation says.

Yet God's self-revelation as the Triune One overturns foreign assumptions about divine perfections. In the Gospel narrative God's power is revealed in the weakness of the cross, and God's righteous-ness is revealed as delivering us from sin, not giving us what we deserve.

God is wonderfully different from what our natural thinking tells us, for this God delights in social existence, ecstatic dance, creativity and spontaneity. This is why we humans love to play in the midst of the seriousness of ordinary life—play bespeaks eternity. Play is a gesture of hope. It takes us momentarily out of the realm of suffering and lets us glimpse deathless joy. It is a gesture of hope in the face of ugliness and destruction.[49]

God is not an absolute Ego, unchangeable and all-determining. God is not a single self, isolated and solitary. God is a beautiful and alluring relational and dynamic community of love who does not alienate but fulfills us. God's glory does not lie in self-aggrandizement but in self-giving. God glories not in domination but in loving. What we see most centrally in God is the shining radiance of love.[50]

According to self-revelation, God is not an Unmoved Mover but the God of Jesus Christ, who goes out of himself and acts in history, who becomes involved in the affairs of his people and enters into conversation with them. God is closer and more intimate to us than we allow ourselves to believe. God is not preoccupied with himself, not unable to give himself away. It is the essence of God that he go out from himself and overflow for the sake of the other. In his very being as triune, God moves outward toward creation and incarnation. Giving us life and taking us to his own bosom are not afterthoughts but accord with God's nature and purpose.[51]

It is natural for God to make a world that would reflect relationality back to him. It is natural for God as social Trinity to create beings capable of hearing and responding to his word and capable of relating to each other also. It is natural for God to create a world not wholly determined but one peopled with creatures with whom God can freely share his life. It is natural for God to humble himself in the making of such a world, willing the existence of beings with an independent status alongside himself, and to accept limitations on his sovereignty voluntarily, not by external imposition. It is natural for God not to have to be all-determining but to be Ruler over a world of finite agents. Such a world is more difficult to manage but offers God items of much higher value.

The Trinity underlines the fact that the world exists by grace. It was not strictly necessary. It did not have to exist. God did not need it, since he exists in trinitarian fullness. The world exists not necessarily but freely, because God takes pleasure in it. God is like an artist who makes the world because he delights in self-expression. We see this in God's rest on the seventh day of creation—a rest not of fatigue but of satisfaction. God took pleasure in the world and delighted in what was made. We delight in it too, because it exists by grace, as a gift. We extol God's name and celebrate before him on account of it. When we dance and make melody to the Lord, we begin to experience on earth the joy of triune life in heaven, in anticipation of participating in union with God.[52]

Though complete in trinitarian fullness, God does not choose to be alone. Barth says, "God wills and posits the creature, neither out of caprice nor necessity, but because he loved it from eternity, because he wills to demonstrate his love for it, and because he wills, not to limit his glory by its existence and being, but to reveal and manifest it in his own co-existence with it."[53] God is bound together with us by choice. This is why he acts in history and relates to creatures. He loves to exist in dynamic relationship with the world. God has pledged himself to this situation so full of promise and of risk.[54]

The love of God grounds creation. His purpose for it has always been union and communion. God loved the world before it fell into sin. His initial relationship with it was not a legal but a loving one.

In federal theology it was said that after creating us God placed us in a covenant of works, demanding obedience and showing no grace. Federal theologians spoke as if the world was not the creation of a gracious God. But love is not secondary among God's purposes. The purpose of creation was to open a sphere for a covenant with humanity. It has always been the Father's purpose to create a people corresponding to the Son and together-bound with him. As Barth says, creation is the external basis of the covenant, and covenant is the internal basis of creation. Creation made the covenant possible through the formation of creatures who could echo triune life. God elected humanity from eternity to share his glory and is so intent on doing this that he even willingly took on himself rejection. God created the world and acts in history to advance the purpose of fostering a community of personal relationships, modeled on the social Trinity, where the gifts of each person are celebrated and nurtured.[55]

The Trinity may even be thought of as providing the place for creation to occupy. Some posit that the distance, as it were, between

Father and Son creates room for the world to exist. Hans Urs von Balthasar, for example, thinks of this as the space in which the world exists. God did not need the world to realize himself, since the Persons are already fulfilled in one another. At the same time the Trinity does not hoard its love. Its love is ecstatic and open to the world. Humanity is chosen in the context of the Father's love for the Son. We are loved in the Son. One could say that the plurality of the Trinity makes possible the existence of the world and the incarnation of the Son. Creation and redemption spring from the gracious dynamics of divine life, from the giving and receiving, the loving and surrendering, the interactions of love.[56]

Our desire for God did not originate with us. We did not initiate the possibility of this relationship. The Trinity made it possible and kindled the desire within us. We do not initiate this relationship. It is God who invites us to join the trinitarian conversation already occurring. The triune God invites us to share in intimacy with God and summons us to enter the communion of self-giving love. The dynamism of mutuality and self-giving goes on everlastingly in the being of God, and we are being drawn in. Prayer is joining an already occurring conversation. The Spirit calls us to participate in the relationship of intimacy between Father and Son and to be caught up in the dance already begun. In prayer on this earth we join the dance and begin to experience the movement and interplay of the trinitarian Persons.[57]

We tend to be biased in the direction of reason as the way to know reality, even in the postmodern situation. But music also speaks to us of the richness and depths of reality. Think of the unity, the harmony, the patterns, the delicacy, the surprises, the delight in music. Even Jesus piped a tune for people to dance to. Was Handel not right to say in his "Ode for St. Cecilia's Day" that harmony was the source of the world and its goal? The text says that nature's heap of atoms hear the voice on high summon them to arise, and they leap to their stations. And in the end they will hear the last trumpet sound, and music will fill the whole universe. It should not surprise us that music thrills us so much, because it draws us to the celestial sounds of the Spirit within us.[58]

By the Spirit we access the presence of the Father through Jesus Christ. Baptized into the triune name, we are adopted into the relationship everlastingly enjoyed by the Son with the Father through the Spirit. We are swept into a divine world of mutual love and begin to experience the very goal of our nature as spiritual and social beings. Designed for mutuality, we are destined for the dance, destined to be married to Christ and share in the triune life. The fellowship experienced on earth is destined to be raised a notch to the level of the Trinity.

Being a Christian is knowing Father and Son and walking along the pathway of cross and resurrection through the power of the Spirit. The loving communion between the Persons of the Trinity is diffusive—it tends by nature to radiate out from the center. Its diffusiveness manifests itself in our existence as loving and lovable creatures and alerts us to our destiny, which is to participate in God's love.

Here, then, I have laid the foundation for the next chapter. In the act of creation God is wanting to effect an echo of trinitarian life on the finite level and to produce beings that will share in the life of the Father with the Son by the Spirit. The other chapters follow from this. To deal with sin, stemming from the human refusal of love, God assumed our nature in the incarnation and incorporates all who believe into the body of Christ and new humanity by the Spirit (chapter three). From cross and resurrection comes the community that prolongs the anointing of Jesus by the Spirit and anticipates the new humanity. The church is a foretaste of the new race, the colony of heaven, the embodiment of the koinonia that God is and that the world will become. God does not will to be alone, so his love overflows in creation and redemption, and he seeks a community into which to pour the Spirit (chapter four). By the Spirit humankind is now being drawn in the direction of the wedding banquet and into union with God (chapter five). By the Spirit too, the invitation becomes genuinely universal (chapter six), and the church is healed of its brokenness as it is led into the truth (chapter seven).

Loving mutuality and relationship belong to the essence of God. In recognizing this, theology makes explicit what the heart has always known. Let God not be defined so much by holiness and sovereignty in which loving relatedness is incidental, but by the dance of trinitarian life. And let us see Spirit as effecting relationships, connecting Son to

Father, and us to God. Spirit is the ecstasy of divine life, the overabundance of joy, that gives birth to the universe and ever works to bring about a fullness of unity.

When we render God in this way, not only atheists might come to love him, but even Christians, for we ourselves often lack a sense of God's beauty and adorableness. God is the ever-expanding circle of loving, and the Spirit is the dynamic at the heart of the circle. Through him we all have access in one Spirit to the Father, on behalf of whom Spirit and Bride say, "Come!" Let us all join in the dance.

TWO

SPIRIT IN CREATION

*T*HERE IS A COSMIC range to the operations of the Spirit, the Lord and giver of life. Pope John Paul II speaks of "the breath of life which causes all creation, all history, to flow together to its ultimate end, in the infinite ocean of God."[1] Yet theology has often diminished the Spirit's activities to much smaller proportions, in effect marginalizing the Spirit to the realm of church and piety. H. I. Lederle remarks,

> For too long the Spirit and his work has been conceived of in too limited a sense. There was a capitulation at the beginning of the modern era in which faith became restricted to the private devotional life and the latter was then described as "spiritual." The Spirit should not be limited to spiritual experiences and charisms—even though it needs to be recognized that this element still awaits acknowledgment in much of Christianity. We need, however, to set

our sights much higher. Not only the realm discovered by pentecostalism needs to be reclaimed but also the cosmic dimensions of
the Spirit's work. The Spirit is at work in the world and should not
be degraded to an ornament of piety.[2]
After its inception, the creation unfolded under the presidency of the
Holy Spirit, who brooded over the primeval waters and turned chaos
into cosmos (Gen 1:2). The deep ocean stirred, and diverse creatures
began to emerge. Most fundamentally the Spirit is associated with the
gift of life and with every new beginning. God breathed into Adam's
nostrils, and the mud sprang to life (Gen 2:7). There would be no life
at all if matter had not been breathed upon by the Spirit of life.

Spirit is truly the life-giver, as Jesus said: "It is the spirit that gives
life" (Jn 6:63). The breath blows on everything, bringing life from
death, beauty from ugliness and peace from confusion. The Spirit
infuses the world with love and flies on the air (Job 12:10; 33:4). "The
Spirit brooded over the still earth as a bird broods over its nest,
warming the dormant life within, wakening it, releasing it, so that the
tiny creatures can come to birth." We encounter Spirit in the life of
creation itself, in the vitality, the joy, the radiance, the music, the
honey, the flowers, the embrace.[3]

Spirit is the ecstasy that implements God's abundance and triggers
the overflow of divine self-giving. Power of creation, the Spirit is aptly
named "Lord and giver of life" in the Nicene Creed. This phrase calls
on us to think of Spirit as active in the world and history, especially
in its development and consummation. The universe in its entirety is
the field of its operations, which are so fundamental for Christology,
ecclesiology, salvation and more. This is the power that caused Christ's
birth, empowered him for ministry and raised him from the dead. None
of these things are possible for the flesh. And the Spirit is present
everywhere, directing the universe toward its goal, bringing to completion first the creational and then the redemptive purposes of God. Spirit
is involved in implementing both creation and new creation. There could
not be redemptive actions unless first there had been creative actions.
The creative acts underlie the salvific acts. The Spirit who brings salvation
first brooded over the deep to bring order out of chaos.[4]

Granted, the Bible says less about creative functions of the Spirit than it does about redemptive functions surrounding the new creation. But the creative functions are presupposed in what is said about the redemptive functions. Emphasis on the Spirit's work in salvation should not be read as a denial of the creative work on which it is based.

For example, Jesus could assume that his listeners knew the Father was the Creator; he did not have to repeat it or dwell on it. There was no doubt in Hebrew thinking that the world and all creatures are dependent on God for life and strength. Hope for the future, for the coming of the kingdom, for the resurrection of the dead—such hope is plausible only because the God who promised them is the Creator of the world. There cannot be new creation without creation first. Paul says, "The creation waits with eager longing for the revealing of the children of God" (Rom 8:19). The promise of cosmic liberation would be unintelligible apart from the original gift of life. The God who saves us is none other than the God who created all things (Eph 3:9). His deeds of creation (power in the skies) are matched by his deeds of salvation (majesty over Israel) in history (Ps 68:34).

Let us explore in this chapter the link between Spirit and creation. Let us reaffirm its importance and overcome its neglect. The Spirit as life-giver and universal divine presence, while not an oft-repeated theme, is nonetheless a weighty concept in the Bible. God is not just *before* creation as its initiator but also *with* creation in its development as its director. Spirit is the ground of the world's becoming and brings God into an intimate relationship with the world. Spirit introduces love into the world, sustains life and gives meaning. The Spirit is with humanity on its journey through time and with the creation in its groaning and longing for deliverance. We are surrounded by the mystery of God, "in [whom] we live and move and have our being" (Acts 17:28).[5]

Theology would not think of denying the omnipresence of God but may overlook the omnipresence of the Spirit. "Where can I go from your spirit?" (Ps 139:7). We may not completely forget it, perhaps, but we tend to forget that the Spirit is present, not as a vague power sustaining the world but as the Spirit of the triune God. In failing to recognize the Spirit's presence, theology may fail to reflect also on the positive implications that flow from it. The power of love is at work everywhere in the world, not just in the churches. The redeeming God is the Creator God. There is a unity to God's work in nature and history, not a dualism. It is not as if creation before the Fall was graceless. Spirit is moving the entire process toward participation in the love of God, and the whole creation is caught up in it.[6]

Spirit and Creation

A number of texts connect Spirit and creation. Elihu says, "The spirit of God has made me, and the breath of the Almighty gives me life" (Job 33:4). He adds,

> If he should take back his spirit to himself,
>   and gather to himself his breath,
> all flesh would perish together,
>   and all mortals return to dust. (34:14-15)

His language reminds one of God's breathing life into Adam's nostrils, making him a living soul (Gen 2:7). The implication is that Spirit is the source of life in both body and soul.

On a broader scale, the psalmist states, "When you send forth your spirit, they are created; and you renew the face of the ground" (Ps 104:30). In another place David declares, "By the word of the LORD the heavens were made, and all their host by the breath [spirit] of his mouth" (Ps 33:6). At Athens Paul affirmed, "[God] gives to all mortals life and breath and all things" (Acts 17:25). Such texts tell us that Spirit gives life to creation at the most fundamental level and that our very life is a gift, not ours by right.[7]

The relative scarcity of such texts does not make the truth unimportant. Creation as a doctrine generally tends to be taken for granted and is treated infrequently and cursorily in biblical study. Even the "creation out of nothing" that theologians consider important goes unmentioned in the Bible. It is deduced from other verses. But the importance of a truth cannot be measured by counting verses. The fact is that the doctrine of creation and the Spirit's role in it is supported both by scriptural texts and by theological reflection on them. Scripture makes it clear enough that God created all things and that the Spirit is present everywhere in the world. The point does not have to be repeated often to hold true. The Spirit is present and active in creation—in its inception, continuation and perfection.

The paucity of texts may be due not only to an emphasis on new creation but also to the fact that the truth is treated in other ways, with other language. The book of Proverbs, for example, extols the creative role of wisdom. We read,

When [God] marked out the foundations of the earth,
    then I was beside him, like a master worker;
and I was daily his delight,
    rejoicing before him always,
rejoicing in his inhabited world
    and delighting in the human race. (Prov 8:29-31)

Wisdom is described as God's agent in creation, much the way Spirit could be described. Like Spirit, playful wisdom is sent into the world to bring God's plans into effect.

The link between Spirit and wisdom continues in the intertestamental period. In the Wisdom of Solomon wisdom is described as the fashioner of things and is linked to the Spirit as being universally present throughout the world (7:21-30). The writer says, "The Spirit of the Lord fills the world, and that which contains all things has the knowledge of his voice" (1:4-8). The Spirit, together with wisdom, is portrayed as the agent of divine creativity.

This gives us an exalted perspective on God's relationship to the created order and inspires in us wonder and gratitude for the gift of creation. It lets us think of God as present in everything, in the ordinary and the extraordinary, and it lays the foundation for observing inspiration both in the craftsmanship of a Bezalel and in the prophecies of a Jeremiah. It allows us a broad sympathy for detecting the presence of God everywhere we look and fighting off dark thoughts about God's absence.

Even the doctrine of providence does duty for the cosmic work of the Spirit. Under this category too we reflect on God at work within history and the world. *Providence* refers to God's sustaining and governing all things and therefore indirectly to Spirit's moving in continuing creation.[8]

When the New Testament speaks of resurrection and new creation, it assumes the creative power of the Spirit. Only the Spirit who brought life to the world in the first place can bring new life to it. Redemption does not leave the world behind but lifts creation to a higher level. The Spirit has been implementing God's purposes for creation from day one and is committed to seeing to it that they issue in restoration. Creator Spirit inspires hope for a world beyond the reach of humanity, in which God's power raises the dead and makes everything new. The prophet asks, "Can these bones live?" and God tells him to say, "I will cause breath [my Spirit] to enter you, and you shall live" (Ezek 37:1-6). Another prophet says that creation will be desolate "until a spirit from on high is poured out on us, and the wilderness becomes a fruitful field" (Is 32:15). They can speak of the Spirit in this way only because he is the power of creation.

It is unfortunate when Christians forget the cosmic and creational role of the Spirit. W. H. Griffith Thomas, for example, denies the cosmic functions and associates the Spirit solely with redemption. He opposes contemplating the Spirit's work on such a universal scale. As an evangelical, he fears theological revision were he to do so. What if people thought they detected stirrings of the Spirit in the heathen world? What if the uniqueness of Jesus Christ were diminished as too much thought was given to the Spirit's global presence? Thomas prefers to bypass the cosmic activities of the Spirit rather than deal with the challenges it would pose to traditional theology. But the effect of neglecting these activities is to break creation and redemption into separate spheres and to draw a line between them. The unity of God's action is thus broken, and creation is downgraded to an event preparatory to redemption.[9]

Not all theologians neglect the Spirit's cosmic functions, however. Calvin, reflecting on Genesis, attributes the beauty and form of the universe to the Holy Spirit and sees them as proof of the Spirit's divinity. He gladly acknowledges the Spirit as breathing life into all things (*Institutes* 1.13.14). Abraham Kuyper, following Calvin, lifts up the cosmic dimensions of the Spirit even more. He conceives of the Spirit as exercising a steady influence on creation from the beginning and to be leading the world to its destiny. He even notes that the Spirit bestows gifts and talents on human beings, thus gracing the whole world. A theology of the Spirit needs to include this dimension, and a fear of abuse must not prevent its proper use.[10]

Trinitarian Creation

Why is there a creation at all? God does not need it, yet paradoxically it exists. Perhaps we can answer this question with another: Why do paintings and symphonies exist? We do not need them either—not the way we need food and drink. Such things exist because of a creative impulse. Works of art flow freely and overflow out of a rich inner life. They arise from celebration and sheer delight in existence. In a similar way, the creation exists as a work of art in which God takes pleasure and through which he gives pleasure. God is like the artist who loves to create and who delights in what is made. Creatures in turn share God's delight when they are struck by the giftedness of their own existence. It makes them want to dance and play.

Something of the why of creation is revealed by the nature of God. He creates in a way that is consistent with his loving nature as a relational being. Not narcissistic or self-enclosed, God is inwardly and outwardly self-communicating, a gracious being. Creation arises from loving relationships in the divine nature. God creates out of his own abundant interpersonal love—it is the expression of his generosity. No outside force compels it; no need drove the decision.

God graciously gave life to the creature and allowed the creaturely other to exist alongside himself. He made room for the creature because of a disposition for abundant communication. God's nature is overflowing, and creation is a fruit of it. God loves relationships, not solitariness. He is not at all like Aristotle's god, thinking only about thinking. God is pure ecstasy—each Person exists in loving relationship with the other Persons, and the joyous fellowship spills over into giving life to the creature. God does not hoard his interpersonal life but gives it away, and his Spirit fosters communion both with God and between creatures. The Spirit's presence in the world also enables it to be sacramental of the divine presence.[11]

Expressed in the act of creation is a will for community. God's being as shared love favors the coming into being of created communities. Daniel J. Migliore says, "God is eternally disposed to create, to give and share life with others. The welcome to others that is rooted in the triune life of God spills over, so to speak, in the act of creation."[12] We should associate God's self-emptying not only with incarnation but also with creation, where we also see God's disposition to make room for others to live. Creation is an act of self-limitation too, the willingness for a relatively independent world to exist alongside God. God creates for his own pleasure, and his pleasure as a triune lover is to admit new partners to the dance. For this reason God embarks on the risky adventure of creating a nondivine, significant created order and even pledges to be involved in it.[13]

The triune nature helps us think about the relative autonomy of the world and its relatedness to God. The world is created in distinction from the Father, to be able to relate and respond freely to God. It is a distinct though dependent reality, made for relationship, and a world in which the Son can become incarnate, both as the fulfillment of God's desire to disclose himself and as redemptive sacrifice (if required). God's nature is an order of loving relations in which, though there is no need to create, there is the possibility of creating a world to which God would relate through Son and Spirit.

History is not the playing out of a timelessly fixed decree but a theater where the divine purposes are being worked out by the resourcefulness of God in dealing with the surprises of a significant creation. History is neither random nor predetermined. The Spirit is active in everything but in ways that are respectful of the dignity of creation. One might think of Spirit as choreographing the dance of creation by analogy to what he does in the fellowship of the sublime Trinity.

God creates out of his relational fullness, out of a love that is not closed but rather open to embrace the universe. Ecstatic, God's love overflows itself and makes room for a creation. Being love, God ever seeks to share being and communicate presence with it. As bond of love, as One who fosters fellowship, the Spirit opens up the relationship between God and world. God is not against us but for us, ever seeking to share his life. God creates freely, not by way of necessity or emanation. God creates by the Word—by a free and conscious act. God, who loves the Son from eternity, loves creatures in the Son and perfects the world through the breath of his Spirit. Spirit makes possible a fellowship among creatures corresponding to God's triune love. By bringing into being ever more complex entities, the Spirit is moving reality toward a manifestation of God's likeness in history and toward the participation of creatures in God's love beyond history.[14]

God rested on the seventh day not because of exhaustion but in order to take pleasure in the creation (Gen 2:3). Creation is a piece of divine self-expression which brings delight. God's self-expression is free and playful. Ontologically distinct, God enters into the world and receives pleasure and derives value from it. The joy comes especially from the fact that the love of the trinitarian community can now be echoed in a world capable of interpersonal love. God's purpose from the beginning was to have creatures in his image with whom he could be united in love. In emphasizing redemption, then, we should not forget that it has always been God's purpose to be "for us" and "with us," even before sin entered.[15]

Creation has value for both God and humanity in a dialectical way. For God there is the joy of self-expression and interpersonal communication. God is delighted by the way that nature can mirror the divine and exhibit its traces. The heavens declare God's glory, and the world reflects his power. Creation itself intimates an ultimate power that fosters openness and spontaneity among creatures. It is also a realm where reciprocal relationships can be enacted on a finite level and where the Trinity can be reflected in the communion of social creatures. These image-bearers can mirror God's image in the sphere of nondivine reality and reproduce the filial relationship that the Son enjoys with the Father. From this world the Father longs to hear the very *yes* from the creature that he hears eternally from his beloved Son.

For the creature too, the world has obvious value. It is a benefit just to be graced with existence. Creation also makes possible a covenant between God and humanity, holding out the promise of union with God. It means that the love that flows between the Persons of the Trinity can flow among all those who allow themselves to be touched by God. So God's joy in creation is certainly not achieved at our expense. God may want a creature who can respond to his love, but we are the recipients of the gift, and we are the ones who are destined to attain the unimaginable fulfillment of our being in God. Community as the goal of creation benefits both God and ourselves.[16]

Creation is not finished yet. Spirit has it on the track of new creation. Paul says, "If there is a physical body, there is also a spiritual body" (1 Cor 15:44). In one sense creation is complete, in that God has called it forth and it exists. But its goal has not been reached, and it is in that sense incomplete and unfinished. Only at the end of history will it be clear what the creation was meant to be, because it will have reached the goal. At present we see much brokenness and provisionality, but at the consummation we will see the complete picture. Until then our knowledge remains partial, and not every question has an answer.[17]

The Two Hands of God

Creation was made to echo the relationality so central to the being of God and is intended to issue in fulfillment for the creature. The way God brings this to pass is through the Son and Spirit. Let us consider now the double mission of Son and Spirit in relation to creation, the two hands with which God creates and perfects (Irenaeus *Against Heresies* 4.20.1).[18]

We should associate God's love for the creature with God's love for the Son as the sense in which God creates through him. God predestines us to be his sons and daughters alongside the Son, that he might be the firstborn among many (Rom 8:29; Heb 2:10-13). Human destiny is to be united to Christ and share God's life with him. God turns to the creature through the Son. They become objects of love as love for the Son is manifested in them. The origin of everything that differs from the Father lies in the Son's self-differentiation from the Father, who loves the creature in the context of love for the Son, its primary object.[19]

Oriented toward the Son, the creation might be pictured as standing alongside the Son. In loving the creature, God is at the same time loving the Son. The Father and Son relationship creates room, as it were, for creation to exist. Creation exists on another level of being from God but is not in every sense outside God. The Father desires union with the creature as he desires union with the Son. As Christ is a perfect expression of the Father, the creature is called to share his likeness. In the Son we see what the creature is meant to be, and in the Son we are invited to become God's sons and daughters alongside him.

Creation is related to the reality of the Son, and by incarnation the Son became part of creation. What the creation is meant to be is seen in the loving response of the Son to the Father. The Son does not live for himself—he does not consider equality with God as something to be exploited; instead he gives glory and thanks to God. The Son gives focus and direction to the creative process. He shows that humans are destined for community, mutuality and relationship. Since God is a community of Persons, his image is vested not in isolated individuals but in persons as community. The image of God is really seen in Christ together with his brothers and sisters.

The creation exists in the space between Father and Son. The otherness we call the Son makes possible the otherness of the world. The Son is the archetype of creation, and the world exists in the space between Father and Son, between the Persons who share in divine life. Augustine prayed, "Thee, O Lord, I imagined on every part environing and penetrating [the world], though every way infinite, as if there were a sea, everywhere and on every side" (*Confessions* 7.7).

Creation exists in relation to the Son because the Son models the other as distinct but in relationship with the Father. The self-differentiation of the Son from the Father is the basis of creation. The Son mediates creation as the ground of its existence, as differentiated from but in relationship to the Father. The Son is the exemplar of creation, independent from but in relationship with God. God is other than the world and transcendent, but the world also fulfills its destiny in relation to God. What was created through the Son finds its destiny in its being returned to the Father by the Spirit. When we worship in the Eucharist, we offer creation and ourselves back to God.

The Trinity is a fellowship of giving and receiving, and creation is intended to echo mutuality. Even though humanity in Adam refused to live in the pattern of giving and receiving, God did not cease to give but instead rendered a perfect offering of praise and obedience in the Son. Christ redeemed the world by restoring its capacity to praise God and restored its otherness in relationship with God. Now through the Spirit, the creation is being enabled through the sacrifice of Christ to offer the praise and thanks that are due.

God freely wills creation and expresses himself in the Son, his Word and image, and also in the creation. We might view creation as a continuation of a movement that transpires between Father and Son. Within God the movement of self-expression is necessary, while in creation it is voluntary. But God's expressing himself in creation is also a movement in God's experience. The fact is that the triune God has made room for the otherness of the creature. Choosing to share their love by creating, the Persons have inserted creatures into the open spaces of the divine life. The immanent Trinity is the economic Trinity—the God who is for us is indeed the triune God.[20]

Creation by the Spirit

Creation is related to the dynamics of trinitarian life in relation to the Spirit also. Spirit is the ecstasy by which God, without leaving himself, can enter the world and be present. The world, created by God through the Son, is also a result of the breathing of the Spirit. Spirit mediates the presence of God in creation and enables the creature to participate in God. The creature, distinct from the Father in the Son, is united to God by the Spirit.[21]

The Trinity may be pictured as a spiral action, spinning and releasing the power of its momentum outward, producing circular motions outside itself. Spirit produces within the world the dynamic movement within God. As the Spirit mediates the relationship between Father and Son, he also mediates the relationship between creatures and God. The goal is that we may enjoy the responsive relationship that the Son enjoys with the Father. The Spirit seeks to reproduce in the world the interior mystery of God, ever spiraling it back toward God. Bringing creation to its goal is the main task of the Spirit. The Son is the Logos of creation, the origin and epitome of its order, while the Spirit is the artisan who by skillful ingenuity sees to it that creaturely forms arise and move toward fulfillment.[22]

I see Spirit as the power that brings God's plans into effect, as a gentle but powerful presence, communicating divine energies in the world and aiming at increasing levels of participating in the fellowship of love. The universe came into being through the Spirit's power, when he hovered over the deep like a mother bird (Gen 1:2 NIV). The Spirit continues to energize and sustain the world through the sweep of history. Like a true artist, he expresses himself in the universe in ways that respect the integrity of its forms and materials. The Spirit aims to bring about the sabbath rest of new creation and the joys of the kingdom of God.

Spirit is perfecter, then, of the creation of which Jesus is the highest expression. Spirit is at work in history, first bringing humankind into existence and then moving it toward the goal of union. Spirit is the power released to bring the divine plans to completion. He is Spirit of creation and new creation, concerned with creating community and bringing about the kingdom. Spirit is the power by which this present age will be transformed into the kingdom and which ever works to bring about ultimate fulfillment. As the power of creation, the Spirit does not call us to escape from the world or from history but keeps creation open to the future.[23]

The scope is breathtaking. God's breath is on the whole creation— we live and move and have our being in an ocean of love. Athanasius says,

> Like a musician who has tuned his lyre and, by an artistic blending of low, high and medium tones, produces a single melody, so the wisdom of God, holding the universe, adapting things heavenly to things earthly, and earthly things to heavenly, harmonizes them all and leads them by his will to make one world order in beauty and harmony. (*Contra Gentes* par. 42)

Spirit challenges everyone to relate to God by means of his self-disclosure to every nation in the course of history. God is revealed in the beauty and order of the natural world and is the prevenient grace that benefits every person (Jn 1:9). God is not a Being who dwells at a distance from the world, nor is God a tyrant exercising all-controlling power. Of course God is not the world and the world is not God, yet God is in the world and the world is in him. Because he is at the heart of things, it is possible to encounter God in, with and beneath life's experiences. By the Spirit, power of creation, God is closer to us than we are to ourselves.

Useful Implications

What are some of the implications and applications of this doctrine of the Spirit? First, appreciating the Creator Spirit lets us see that God is involved in creation down to the last detail. Everything that exists, from spiders to galaxies, manifests the power of the Spirit. The world is not empty of meaning but is actually full of mystery. Anyone who has wondered at the beauty of the sunset has experienced the Spirit's creativity. The Spirit is not nowhere (as secularists tell us) but everywhere, and our lives can be immeasurably enriched by taking account of this. The Spirit is present in all human experience and beyond it. There is no special sacred realm, no sacred-secular split—practically anything in the created order can be sacramental of God's presence.

God is present to us in the creation, and the world is a natural sacrament. We meet Spirit in moments of joy and sadness, hope and yearning, suffering and struggle. Spirit is at work in the world and not "an ornament of piety." Our experience has the potential to mediate his presence. Spirit is "the mobile, pure, people-loving Spirit who pervades every wretched corner, wailing at the waste, releasing power that enables fresh starts. Her energy quickens the earth to life, her beauty shines in the stars, her strength breaks forth in every fragment of shalom and renewal that transpires in arenas of violence and meaningless."[24]

The phrase "in arenas of violence and meaninglessness" is important. Spirit is not only everywhere present but everywhere up against the human negation of God. The world does not know or receive the Spirit (Jn 14:17). There are powers of resistance with whom the Spirit is locked in mortal combat. Spirit is present in the struggle to make creatures whole, giving hope to the hopeless and working at reconciliation to bring about newness. Spirit renews the face of the ground and works to restore brokenness. For when sin abounds, the Spirit's grace does much more abound.[25]

Second, Creator Spirit keeps the link between creation and redemption open and alive. Theology has the unfortunate habit of drawing a line between creation and redemption, distinguishing them too sharply. This loses sight of the truth that redemption is a restoration of creation, not its denial. The cosmic functions keep before us the unity of God's work in creation and redemption. Spirit is the power of redemption only because he is first the power of creation. Only the Spirit of creation is strong enough to be the Spirit of resurrection. The role in creation is primary and undergirds the other work. The whole creation is a field of the Spirit's operations and thus sacramental of God's presence.

Let us stop demoting the Spirit, relegating him to spheres of church and piety. His role in the creation is foundational to these other activities. The whole creation is home to the Spirit's operations, and the cosmic fruits issue in new creation. The Spirit is the perfecter of the works of God in creation.[26]

Neglecting Creator Spirit gives us a narrow perspective on God's operations in the world. While recognizing revelation beyond the Bible and providential activity outside the church, theology often has little inclination to associate grace with them or see any beneficial, preparatory role in them. I suppose this reluctance is motivated by the desire to protect the uniqueness of salvation through Christ, as though admitting a preparatory work would overshadow its fulfillment in Christ. By acknowledging the work of the Spirit in creation, we are actually allowed a more universal perspective where Spirit can be seen as seeking what the Logos intends and where one can believe and hope that no one is beyond the reach of grace. A foundation is laid for universality if indeed the Spirit pervades the world and if no region is closed to his influences.[27]

Spirit prepares the way for Christ by gracing humanity everywhere. In such global activities Spirit supplies the prevenient grace that draws sinners to God and puts them on the path toward reconciliation. What one encounters in Jesus is the fulfillment of previous invitations of the Spirit. God's love is the ever-present ground and goal of created things. We know this from Jesus Christ, but this truth has always been so, always a possibility. One does not properly defend the uniqueness of Jesus Christ by denying the Spirit's preparatory work that preceded his coming. Let us try to see continuity, not contradiction, in the relation of creation and redemption.[28]

Third, if the whole world is the field of Spirit activity, recognizing

Creator Spirit gives us the opportunity to relate theology to origins and environment in fresh ways. Spirit is the field of power that lifts the material world above and beyond itself. Spirit is the reason that nature produces more than one would expect from a natural order. The Spirit's work allows us to speak more intelligibly about creation and even helps us with ecological responsibilities and our stewardship of the earth.[29]

Science and Theology

Before relating Spirit to human origins, let us consider the underlying issue of the relation of theology to science. It seems to me most natural to regard them as two forms of human response to reality. We investigate the world, God's creation, and we study the Bible, God's Word. The two activities interact, each investigating things in its own way and surveying reality from its own perspective. Ideally one hopes that they will prove to be complementary activities and not antithetical, partners rather than enemies.

No doubt science has important things to say to theology, and theology to science. The information each gleans in its own manner merits our respect and requires some integration. What God tells us in the book of nature should interact with what God tells us in the book of scripture. Ideally theologians would read the book of nature and scientists would read the Bible, each in the light of the other, because both deal with and describe God's world. The dialogue of theology with science is important if we aim to make sense of Christian truth claims. As Einstein said, religion without science is blind—science without religion is lame.[30]

Some recent interaction has not been helpful. Certain advocates of creationism and certain advocates of evolutionism have been twisting science to make it serve their purpose. Carl Sagan, for example, deceives when he states at the beginning of his television special that "the universe is all there is, was, and ever will be." This is unsubstantiated dogmatism, since science does not and cannot tell us such a thing.[31] Creationists, on the other hand, do something of the same when they twist the facts of nature to fit literalistic interpretations of the Bible. Both sides sometimes hold science hostage to dogma.

Evolutionists are blind to design in nature even when it is apparent, while creationists ignore the age of the earth and the developments in nature since creation and are also insensitive to the teleology at work in the natural processes. Recognition of the Creator Spirit might help this discussion.[32]

Theology should capitalize on opportunities now afforded by modern science by recovering the truth of Creator Spirit that allows us to place the discussion in a positive light. It allows us to consider science in the framework of theism and notice God at work in nature, bringing about the future of the world. To oppose naturalistic evolution, we need not deny the evolutionary continuity of forms in nature. A theory of progressive creation can make sense of what we know about nature's history. God not only created the world in the beginning but also works within and through everything to bring about his goals. God is at work in the ordinary ways that science tracks and also in extraordinary ways that anticipate the kingdom.[33]

The theory of evolution is a working hypothesis in science. It cannot answer every question and is not immune to criticism. But it is a well-researched and thoughtful proposal based on a wealth of observation which theology should seek to integrate properly.[34]

Theology and science should be partners in search of truth. Science helps theology understand the physical world, and theology helps science detect the meaning and mystery of what is. Theology is fruitful for science because it raises issues that go beyond science; science is important for theology because it helps us connect the biblical text with created reality.

Theologians and scientists both exegete God's world, which we have been given to study and appreciate. Contemplating this world fills us with wonder and gratitude. Science, based in the freedom of the knower, can along with theology contribute to our understanding. The Spirit itself has formed within us the creative capacity not only to understand the world but also to give it voice and offer it back to God with thankful praise.[35]

Creation is an ongoing process as well as a past event. The world was brought into being and is now being sustained by God's creative breath. The Spirit is the field of creativity shaping the process. He is active in natural processes as well as in domains of piety and miraculous events like Jesus' resurrection. Acknowledging the Spirit's continuous activity throughout the universe adds great meaning to our awareness of God's care for the human and nonhuman world. The Spirit is the One to whom all creatures owe their life, movement and aspiration. Recognizing this can lead us into a spirituality of the present and the ordinary, a celebration of God here with us and our dwelling in God. It helps us develop a heart of thanksgiving for creation and every part of it.

The Spirit of God indwells creation and works on the inside of it by means of subtle operations. Pierre Teilhard de Chardin helped us to see that things have an outside that can be measured and an inside that cannot. Theology tells us of a power of love within the world that is pushing things forward. It tells us of the Spirit who strives to create a greater awareness of God and a greater Christlikeness in the creature. By the Spirit, through a series of leaps and breakthroughs, the invisible becomes visible. Theology can illumine what science discovers by naming the bias toward order within the world. It identifies Spirit as working within nature, unfolding God's purposes by immanent operations. It can point to grace at work within the structures of the world, facilitating the self-transcendence of the creature and bringing a groaning creation to birth.

Spirit and Origins

Integrating scientific learning with theological insight is an important challenge for serious theology. The contemporary scientific picture of the world calls out for theological reflection. Let us consider how theology may shed light on nature as God's continuing creation and how the Spirit may be understood as working in this context.[36]

Science has made this task easier by correcting some of its own presuppositions about nature as a determinate mechanism, static in character. It is now offering a more holistic and dynamic concept of nature as an expanding process. Matter is being viewed more as imbued with life, restless and insurgent, and inclined toward ever greater organization. This may make it possible to make the divine-world relationship more intelligible. Recent views in science support an understanding of the universe as an entity whose processes are imbued with mystery and make the time propitious for rapprochement between science and theology. The time is right for perspectives informed by what is known scientifically and also sensitive to the religious dimensions of reality.[37]

Belief in the Creator Spirit gives a perspective that is consonant with the biblical witness and new understandings of the universe. The doctrine of the Spirit may provide a conceptual way for understanding the continuing creation. Spirit is the power that transcends and operates within nature, guiding it to its destiny. Theology, informed by scientific insight, has a framework for dealing with questions of origins.[38] Theology and science can be better integrated with the help of Spirit. The dynamic order that we are glimpsing in science calls out for understanding in terms of the wisdom and creativity of God. On the horizon is a reinvigorated natural theology based on the life-giving work of the Spirit.[39]

A certain correspondence exists between belief in creation and the scientific picture. Both posit a creation event, an incredible singularity, that issued in the dynamic process we call nature. It is not easy to account for the existence of the world on naturalistic grounds nowadays. The big bang calls for a nonnatural explanation. Why the world even exists is a mystery. How could the universe have come into being apart from creation? Thus science today points us to a Creator. Spirit has the power of creation and the energy for the creation event. The Spirit is the temporal first cause of the world, which had its beginning in time.[40]

Beyond that, the orderliness of the world is amazing—especially the capacity of nature to produce living, conscious, personal beings. This is not a question only of complex phenomena such as the eye or the brain, but of a world order that produces intelligent life. A power of creativity is at work in the universe, which can be viewed as a creaturely perichoresis of dynamic systems echoing the trinitarian mystery. Apart from divine intelligence, it is very hard to account for it.[41]

The term *creation* is firmly and mistakenly fixed in people's minds as referring to the initial creative event, not to subsequent history and developments. People too often have the impression that God created the world and then let it run more or less on its own, as though God was active in the world's beginning but not subsequently. As a result the action of the Spirit in natural history is eclipsed.

The world has a history and a destiny as well as a beginning. It has a beginning, a middle and an end. If we were aware of this, a door would open for relating the Spirit to the natural processes studied by science. Neglecting this truth, on the other hand, prevents us from interpreting the processes of development in a meaningful way religiously. It is possible to transcend the fruitless debates between creationism and evolutionism by linking the Spirit with continuing creation and natural history.[42]

The link of Spirit with nature is most convincing in relation to the serendipitous creativity that seems to be at work in nature. *Serendipity* refers to the tendency of natural processes to produce more than would be expected from development based on chance and to be moving in the direction of increasingly complex forms. This is especially true in the appearance of the human race and in the trajectories toward humanization within nature. There appears to be much fine-tuning of detail in the natural process which favors the rise of humanity. Nature seems to be biased toward our existence, and humanity in turn may be the clue to what is happening in nature.[43]

Darwinism has much to say about how natural selection preserves and refines organisms, once they have appeared, but it sheds less light on how and why positive new features originate. The origin of species is the problem, and theology can help with it. It helps by identifying the power of the Spirit as that which brings order out of chaos and summons forth ever higher forms of life. The Spirit is the perfecting source of the dynamism evident in the cosmos. Natural processes reveal the orderliness of the physical world and show many signs of divine intelligence. The work of the Spirit is almost visible in the dynamics of natural occurrence and in the sequence of forms.

Although scientists are methodologically loath to acknowledge that nature is dependent on something higher than itself, for so complex a world to have uncaused existence and undirected history would be nearly unintelligible. The idea of the creative Spirit at work in nature has much plausibility, because it can account for the teleology that has been creating the preconditions of a life-filled world. At every stage the Spirit creates conditions for cooperation and community.[44]

Moltmann summarizes: "The Spirit is the principle of creativity on all levels of matter and life. She creates new possibilities and in these anticipates new designs and blueprints for material and living organisms. In this sense the Spirit is the principle of evolution."[45]

As a theologian untrained in science, I must listen to scientists who name the conditions necessary for the emergence of life and for its continuance. They speak of the initial heat of the big bang, the distribution of gases, the weight of neutrinos, the total mass of the universe, the value of certain constants, the force of gravity, the strong nuclear force, the temperature of the interior of stars, the constancy of climate, the salinity of oceans, the depth of the ionosphere, the rate of expansion, the formation of elements, the particle-antiparticle ratio, and so forth. They say that a small change in physical conditions would have resulted in an uninhabitable world. From this I conclude that the world seems to be fine-tuned for life and to have known (in a manner of speaking) that we were coming and were supposed to be coming. The world itself bears witness to a Creator who is interested in human beings and to a power capable of producing them.

The concept of Spirit active in creation makes sense as a power at work, supervising and fine-tuning the world. It seems unlikely that life could have come about by chance. A few of the preconditions might have come about by chance, but not so many of them. There seems to be a power at work in the immensities of time and space which values human persons. This is not just any world—it is a world right for life and a world designed for us.[46] The world is just too complex to be explained as a product of mindless forces. The signs of intelligence are too strong for that. Biological life, for example, requires too much information for physical causes to have generated it. The naturalistic outlook stumbles over many such realities.[47]

The argument from design has taken on new life in our day. It has always been a popular argument, because few have been able to accept that the universe is the product of chance. Recent science has only strengthened this conviction. It has become even more difficult to accept on purely naturalistic grounds such realities as human freedom, openness, creativity, rationality and sensitivity to aesthetic, moral and religious values. Something in nature is moving things from simple to complex, from nonliving to living, from unconscious to conscious life, from animal to human. It is difficult to account for this without reference to the Spirit.

The scientific outlook presents a dynamic picture of a world of entities involved in change. And it is natural to view God the Spirit as continually creating, ceaselessly active in processes of the natural world, directing and fine-tuning. This understanding sheds light on the delight God takes in the world and its abundant variety. What a splendid open-endedness, what a remarkable ecology of free creatures! Humans become for God a responsive partner to whom he can in turn respond.

Spirit can be viewed as a ballet dancer who leaps into the air and lands in perfect balance in relation to a partner. In God we live and move and have our being. He is like an ocean containing the world, like a boundless sea environing it on every side. Our time is within God's time, our space within his space. God has access to the world from every point that is open and subject to the Spirit that pervades it. The whole world process is like the unfolding music of a divine composer.[48]

The Spirit animates and interpenetrates the world, which is not a mechanistic order. Spirit broods over the waters and sustains the world. Divine creativity is everywhere active, forming new possibilities and patterns. It fosters interaction and presides over the systems of life.

The universe is not closed but open to God and to the future. Creation is not finished until it has reached its goal. God transcends the world as its Creator but is also immanent in the world as its perfecter through long developments. Theology can understand the natural order in a new context: Spirit is the creative ground of all new possibilities. It is God that gives the world a future and the Spirit that brings it to pass.[49]

The Anthropic Principle
On the sixth day God made humans in his image and likeness. Here

is a creature capable of having a relationship with God and able to mirror the love of the Trinity in social relationships. Not only the Bible but also our own observations place humans in a special position. The universe is finely tuned to bring forth human life, and the system is oriented to its emergence. There is a contrivance at work that not only favors life but indeed favors personal, moral, spiritual life.

The process has gone much further than would reasonably be expected on a naturalistic basis. It could have stopped with animals, which in order to survive and flourish would need to know aspects of the workings of the environment, but not what we know. Nature did not stop with animals but proceeded to come up with creatures with the capacity for religion and philosophy, art and music, literature and morality. What a rich surplus to produce a creature who searches for meaning, for beauty, for intelligibility! The existence of such a creature is remarkable—a rational and personal, moral and spiritual, free and aesthetic creature. Theology declares that humanity is the goal of creation; science must agree. For both, humanity is the glory and goal of the process.[50]

It is extraordinary that sentient, conscious, thinking, moral and spiritual beings should exist. Imagine a creature who can speak, use symbols, employ language, make sentences, reason—so different from other animals qualitatively as well as quantitatively. It is hardly what one would expect from a purely material process. We seem to be the work of something different from mere natural causation. The likelihood of our happening is small in terms of natural or random process.[51] What does make sense of it is the Spirit, who wants such a creature to come into existence. The psalmist sensed this:

> It was you who formed my inward parts;
>> you knit me together in my mother's womb.
> I praise you, for I am fearfully and wonderfully made.
>> Wonderful are your works;
> that I know very well. (Ps 139:13-14)

The universe has produced a creature able to understand the process that created it. It is a marvel to think that the world can be comprehended at all, but even more marvelous that *we* can grasp its purpose.

The process has produced a creature who is able to look into the intelligibility of the process itself. Though children of the system, we are semitranscendent to it and able to reflect on it.

The gift of intelligence is a fact of great significance. How can it be an accident? Paul Davies comments, "Through conscious beings, the universe has generated self-awareness. This can be no trivial detail, no minor byproduct of mindless, purposeless forces. We are truly meant to be here." It makes good sense to interpret the world and humanity in a religious way. We are not simply intelligent animals but the goal toward which the process has been aiming all along.[52]

A good deal of suffering has been involved in creating after this fashion. Life depends on regularities of nature. Minor variations in them could bring the human species to an end. The water that makes life possible can also drown us. There are rules in place that hurt us if they are violated. Our lives occur in an environment that can turn against us. The created order is an expression of God's love but entails suffering too. There is waste, there are dead ends. Higher levels emerge amidst pain and death.

We feel the created order is a good order, an order in which high values can be realized. We assume they could not have been realized in less costly ways. We fall back on our faith that God is at work in the situation to bring about his purposes. Jesus said, "My Father is still working, and I also am working" (Jn 5:17). The process of nature involves sacrifices. Nature is unfinished and groans in the pangs of childbirth. A cross is woven into its creation.

For some these ideas may involve a new way of thinking of things. Such a framework posits a slower divine strategy for forming human persons than we have previously imagined and envisages a process where death was operative long before human sin (at least) entered the world. It requires us to think of death in different senses: death as the termination of life, which is part of the created order, and death as the ending of human life in fear and guilt, which is not. It suggests that Adam, had he not sinned, would still have reached the end of life and entered God's presence; however, he would not have died the way sinners die, with a troubled conscience.[53]

The Human Spirit

Having made the earth habitable, Spirit called forth living creatures. God breathed into man's nostrils and gave him life (Gen 2:7). God made human beings living images of God, with the capacity to relate to him and hear his word. He made creatures who could live in relationship with God. He brought into being a human "I" capable of responding to a divine "Thou." Spirit, who facilitates God's relationship with the world, called forth a creature capable of loving God, a personal subject whose nature is to engage the world and its Maker.

As spirit, as persons, we are creatures of God's Spirit. The Spirit has brought forth a human spirit and created the possibility of a dialogue with itself: the Spirit "bears witness" with our spirit (see Rom 8:16; 1 Cor 2:11). Humankind has spirit by nature, not only through redemption. Spirit is fundamental to human identity. This is what makes a relationship with God possible: the created human spirit can encounter the uncreated divine Spirit. The Spirit of God graces us with a capacity to know and respond to God's initiative.[54]

Though everywhere present, God is nowhere more present than in human beings. Because of our intelligence, our deeper and richer experiences, our freedom and openness to God, we stand at the pinnacle of creation and serve as a fuller dwelling place for God than other forms of life do. Created in God's image, we bear a resemblance to the divine Subject and are able to be more conscious of the divine presence. Though we reverence God's presence in all creation, we do so especially in human beings. They are of more value than many sparrows because they have spirit that can reach out to Spirit and experience God in creaturely life. We are by our creation naturally religious. We are constructed so as to be able to see God's hand at work and interpret events religiously. As spirit, we are made for encountering God and responding to his love. The greatest issue is whether when the Spirit approaches human spirits, he receives a welcome or not.[55]

One encounters the Spirit not only in religion but in experiences of every kind. God is in the love we feel for one another. God is present in the give-and-take of relationships. God comes in the compassion we feel in the midst of brokenness. The Spirit is not restricted to religious spaces; he is the giver of life itself and present in all aspects of it.

> The breadth and depth of experience that may mediate holy mystery is genuinely inclusive. It embraces not only, and in many instances not even primarily, events associated with explicitly religious meaning such as church, word, sacraments, and prayer, although these are obviously intended as mediations of the divine. Since the mystery of God undergirds the whole world, the wide range of what is considered secular or just plain ordinary human life can be grist for the mill of experience of Spirit-Sophia, drawing near and passing by.[56]

The direction of Christian existence is to become Christlike, to enter with him into union with God and to become more aware of the liberty of the children of God. Having been born of the flesh, we need to be born of the Spirit (Jn 3:5). Now with a psychic body, we are destined to receive a spiritual body (1 Cor 15:44). Spirit is leading the natural world to a higher condition. Creation is destined to obtain the glorious freedom of the children of God (Rom 8:22). Matter is becoming spirit. It is not going to regress into entropy but is on the march toward resurrection. The purpose of cosmogenesis is Christogenesis; the goal of creation is new creation in Christ.

The Risk of Freedom

Suffering and struggle are involved in the creaturely process. Anxiety, loneliness, limitation, temptation are all part of it. We are not protected from challenges and trials. This is not a struggle-free world order. God wills good for the creature, but also a creature who corresponds with God in terms of love. Only a free creature can fulfill such a destiny. It cannot be preprogrammed. Alongside the freedom to love is the freedom not to love. Alongside the freedom to be responsible is a freedom to be slothful and disobedient.

God took risks in creating this sort of a world. Evil is not even only of human making. Genesis shows us that even in the act of creation God confronted formlessness and darkness and had to establish a life-sustaining order against it. There is a vulnerability and fragility to the creation, and part of our calling as human beings is to join with

God in preserving it in the face of dark possibilities.[57]

Humans are unique among creatures in their openness to new possibilities. They are free to move beyond present situations and experience the world in ever new ways. Much less limited by inherited factors than animals, more malleable and adaptable than they, we are spirit.

Though we are already human, there is a sense in which we are still becoming human. As Orthodoxy says, though we are created in the image of God, we have still to attain the likeness of God. We are always on the move and never wholly satisfied. The finite world cannot satisfy us completely, because we are spirit and directed toward a goal that lies beyond the world. As God's kindred spirits, we find our hearts restless until they rest in him. Our goal is to participate in the filial relationship between Father and Son.

God's promises are affirmative in Christ, but he longs to hear the "amen" from our lips (2 Cor 1:20). God is a lover wanting to be loved. He awaits a response to the love that gave us being. Having said, "I love you," God asks, "Do you love me?"—and gives us countless chances to say yes. God delights in hearing the yes that Mary, the mother of Jesus, gave him long ago: Yes, I love you, Lord; I put my life in your hands.[58]

Such beings are both a wonderful and a risky experiment. The freedom that makes yes possible also makes no possible. To the invitation of love, one may respond gladly or refuse. Forced love is a contradiction in terms, and God does not force his love on us. God took risks in the decision to make significantly free creatures. Though he does not abandon creatures to their own choices when they fall, God also does not stop them from deviating from his purposes and the consequences. There was a risk in granting independence to the creature, but it was a risk required for the fulfillment of God's plan.[59]

Human beings are placed in a position in which it is possible to be aware of God or not be aware, to respond to God or not to respond. We have been placed at the right epistemic distance from God to make it a real decision. From this point we can move toward God or turn away.

The evidence for God's reality is sufficient but not excessive. We can move into God's presence or choose to go the other way. We may decide to immerse ourselves in the material world and live apart from God. We may try to secure our life as a response to the anxiety we feel in the face of our mortality.

Indeed, this possibility has become the common choice. Rather than anchoring our lives in God's love and finding our security there, we have moved in the opposite direction, resisting God's call and refusing to go forward with him. We have placed our trust in the creature more than in God and have embarked on a path to self-destruction. The defiant no of humanity has had terrible consequences, and thus our movement from divine image to divine likeness has been made much more difficult.[60]

The Spirit grieves and suffers with creation, not only with those sufferings involved in natural processes but also in the new ways brought about by sin. Because of it creation groans in travail, but Spirit keeps hope alive in humanity even in the midst of suffering. Such sufferings are the birth pangs of a new creation, when we along with creation are united with the life of God. Despite everything, Spirit persists toward the goal of freeing us along with the universe (Rom 8:23).

The origin of evil is a great mystery, but it will be resolved—not altogether now, but in the future by the action of God. The world is incomplete and unredeemed at present, and we can find no adequate answer to evil in its totality. This will require the fulfillment glimpsed in the resurrection of Jesus Christ, where God takes responsibility for the world and offers humanity hope.

In the meantime, providence often has a scandalous appearance. Babies are massacred in Bethlehem with no one to rescue them. God's Son cries out in agony in Gethsemane and from the cross—and hears silence. God's heart is broken, but he does not act in the hoped-for way. There is something posing a threat to God's rule, to a certain extent limiting what God can do as ruler of the world. Therefore God does not now eliminate suffering but redeems by means of it.[61]

Human destructiveness wreaks havoc on the world of nature also. As shaper of the environment, Spirit is ecologist par excellence, forming and sustaining all habitable space. The Spirit makes the earth rejoice and cares about the natural world as well as human history. Spirit vivifies the cosmos and gives the universe its order and beauty. The world is filled with its energy. There is no split between nature and history, because creation itself (nature and history) is destined to share the glory of God.

This is why it is practically blasphemous to do violence to that which has been made habitable. The universe is not divine but is filled with God's presence. The destruction of nature is hurtful to the God who formed it and loves it. The Spirit suffers along with nature and struggles against powers that despoil. God delights in creation and grieves over its despoliation.

This does not mean that the Spirit will rescue us by unilateral action from what we have done. Spirit-shaped ecology does not take away the freedom of those who are threatening it. Though sharing the pain, Spirit does not rescue us from the consequences of our actions. Ecological damage is our doing, and we will suffer the consequences. We are trustees of the earth and fellow creatures with its inhabitants. Spirit calls us to ecological consciousness. We are dependent on nature and belong to the natural order. It is not simply an object for domination and exploitation, but the Spirit's project, to be redeemed along with us. Nature is our home, blessed by God who took flesh, and it is destined for renewal.[62]

Spirit is a beloved guest in our hearts, but not only there. He was at work in the beginning, presiding over the world, turning chaos into cosmos, bringing life out of death and beauty out of ugliness. Spirit is at work now in the far reaches of the cosmos. Let us not forget that the power that brought the universe into being is the power at work in our lives, the power that can change ugliness into something beautiful for God.[63]

THREE

SPIRIT &
CHRISTOLOGY

*A*NOINTING BY THE SPIRIT is central for understanding the person and work of Jesus—more central than theology has normally made it. Christology must not lack for pneumatology. The Gospel narratives portray the Spirit as working actively in every phase of Jesus' life and mission. The title "Christ" itself signifies anointing—in this case by the Spirit. Jesus is the Christ, the Anointed One, and therefore he said when inaugurating his mission in Nazareth, "The Spirit of the Lord is upon me, because he has anointed me to bring good news to the poor" (Lk 4:18). Jesus was a man of the Spirit. Peter sums it up: "God anointed Jesus of Nazareth with the Holy Spirit and with power; . . . he went about doing good and healing all who were oppressed by the devil, for God was with him" (Acts 10:38). The theme is caught by John: God "gives the Spirit without measure" to Jesus (Jn 3:34). It may be that if this truth is given its due, we will gain insight into the person and work of Christ. To hint at the result, it offers a "last Adam Christology" in which Jesus is empowered by the Spirit to recapitulate the human journey and bring about humanity's fulfillment.[1]

In the past theology has preferred to think in terms of Logos Christology. By that I mean it has chosen to interpret the event of Jesus Christ in terms of the divine Logos becoming flesh, in preference to other ways. Logos Christology towers over the other interpretive possibilities. It should not do so. The term *Logos* is used only in the Fourth Gospel, and Logos Christology became central because this was a category prevalent in the context of the church's early development. It served theology well in the Greek world. But it eclipsed other possibilities, including Spirit Christology.

Just as there has been neglect of the Spirit as Creator, there has been neglect concerning the work of the Spirit in relation to Christ. The effect of such neglect has been to exalt Christ above Spirit and direct attention away from certain aspects of Christ's work as the last Adam, representative of the human race.

I have a suggestion. Let us see what results from viewing Christ as an aspect of the Spirit's mission, instead of (as is more usual) viewing Spirit as a function of Christ's. It lies within the freedom of theology to experiment with ideas.[2]

I am not suggesting a rejection of Logos Christology, only contesting its dominance over other models. It is understandable historically why theology would prefer Logos over Spirit Christology. There was the fear of adoptionism (the heresy that saw Christ as only a Spirit-filled man), and there was the apologetic attraction of Logos in the context of Hellenism. But we are not driven by these factors now, and we must not emphasize one biblical idea to diminish another, especially when the result is one-sidedness in our thinking.[3]

It is simply not right to emphasize the descent of the Logos and ignore the work of the Spirit in the Son. Yet it is striking how systematic theologies, in explicating the divine-human person of Christ, forget altogether about the Spirit. It was anointing by the Spirit that made Jesus "Christ," not the hypostatic union, and it was the anointing that made him effective in history as the absolute Savior. Jesus was ontologically Son of God from the moment of conception, but he became Christ by the power of the Spirit. When Satan tempted him to misuse his powers, the Son refused, choosing the path of dependence on the Spirit.[4]

The Almighty has inserted himself into history and humanity in Jesus—as weak, powerless and dependent on the Spirit—in order to become what we were meant to be, the communion of God and humanity. By the Spirit he has also become through resurrection the firstfruits of a new humanity. As a result of his assuming our human nature as last Adam, Jesus has created a new human situation ("there is a new creation," 2 Cor 5:17). As a result, we all in union with Christ by the power of the Spirit are enabled to participate in divine life. By faith and baptism we enter the new human situation by virtue of solidarity with the One by whom it was accomplished by God. The last Adam has fulfilled the destiny of humanity by recapitulation and will bring it to its destined position in the life of God.[5]

By taking on our nature and becoming human, Jesus raised humanity to the level of the Son in relation to the Father. God has made us alive together with Christ and seated us with him in heavenly places (Eph 2:4-7). As the Athanasian Creed says, in Jesus Christ humanity has been assumed into God (par. 35). A door has been opened for humanity to enter God's presence, transformed and glorified. God, having united himself to humanity, invites us into unity with God, which is the destiny of creation. In Christ the last Adam, first of all, the goal is realized—the divine is joined to human nature. And through the Spirit, second, the divinization of the world is beginning to be realized. In Christ, humanity is elevated to the life of God. What was intended in creation is accomplished by incarnation. By sharing flesh and blood, he has become the inauguration of a new humanity. Our healing has been accomplished by God's becoming human and restoring our brokenness from within his incarnate human life. All this is made efficacious by the Spirit, because the power that raised Christ is now at work in us.[6]

The point to stress here is that the Spirit is more central to the story of Jesus than theology has usually acknowledged. It was by the Spirit that Jesus was conceived, anointed, empowered, commissioned, directed and raised up. We emphasize God's sending the Son and must not lose the balance of a double sending. God sends both Son and Spirit. Irenaeus spoke of them as God's two hands, implying a joint mission (*Against Heresies* 4.20.1). The relationship is dialectical. The Son is sent in the power of the Spirit, and the Spirit is poured out by the risen Lord. The missions are intertwined and equal; one is not major and the other minor. It is not right to be Christocentric if being Christocentric means subordinating the Spirit to the Son. The two are partners in the work of redemption.[7]

Universal Preparation

This chapter falls into two major parts: Spirit Christology and its relevance for the work of Christ. We begin by placing Christology in the context of the Spirit's global operations, of which incarnation is the culmination. In a nutshell: "the true light, which enlightens everyone, was coming into the world" (Jn 1:9). Luke gives us a hint of this in his birth narrative. He describes the Spirit as hovering over Mary in a manner that reminds us of the Spirit that brooded over the waters of creation in the beginning (Lk 1:35). Luke is telling us that the Spirit who brought about the birth of Jesus has always been present and working in the world. Spirit is thus the source of creation *and* redemption. Active in creation, Spirit is active also in steering the world toward the goal of union with God.

Spirit has always longed to make human beings the friends of God, sons and daughters alongside the Son by adoption. Spirit longs to fill every heart with love and always has in mind participation in God. What is being offered by Jesus' birth is the same grace that has always been there since the foundation of the world and now is being decisively manifested. In this baby we glimpse not just creation, but new creation.

The Old Testament stories of Melchizedek and Job show that grace was prevenient and faith was possible even for them as pagans living outside Israel and before Christianity. Long before Moses, long before Christ, the heavens were proclaiming the glory of God. Hope did not begin to be a human possibility with Abram, as if during thousands of years before him sinners had been abandoned to despair.

The event of incarnation is the definitive word of everlasting love by way of fulfillment. There is continuity in the work of God the Creator and God the Redeemer. God's presence is everywhere, and Spirit is preparing human hearts to know him. Spirit's activity in creation underlies his activity through Jesus Christ. The power of creation presses toward new creation. God's work in the continuing creation is not the work of an alien, but the work of the Father of Jesus. Redemption through Jesus is an action of the Spirit of life actualizing the original creative purposes of God.[8]

The Spirit's work in creation anticipates the work of redemption. The Creator Spirit brought forth intelligent creatures for communication and fellowship with God. The great musician who composed the music of the spheres wanted creatures capable of appreciating more dimensions of the sound. Therefore the world has been populated with creatures capable of hearing God's word and responding. One can almost anticipate the incarnation from what went before. One might expect God, if the world is his self-expression, to make his purposes further known and communicate with his creatures. Such a perspective leads us to expect a word that would address the human condition.[9]

Paul states that God has never left himself without witness (Acts 14:17). He worked with Melchizedek as well as Abraham, with Philistines as well as Israelites (Amos 9:7). As Irenaeus put it, "God by various dispensations comes to the rescue of humankind" (*Against Heresies* 3.12.13). The Spirit is ever working to orient people, wherever they are, to the mystery of divine love.[10] Nowhere in history is grace completely absent. God has never failed to draw sinners to himself from the beginning of time. There is one world, and God has a claim on it. There is a history of grace that has now reached its climax in Jesus Christ, the sacrament of salvation, the revelation of God's unambiguous love for the world.[11]

Preparation in Israel

God created a risky world when he made it his goal to hear a yes of love from creatures. It meant that a no was also possible. So when human beings turned from their lover, God had to let them go in grief.

Love lets children leave the Father's house to seek fulfillment where, ironically, it cannot be found. The father of the prodigal did not force his son to stay home. In spite of the pain to them both, he allowed his son to seek a life of his own. Love is not forced on the beloved, who is allowed freedom to make his own choices, even if it means siding with the darkness.[12]

The decision grieved the Father, but he did not give up. Instead he bared his holy arm to save the lost (Is 59:16). God shouldered his own responsibility for evil by making salvation available and creating hope. Though human disobedience was a significant cause of evil, God, having permitted evil, did not abandon the world but sent Son and Spirit to redeem it. God did not leave us to perish but reissued the invitation to participate in glory.

A history of the Spirit preceded Jesus. Ancient Israel first experienced the Spirit as the shaper of a nation. The Old Testament often refers to spiritual gifts that sustain community: gifts of courage for leaders, wisdom for teachers, creativity for poets, inspiration for prophets. In Israel's early history, the nation experienced the power of the Spirit again and again, delivering it from danger and distress. The Spirit rescued Israel and held it together as a people.[13]

But as time went on, the hope grew for a greater outpouring of Spirit in the future. The prophet Isaiah announced that the Spirit would rest upon God's servant and through him mercy and justice would flow to all nations. Because of the Spirit, this servant would be instrumental in the coming of God's kingdom. Other prophets such as Joel also spoke of the Spirit's being poured out from heaven in an unheard-of intensity (Joel 2:28). Through such prophets, hope was born for an outpouring of the Spirit and an anointed servant of God. The hope began to be articulated that the activity of the Spirit among the people of Old Testament times would transfer to an anointed servant who would implement God's ultimate mission. Isaiah put it in a nutshell: "The Spirit of the LORD shall rest on him" (Is 11:2; 42:1). There would come a uniquely equipped charismatic leader and a special anointing of the whole community. Israel's messianic hope included the expectation of Pentecost.[14]

According to Jewish belief during the period of the second temple, the Spirit was withdrawn because of the sins of the people. There was an "echo of his voice" *(baṭ qôl)* but not the Spirit. The birth narrative in Luke is alive with manifestations of the Spirit in order to signal a reversal. It signifies that the Spirit has returned and the time of barrenness is over. The Spirit has begun a new activity, heralding end-time salvation. God's wisdom (the Son) is pitching a tent in history, and God's presence (the Spirit) has come to dwell in new and unexpected ways.[15]

Jesus and the Spirit

A central claim and early attempt to understand Jesus makes reference to the Spirit. Jesus saw his own ministry in these terms. He had an anointing to preach good news to the poor and rescue people from all sorts of bondage (Lk 4:18). He declared, "If it is by the Spirit of God that I cast out demons, then the kingdom of God has come to you" (Mt 12:28). Jesus was conscious of a joint operation with the Spirit to bring God's kingdom near. To do this he was anointed with Spirit and power (Acts 10:38).[16]

This was the first impression many people had of Jesus. They marveled at the way he taught with authority and healed the sick. It made them think of him as a prophet. Some said, "A great prophet has risen among us!" (Lk 7:16). Peter said what everyone knew, that Jesus was "a man attested . . . by God with deeds of power, wonders, and signs that God did through him" (Acts 2:22).[17]

The Gospels go out of the way to connect Jesus with the Spirit on all kinds of occasions in his life—birth, baptism, temptation, preaching, healing, exorcisms, death and resurrection. Overall they reveal Jesus as a gift of the Spirit. He was the Son of God who nevertheless emptied himself to live in solidarity with others, as dependent on the Spirit as any of them.

The Gospels present Jesus as dependent on the Spirit. They depict the Spirit as helping him trace out his human path. Spirit prepared for his coming, was instrumental in his birth, guided him through life and by his death and resurrection opened up the door to salvation for everyone. The Son emptied himself, was dependent on the Spirit and suffered out of his love for us. The Gospel writers want their readers to identify with the Spirit-filled Jesus as a paradigm and live out of this very baptism in the Spirit.[18]

Considering how central the Spirit was in his experience, Jesus spoke about it rather seldom. In other ways, however, he bore witness to it. He demonstrated the reality of the Spirit, if he did not develop a doctrine. He did not minister in word only but with power. Jesus preferred to act out of the power of the Spirit rather than to speak about it. Even today, the way to teach about the Spirit is to live in dependence on the Spirit.[19]

At the beginning of Luke's Gospel, the angel says to Mary, "The Holy Spirit will come upon you, and the power of the Most High will overshadow you" (Lk 1:35). Reminiscent of Genesis 1:2, this language indicates that the conception of Jesus is an act of creation, the sign in fact of new creation. It tells us that God is powerfully at work in Jesus' birth. It is not a sexual reference—the angel is not speaking of a begetting of a child by the gods. It is the picture of the same Spirit, who was and is active in creation, as being active now in new creation. The virginal conception speaks of the coming of Christ as a gift of the Spirit. The Spirit's earlier creative activity is coming to a head in his birth. This child, more than a fulfillment of human love, is the very embodiment of messianic expectations.

Jesus is already anointed by the Spirit as Christ in Mary's womb. The human vehicle for the Son of God is being readied. The event will mean a fresh start for humanity. Humanity will be restored to communion with God. Spirit is prominent in the birth because it points forward to Pentecost and new creation. This explains why prophecy and praise abound in response to Jesus' birth.[20]

We know little about Jesus as a youth except that he grew in grace and wisdom (Lk 2:40-52). On one occasion in the temple at the age of twelve, he revealed great understanding. It is likely that Jesus was becoming more aware of his special relationship with God and his unique calling. He had to be about his Father's business in the temple—this awareness shows the Spirit was with him in the formative years. Truly as the prophet had said, a Spirit of wisdom and insight rested on him.[21]

The Spirit came upon Jesus in power at baptism. As he was about to begin his ministry, the Baptist was calling people to repentance and announcing the coming of One who would baptize with the Holy Spirit. Jesus heard him preach and responded. He must have viewed John's baptism (as John did himself) as the inauguration of something new by way of salvation, and so he allowed himself to be baptized. On that occasion he received the Holy Spirit while he was praying (Lk 3:21-22). This was his anointing as Messiah, not with oil but with Spirit. Through the waters of baptism Jesus entered into a solidarity with sinners and took their cause upon himself. In baptism he experienced God as his Father and was conscious of his own sonship. He was God's Son in a special sense but would invite others into that relationship by adoption.[22]

Being baptized in the Spirit meant he was endowed with power and equipped for mission. In this account the Spirit is pictured as a dove descending upon him. Why is this? Perhaps it is meant to remind us of how after the flood of Noah, a dove returned with a fresh olive branch in its beak. The dove symbolized the renewal of creation after judgment. In this instance the dove speaks of messianic time and new creation. It is important to note that baptism in water and baptism in Spirit coincide. The spiritual and the physical flow together. This became important for the Catholic tradition, which wants to keep the connection and give baptism a sacramental meaning. As physical birth takes place in water, new birth by the Spirit also normally takes place in water. Here we see the beginning of a sacramental principle.[23]

Following the baptism, Spirit took the initiative and drove Jesus into the wilderness to be tested. As representative of the human race, Jesus was going to have to experience what Adam suffered and conquer it. The temptations were aimed at his vocation as the anointed representative of humankind. Spirit knew that Jesus had to endure trial and repudiate all paths contrary to the Father's will. Therefore Spirit gave him wisdom to rebut Satan's deceitful questions and strength to repudiate worldly power in favor of the path of suffering and love. So it was that immediately after his baptism, Jesus began to feel the opposition that would take him to the cross. Spirit led him down the path of suffering and would not let him avoid it. Spirit does not let us avoid it either.[24]

It is important to recognize that Jesus was dependent on the Spirit. He had to rely on the Spirit's resources to overcome temptation. He was weak and human and did not know the life of undiminished deity. He suffered real attack in the temptations and was not play-acting. It was not through confidence in his own power that he put himself at risk. Victory over temptation was not achieved in his own strength. He overcame sin by the power of God and in so doing modeled the lifestyle of faith for us all. Jesus surrendered himself in trust and conquered the powers of evil by the Spirit, as we all must.[25]

According to Paul, Christ came in the likeness of sinful flesh (Rom 8:3). He did not protect himself but took on fallen human nature. As mortal and corruptible, not immortal and incorruptible, he struggled against sin. His sinlessness was really due to his relation with the Spirit, not his own deity. It was a real, not pretend, victory that he won over sin, flesh and devil. He conquered in the power of the Spirit.[26]

In becoming dependent, the Son surrendered the independent use of his divine attributes in incarnation. The Word became flesh and exercised power through the Spirit, not on its own. The Son's self-emptying meant that Jesus was compelled to rely on the Spirit. In a sense, self-emptying comes naturally to God. Creation was a kind of self-emptying when God made room for creatures. Self-emptying is characteristic of God, who is self-giving love itself. Spirit is important for understanding the kenosis. Spirit enabled Jesus to live within the limits of human nature during his life. The Son decided not to make use of divine attributes independently but experience what it would mean to be truly human. Therefore he depended on the Spirit for power to live his life and pursue his mission.[27]

Empowered for messianic vocation, Jesus inaugurated his ministry in Nazareth. It was evident that the power of the Spirit was on him for the benefit of the world. Jesus came as the Anointed One, preaching the gospel of the kingdom and performing signs of new creation. He proclaimed good news to the poor, mercy to the sick, liberty to captives, sight to the blind. By the power of the Spirit, Jesus announced a God who wills human wholeness. Therefore he went not to the righteous but to the sick and the outcast, to gather them under God's wings. By the Spirit he set people free from entrapment.

He brought them hope and liberated their relationships. Demonic powers were driven out, and creaturely life was restored. All this happened because the energies of the life-giving Spirit were at work in Jesus.[28]

A text that many find difficult actually points to the importance of Spirit for Christology. It is the verse where Jesus says that every sin can be pardoned and words against him forgiven, but "whoever speaks against the Holy Spirit will not be forgiven, either in this age or in the age to come" (Mt 12:32). What can this mean? Why would speech against the Spirit be unforgivable but not speech against the Son? The answer confirms the central role that the Spirit plays in Christology.

Blasphemy against the Spirit is serious because it involves a repudiation of the power that is making people whole in Jesus. Here God is at work delivering people, and some people are actually identifying that with Satan's work. What they are doing is negating God's work of salvation, not only for themselves but for everyone. It is unforgivable because even God's forgiveness cannot reach persons so blind.

This highlights the importance of Spirit at work in collaboration with the Son. Because the mending of creation by Son and Spirit is such a crucial move on God's part, attempts to discredit it are judged harshly. Speaking against the Spirit means refusing to celebrate the healing and saving power of God. This is a sin beyond forgiveness because it reveals a person standing deliberately outside the circle of love.

We should ask ourselves if we are on the side of the Spirit. Do we judge the tree not by its fruit but by its label and pedigree? The point is that we grieve the Spirit whenever we side, even temporarily, with powers that resist healing.[29]

The Spirit enabled Jesus to do his mighty works. Not that Jesus was a wonderworker who sought to dazzle and impress. He did not go in for easy victories based on sensations. He would not perform signs merely to satisfy curiosity or even to overcome unbelief. The purpose of his miracles was salvation in body and soul, and they were performed with a view to the kingdom. Though they did accredit his claim, the purpose of the miracles was to set people free and demonstrate that the kingdom was entering the present. They show that salvation is at work and the kingdom of God is inaugurated. They are not evidence of Christ's deity but evidence of the Spirit at work in him.[30]

Jesus' activities of liberation were good news to many but posed a threat to the political and religious status quo. The leaders found him an intolerable threat and conspired to get rid of him early on. Their answer to the invitation to life was to seek his death. It became very clear to Jesus that he would have take up a cross. "He set his face to go to Jerusalem" (Lk 9:51). The power of the Spirit would have to prepare him to give up his life. Martyrdom is a charism of the Spirit (1 Cor 13:3). Only such a gift can enable a person to serve rather than be served (Mk 10:45). The book of Hebrews explains that Jesus would be enabled to offer himself up to God through the Spirit (9:14). Spirit would empower him to confront the powers of darkness and to join the line of murdered prophets. Jesus knew it when he said, "Jerusalem, Jerusalem, the city that kills the prophets and stones those who are sent to it!" (Lk 13:34).

Jesus knew he would have to face death the same way he faced temptation—in the power of the Spirit. Though the Gospels do not say this exactly, Hebrews draws out the valid deduction. Spirit who was with Jesus from birth would be with him at the culmination. Spirit would help him to say yes to God at the moment of his greatest trial. Spirit would give him words to speak before his adversaries and help him pray the prayer of relinquishment and surrender to the will of God. As human, Jesus cried out for the cup to pass from him, but as Spirit-filled he prayed for God's will to be done. In Gethsemane he experienced a crucifixion of will before his execution. He said by the Spirit, "I am yours, Lord; I have come to do your will" (see Heb 10:7).[31]

The Spirit is also the reason the story does not end there. Jesus may have been dead, but the Spirit, power of creation, makes the dead live (Ezek 37:13-14). Spirit was the agent by which God raised Jesus up. Paul says he was "declared to be Son of God with power according to the Spirit of holiness by resurrection from the dead" (Rom 1:4 mg). Resurrection constituted the public accreditation of Jesus. The Spirit was instrumental in it, for Jesus as for us (Rom 8:11); Paul says, "God raised the Lord and will also raise us by his power" (1 Cor 6:14).

Jesus' resurrection marked the beginning of new creation and the commencement of the age to come. Death will no longer have the last word. There is hope for humankind. The cross happened because of the Son's fidelity to God's call by the power of the Spirit. In the Son, the Father participated in the sufferings of the world. The Crucified One was not abandoned in death but was raised to life. The victory was won by the power of love. Spirit, who led Jesus to self-surrender, brought him back from death.

In Jesus the Spirit experienced an undistorted acceptance of God's love and found the ideal receptacle for God's self-communication as the Son. Thus all of the creating and redeeming activities of the Spirit reached their goal in him. The kingdom was inaugurated, the new order had begun, the power could be poured out.[32]

Recovering Spirit Christology

Let us not diminish the importance of the Spirit for Christology. Logos Christology is not the whole story; indeed, if we exaggerate it we may eclipse the mission of the Spirit and effect its subordination to that of the Son. Among other risks, we may strip the self-emptying of the Son of its radicalness and even put his true humanity in jeopardy. At least the early church had an excuse for favoring Logos Christology. There was an apologetic advantage to Logos Christology then, but not today. There is no reason for us to continue to let Logos Christology dominate and marginalize other dimensions.[33]

I am not recommending adoptionism. Against the likes of Geoffrey Lampe and John Hick, I hold that Jesus was more than mere man endowed with the Spirit. My point is that Spirit Christology and Logos Christology are complementary, not antithetical. One complements without replacing the other. Logos Christology is ontologically focused, while a Spirit Christology is functionally focused, but the two work together. Generally speaking, Logos addresses the Person of Jesus while Spirit addresses his work. The deity of Christ is seen only in his humanity as filled by the Spirit, and the incarnation is viewed only on the redemptive-historical plane. Spirit Christology draws us into the life of Jesus and helps us avoid abstract thinking.[34]

We need to make room for the Spirit in our Christology in order to give both Son and Spirit their due. The mission of one is not subordinated to the mission of the other—there is a mutual and reciprocal relationship between them. Neither Son nor Spirit ought to be subordinated to the other. Each can be viewed in terms of the mission of the other. Since I have been stressing the role of Jesus in the mission of the Spirit, perhaps I should add that the Spirit can also be seen the other way around. Apart from the Son, Spirit can be vague and undefined. It is the Spirit of Jesus Christ that we are talking about. If it is true that the Spirit empowers the Son, it is also true that the Son is the criterion of manifestations of Spirit. The relationship is reciprocal through and through.

I realize that "Spirit Christology" might not be the best term to use. *Spirit* is used by liberals to refer to the divine element in Jesus, not to the third Person of the Trinity dwelling in him. "Spirit Christology" as used by them refers to an inspirational, not an incarnational, Christology.[35] When I refer to Spirit Christology, I do so in an orthodox way that preserves the trinitarian distinctions. Spirit Christology enriches but does not replace Logos Christology. It enriches Logos Christology by doing greater justice to the role of Spirit in Christ. It gives better recognition to the missions of both the Son and the Spirit. It neither exaggerates nor diminishes the role of either Person. I am indebted to Eastern Orthodox theology, which has always maintained that Western traditions have diminished the role of the Spirit by giving the Son an ontic role and the Spirit only a noetic one.[36]

God uses his two hands in the work of redemption. Neither is subordinate to the other; neither supplants the other. My desire is to emphasize that the Spirit is active in every aspect of the messianic mission—not as a substitute for Christ nor as an instrument of Christ, but as the third Person of the Trinity. As the bond of love that binds Father and Son together in eternity, Spirit also sustains the relationship between the earthly Jesus and his heavenly Father on earth and actualizes it progressively throughout his walk with God. The Spirit prepares, constitutes and communicates the mystery of the incarnation. From birth through baptism and ministry, culminating in death and resurrection, the Son lived in an intimate and reciprocal relationship with the Spirit. His death and resurrection constitute the event in which the Father saves humanity through Son and Spirit. This is a trinitarian event in which the three Persons experience the mutuality and reciprocity characteristic of the triune God. God is not an immutable essence dwelling in metaphysical isolation from the world. God is self-defined in this historical action.

Salvation by Recapitulation

But what does Spirit Christology signify? What light does it shed on our understanding of Jesus' mission? Let us explore now the meaning of Jesus' saying to the disciples that it would benefit them if he went away, "for if I do not go away, the Advocate will not come to you; but if I go, I will send him to you" (Jn 16:7). Why did the outpouring of the Spirit have to wait until Jesus died and was glorified? What was it about those events that made them a turning point in the history of redemption? How did the mission of Jesus trigger Pentecost?

Paul says that had the rulers of this age known what Jesus' death and resurrection would do, they would not have crucified the Lord of glory (1 Cor 2:6-8). What I am going to propose now is an interpretation of the work of Christ stimulated by the reappropriation of Spirit Christology. The heart of it is that the Spirit facilitated the Christ event in order to save humanity by way of *recapitulation*. This is what atonement looks like when Christology is placed within the mission of the Spirit.[37]

Thomas F. Torrance attempts to name it:

Until he [Jesus] had sanctified himself and perfected in our human nature his own offering for all men, until he had made the once and for all sacrifice to take away sin, until he had vanquished the powers of darkness and overcome the sharpness of death, until he had ascended into heaven to present himself in propitiation before the Father, the kingdom could not be opened to believers, and the blessing of the divine Spirit could not be poured out upon human flesh or be received by sinful men.[38]

In other words, something happened through the total journey of Jesus that literally changed the world and opened the door wide to union with God.

The participatory journey of the Son by the Spirit was what was necessary for God to get a grip on the world in order to redeem it. End-time salvation could not come into play until this mission was completed and this representation had taken place. There had to be the great exchange in which, when one died all died, and the fallen race is raised up to sit with Christ in heavenly places. God had to be represented among human beings, and humanity had to be represented before God. Only this would give momentum to world redemption. It could be the turning point because it affected humanity itself and introduced a new reality into history. Jesus through the Spirit created the space for salvation to go forward, as people are baptized into his death and resurrection and a new community appears which prefigures the kingdom of God. With the glorification of Jesus a process began which will end in the divinization of the world.[39]

The model is participatory. E. P. Sanders remarks, "The prime significance which the death of Christ has for Paul is not that it provides atonement for past transgressions (although he holds the common Christian view that it does so) but that, by sharing in Christ's death, one dies to the power of sin or to the old aeon, with the result that one belongs to God. The transfer takes place by participation in Christ's death." Later he adds, "One participates in salvation by becoming one person with Christ, dying with him to sin and sharing the promise of his resurrection."[40]

The author of Hebrews tries to identify what it was about the Christ event that triggered the end times: the Son had to partake of flesh and blood, had to be tested as we are, had to experience weakness, had to learn obedience, had to bear the sins of many, had to free us from the power of death, so that he could become the source of eternal salvation (Heb 2:14-18; 4:14-16; 5:7-10). Jesus is seen as a forerunner who entered the sanctuary, the pioneer and perfecter of faith (6:19-20; 12:2).

The point is that there had to be a representation before Pentecost could happen. There had to be a participatory journey to realize God's purpose for creation and bring about reconciliation. This would be the means of grace which the Spirit could then apply to sinners to transform them.

This explains why the Spirit had to take Jesus on a representative journey for the sake of wholeness. It encourages us to seek the meaning of atonement not in a rationalistic theory but in the mighty act of God in which sin and death are annihilated and the world begins to be re-created.

This is the theme of Irenaeus and the first theory of atonement: God sent his Son in the power of the Spirit to enact a recapitulation of human history through the life, death and resurrection of Christ, which would give the human race a new start (*Against Heresies* 5.14). This is the means by which God will sum up all things in Christ (Eph 1:10). God would reestablish sovereignty over the world and redeem lost humanity by reenacting the human condition in the experience of Jesus, overcome the pitfalls and open up the future. God would bring about atonement by making Jesus head of a new humanity and in this way would restore unity with the creature. In Paul's language, God saves us by the faithfulness of Jesus Christ (Gal 2:16, 20).[41]

The Catechism sums it up:

Christ's whole life is a mystery of recapitulation. All Jesus did, said, and suffered, had for its aim restoring man to his original vocation. When Christ became incarnate and was made man, he recapitulated in himself the long history of mankind and procured for us a "short cut" to salvation, so that what we had lost in Adam, that is, being in the image and likeness of God, we might recover in Christ Jesus. For this reason Christ experienced all the stages of life, thereby giving communion with God to all men.[42]

Each stage of development and phase of history was lived through by Christ in obedience to God and dependence on the Spirit, so that the effect of Adam's sin was reversed. Through this act of representation, creation is restored. Key is Christ's representation of humanity and our incorporation into him through faith by the Spirit. The idea is that what took place in Christ paradigmatically will be applied to and realized in us. This act of atonement includes and does not replace us; it is a representation that includes rather than excludes.[43]

God effected the conversion of humanity in Jesus, who represented the race and thereby altered the human situation. In his death and resurrection, humanity de jure passed from death to life, because God has included it in the event. Its destiny has been objectively realized in Christ—what remains to be done is a human response and salvation de facto. The possibility of newness must be laid hold of by faith. Christ became what humans are, even in our condition of alienation, so that we might share his justification and victory. Paul says that when one died, all died (2 Cor 5:14). Because Jesus is a representative, others can share in his death and resurrection by the Spirit. A new situation now exists: we have only to accept what has been done and allow the Spirit to conform our lives to Christ.[44]

Much popular thinking about the atonement leaves the cross in the past (relating it to pardon) and does not see it as a dimension of the present. This misses the parallelism between Christ's experience as the last Adam and our salvation through him. Yet the interweaving of these two is a major theme of Pauline thought. The apostle actually says that in the event of death and resurrection in solidarity with us, Jesus Christ was adopted, justified, sanctified and glorified in our place. On the cross he died to sin (Rom 6:10). By the resurrection he was saved from the power of death, which now has no dominion (Acts 2:24; Rom 6:9), and was declared Son of God (Rom 1:4). He was also justified by the Spirit (1 Tim 3:16) that we too might be justified by it (Rom 4:25). In his death we die to sin (Rom 6:11). He was glorified as the last Adam in advance of our resurrection (1 Cor 15:49). Paul sees redemption as first worked out in Christ our representative, and only then in us. As a result of his vicarious humanity, we are adopted, justified, sanctified and glorified in relation to him. Christ became what we are in order that we might become what he is. We are saved by his representative journey. The redemption of Jesus Christ as the last Adam is ours by virtue of solidarity with him, into which we are drawn by the Spirit.[45]

Christ's representation is inclusive, not exclusive. It is not a transaction that affects us only in a legal way. Christ died and rose so that we might die and rise with him. What took place in him is meant to be repeated in each of us, as in baptism we die and rise with him. His dying and rising act as a magnet to draw us in. Old Adam dies in the death of Christ in order to be changed into new Adam (1 Cor 15:49). And it is the Spirit that works out this reconciliation in life.[46]

Four Gospels tell about Jesus, to help us place ourselves in the story of our representative. In the epistles the doctrine of representation is explained by the category of solidarity: Jesus represented humanity in such a way that what took place in him could be repeated in us. This is not easy for us to grasp because of our tendency toward individualist thinking. But it is not beyond us altogether. People serve us by acting on our behalf all the time. Leaders represent us in the corridors of power; doctors and engineers do for us what we cannot do for ourselves. Representation is experienced in every social group.[47]

The Son, by whom, for whom and in whom the world was created, made the decision (this is the "grace" of our Lord Jesus Christ) to partake of humanity in order to implement in history his filial relationship with the Father on our behalf. He lived a life of obedience to God in the flesh vicariously for us, realizing in his humanity what God longs for in our own, setting in motion a process of salvation and healing. Karl Rahner writes, "The effect of the hypostatic union for the humanity of the Logos consists precisely in the thing which is ascribed to all men as their goal and fulfillment, namely, the immediate vision of God which the created, human soul of Christ enjoys."[48]

God must have looked at our plight and decided on this solution. The Son would become human and live a life of obedience in the power of the Spirit, and would by resurrection enable humanity to participate in new creation. Spirit Christology helps us to take seriously the motif of the last Adam's tracing of our human path and directs our attention to a participatory model of atonement, in which the central motif is union with Christ.

I take it that Jesus became the turning point of history because he could represent the race. He could stand in our place and act for our benefit. Because of this representation, those alienated from God receive hope, and the Spirit can conform them to Christ's image. The fall into sin had propelled humanity into a vicious cycle of self-destruction, but the last Adam has given the race a new beginning. Because there was no one else able to enter the breach, the Son became flesh and broke through death and alienation. Now it is possible in the Spirit for us all to participate in the Son's obedience to God. Salvation is via union with him in his death and resurrection.[49]

Pentecost happened when it did—and could only have happened then—because Jesus had by that time completed the journey of atonement, worked out the recapitulation and become firstfruits of a new humanity. The concentration of the Spirit on Jesus alone during his earthly life would be followed by a movement to the nations. He came first only to Israel but now goes on to the world in the Spirit. The promised mission of God to gather the nations can begin, for the Spirit makes ready to transform history. Hendrikus Berkhof states, "It has to become evident that in his person and work he represented us, and that from now on, in virtue of his work, a process toward the renewal of the human race is under way. Therefore, the concentration of the representation is now followed by the centrifugal movement of the winning of people, of the spreading of the renewal everywhere."[50]

Saved by His Life
Through obedience to the Father and dependence on the Spirit, the Son of God recapitulated humanity's history. He reversed the human no that had led to our fallenness and returned the yes that was the divine purpose for humanity. He saved us not by death only, but by death and resurrection. Paul says Jesus "was handed over to death for our trespasses and was raised for our justification" (Rom 4:25). He adds, "If while we were enemies, we were reconciled to God through the death of his Son, much more surely, having been reconciled, will we be saved by his life" (Rom 5:10). Paul also writes that the Son has "abolished death and brought life and immortality to light through the gospel" (2 Tim 1:10); we are thereby "raised with him through faith in the power of God, who raised him from the dead" (Col 2:12). The point is that Jesus acted vicariously on our behalf not only in dying but in living and in rising as well. We must speak not only of the vicarious death of Christ but also comprehensively of the vicarious humanity of Christ.

To make the point stick and be sure readers attend to it, let me begin dealing with soteriology at the point of the resurrection rather than the crucifixion. Among the advantages of such an approach are opportunities to correct the neglect of the resurrection in theology and to affect the way we would regard the cross itself. Once we grasp the fact that we are saved by Christ's life, we may be open to fresh thinking about how we are saved by his death.

On that subject our thinking has gone astray. We have placed such emphasis on the legal dimension of atonement that the resurrection, which does not address that issue as framed, drops away as a saving event. The error of this is plain from the New Testament, which makes resurrection central and ties the cross to it. We say that Christ's work was "finished" on the cross, but it was not. Had Christ not been raised, we would be still in our sins and subject to death (1 Cor 15:17). It is incredible how in systematic theologies dozens of pages are given to theories of atonement (meaning the death of Christ) and hardly any to the soteriological significance of resurrection. The fact is that in certain juridical models of the atonement, resurrection has no significance for salvation. Its significance is apologetic, not soteric. It is not a saving event, only the vindication of Jesus' pre-Easter claims, in which case we cannot speak of being saved *by his life*.

The reason is not obscure. If guilt is the only issue, propitiation is the answer and resurrection the add-on. If on the other hand, death is the problem, then the resurrection is of central importance. Christ's resurrection is a saving event because death and the recapitulation of humanity require it. Again, Paul shouts that Christ "abolished death and brought life and immortality to light through the gospel" (2 Tim 1:10). The work of Christ was not primarily a legal transaction but a power event. Eastern theology grasps this point. *Both* sin and death are problems for humankind, because death entered the world with sin (Rom 5:12). Death must be dealt with if we are to be saved; therefore God saves us by the resurrection. Humanity is taken through death into resurrection by the representative act of Jesus Christ. The goal of creation, to share the glory of God, is now out in plain view.[51]

When we speak of the resurrection as a saving event, we do not see it as a bare symbol for the awakening of faith in the disciples. It refers to something that happened to the body of Jesus. In the resurrection Jesus was transformed to the life of the age to come by the power of the Spirit. By the resurrection God reversed the verdict of the cross, where Jesus' claim to authority was denied by humanity;

thus God makes hope possible for the dead. The resurrection is not just proof of Christ's divinity or confirmation of his sacrifice. It augurs the transformation of the world. By it Jesus became the cause of salvation and transformation. Those who die with him share life with him. The resurrection inaugurated—first for Jesus, then for us—the new creation. The resurrection states that the forces of evil will not prevail. It gives a glimpse of new creation and signifies a glorified existence in human nature in a new environment where what we were meant to be can be realized.[52]

Through resurrection, Paul says, Jesus "became a life-giving spirit" (1 Cor 15:45). He seems to mean that Jesus now can make possible the resurrection of the dead. With a view to atonement, the Father gave the Spirit to the Son, that he might complete a representative journey on our behalf. The Risen One now gives us the Spirit, which had previously been given to him, in order to bring us along with him on the journey that leads to God. All humanity has the potential to be the children of God, because all were included in his representation. What remains is for everyone to be reconciled to God personally and subjectively.[53]

Humanity was transformed by Christ through the power of the Spirit and can share in his representative journey through death to life. God revealed the goal of creation in Christ and offers it as a gift to us. His longing is for the divine likeness to be formed in us. Paul speaks of his fellow believers as "my little children, for whom I am again in the pain of childbirth until Christ is formed in you" (Gal 4:19). We were created in the image of God with a view to growing into the likeness to God. Though lost in Adam, the likeness is restored in Christ. Though still unfinished in us, the likeness is not unfinished in him. The incarnation anticipates the fulfillment of God's purposes for us because the new humanity has appeared in Jesus. The incarnation represents the true divine likeness, and the resurrection signifies what humans are called to become.

The Son came in veiled glory, emptied of divine prerogatives, dependent on the power of the Spirit. As the beloved Son, he surrendered his life to the Father and returned the yes that God longs to hear from the creature. Through Son and Spirit, God is leading humanity to union with himself. He wants us to share the Son's filial relationship with himself.

In Christ, God gave himself a human heart, as it were. To Jesus he said, "You are my beloved Son—I am well pleased with you" (see Mk 1:11). Jesus replied to God, "You are my Father; I have come to do your will" (see Heb 10:9). We are summoned into this relationship, to become sons and daughters in the Son. The Spirit is calling us to this tender filial love.

By his resurrection, Christ preactualized the consummation of the world. Its transformation is anticipated, and all things are sure to be made new. The Risen One is the vanguard and embodiment of the new order. Jesus prefigures what will be true for us also in the new creation. It is the seminal event, the seed from which the new reality grows.

The Lord's human body was not discarded but shared in resurrection, pointing to the salvation of the whole person. Humans are open to the future. They make plans and strive to realize goals. But we are mortal, and ultimately the future lies in God's hands. The incarnation is an event within history pointing to the goal and moving humanity toward union with God. In Christ the world has entered its final phase, and its redemption in that sense is near. In Karl Rahner's words, the incarnation and resurrection enacted "the irreversible beginning of the coming of God as the absolute future of the world." As the firstfruits of the new humanity, Jesus says, "Because I live, you also will live" (Jn 14:19).[54]

The work of the Spirit of creation converges on the incarnation of the Son, in which creation finds fulfillment. Through the incarnation we glimpse the destiny of our union with God, because it has implemented the goal of creaturely existence. One could say that the incarnation is the self-actualization of God in history. The event disclosed the triune nature and reasserted the rule of God. The true relationship of the creature to God has been realized in the incarnation of the Son. Wolfhart Pannenberg states, "Only in the light of the incarnation of the Son in our relation to God may it be said theologically that creation comes to fulfillment in us and that the whole universe was created with a view to us."[55]

Salvation by the Cross

Displaying the goal of creation by preactualizing the resurrection of the dead is not all that was accomplished through Christ. There is also the cross as a saving event whereby our brokenness is healed and our guilt canceled. There is a knowing of Christ not only in the power of his resurrection but also in the fellowship of his sufferings and our becoming like him in death (Phil 3:10).

Here we are still in the vicinity of representation and solidarity. Through incarnation, God entered deeply into the human situation to overcome all our alienation. The goal is that we be brought into unity with God and be enabled to share the divine glory. Spirit Christology invites us to view the cross differently, in the context of recapitulation and participatory journey. It gives us the opportunity to celebrate the centrality of resurrection, conceptualize the cross in terms of recapitulation and give the Spirit back its role in the work of atonement.

One common view of atonement considers the cross a propitiatory sacrifice isolated from the resurrection and from human involvement. This model results from viewing the atonement primarily in legal terms, not in the context of the representative journey of Jesus into which the Spirit is inviting us to participate. I want to challenge this way of thinking and place more emphasis on death-with-Christ and life-with-Christ, on our death to sin through the cross and our life with God through resurrection and union. The popular view is distorted, picturing the Father as judge and the Son as victim. It gives the impression that God values his honor more than he values us, and it threatens the unity of Father and Son in the work of atonement.

Before confronting the issue head-on, let me sketch an understanding of the cross in the framework of representation. The issue is delicate, and it would be good to have described an alternative before addressing it. One can view Jesus Christ as the true prodigal, who left the Father's home not as a rebel but as an obedient son. He identified with sinners in the far country, surrendered everything he had and returned home by way of the cross. Jesus became brother to the transgressors, engaging their alienation and accepting their condemnation. He did this for us all, that we might become like him and return home with him. Having taken our flesh, he made the journey as our representative empowered by the Spirit. He took humanity through the stages of fallen existence and reconciled it. In Christ God took the lost cause of a humanity that had rejected him and ruined itself. He made this cause his own and carried it through to the goal. Instead of allowing us to perish, he humbled himself and became a servant in order to save us. In becoming flesh, God turned the human situation around and started history over again. The atonement tells us that God intends to be God for us, whatever it costs him. God registers his yes decisively against the human no.[56]

Is there perhaps a representative and participatory model of atonement more plausible and biblical than the popular view? It would be a model in which God saves humanity by the representative journey of Jesus Christ. In order to confront the world with the rule of God, Jesus walked into the eye of the storm. His love for humanity was so great and his desire to please the Father so intense that he allowed himself to be rejected. The Spirit led him along a path in which wrath, pain and evil become absorbed by the heart of the suffering Servant King. The incarnate God, anointed by the Spirit, defeated the enemy by an act of defenseless love and by the same Spirit enabled us all to be involved in his dying and rising. Thus the gospel calls us to enter into his journey, united in his death and resurrection, and to grow into his likeness.

The cross loomed over Jesus' life from the beginning. Early in his ministry he met with a degree of success, but before long there was resistance and a hardening of hearts. At a certain point Jesus traveled to Jerusalem to bring matters to a head (Lk 9:51). He must have known this would mean his death but was prepared to love to the uttermost. He would be true to his mission, even if it meant his rejection. He confronted the religious and political leaders and forced them to choose in regard to the kingdom of God. He was prepared even to drink the bitter cup of divine abandonment and suffer its dread and anguish. Eventually he would die all alone, crying out to his Father. He trusted God even unto death, not only a painful death but a death that would have to signify to any onlooker that his mission had been a failure.

The hard part to grasp (at least for me) is the fact that Jesus was handed over to death not only by Roman soldiers and Jewish priests but also by his Father. When Abraham was about to sacrifice Isaac in the Old Testament, at least God relented at the last minute. But in this case God let the Son die and thus welcomed suffering into the triune life. Paul says, God "did not withhold his own Son, but gave him up for all of us" (Rom 8:32).

The sentence of death which the human authorities passed on Jesus ought really to have been passed on them—he died in their place. But what can this mean that the Father gave him up to die? It means that *the cross must be seen as an intratrinitarian drama.* Here the giving and receiving of love within the Trinity take a painful redemptive form in history. The cross was the sign of the Father's love for a world created in and for the Son. He who had always said yes to the Father stood in sinners' place and suffered their fate. He identified with them to the point of abandonment and transformed the situation of humanity by suffering love. Through the Spirit, the Son offered himself to the Father, and on the cross the Father's forgiving love and the Son's suffering love were brought together by the Spirit, bond of love.[57]

Jesus surrendered himself to the Father and said in his dying hour, "Into your hands I commend my spirit" (Lk 23:46). He presented his body as a living sacrifice to God. Sacrifice is best understood not primarily as balancing the scales of justice. It is the surrender of a life and not so much an appeasement. "The life of the flesh is in the blood; and I have given it to you for making atonement" (Lev 17:11). Christ's death was an offering of obedience to God. As our representative, he surrendered himself to God on our behalf. "By the one man's obedience the many will be made righteous" (Rom 5:19). We are saved by the faithfulness of Jesus Christ (Gal 2:20).

"Being found in human form, he humbled himself and became obedient to the point of death—even death on a cross" (Phil 2:7-8). The Spirit enabled Jesus to make a perfect offering for us and now calls us to offer our bodies as living sacrifices (Rom 12:1). Here is the sin offering that wipes away the sins of the world. Here God grants forgiveness by condemning sin and assuming the consequences himself. The God of love wants to be associated with human beings and is willing to bear the pain in order to heal the broken relationship. Because Christ died as our representative, our status before God is changed and a new situation is created.[58]

The circle of love within God is not closed but has been opened by the Spirit. The Son knew that by suffering he could absorb evil and redeem humanity. Therefore he became sin's embodiment and took the sin of the race on himself, to defeat the powers of darkness. The Son, in self-distinction from the Father, entered by incarnation into the situation of the creature and brought it back to fellowship with God. Thereupon the Spirit has been poured forth to implement the reconciliation. By the Spirit we enter into union with Christ and begin the journey toward transformation. The Spirit deals with the powers of sin in us until we share the glory of the risen Lord.[59]

C. S. Lewis noted that while Christians agree that the cross puts us right with God, they do not agree about *how* it does so. We know it is an effective medicine but are not certain how it works. It is hard to find a theory of atonement that can be intellectually mastered. Lewis himself thought in terms of participation. He thought that Christ became human in order to exist vicariously for us, that we might share his life, death and resurrection. In this view we are saved by identifying with him and by becoming like him. We are saved by participating in the life communicated through him. Lewis spoke of Christ as the carrier of a good infection. What we need to do is get close enough to him to catch the virus of new life. Humanity has been saved in principle, but we have to open ourselves to the last Adam. "One of our race has the new life; if we get close to him we shall catch it from him." This is not a rational theory of atonement, but it speaks dramatically of the work of God which saves.[60]

The important thing for me is that seeing atonement within the framework of the representative journey keeps the Spirit in the picture as a vital component. Few theories of the atonement manage that. First, the Spirit led Jesus to death—"through the eternal Spirit [he] offered himself without blemish to God" (Heb 9:14). Second, through the Spirit he was raised from the dead (Rom 8:11). Third, in the aftermath of resurrection, Spirit enables us to share in reconciliation. As our representative, Jesus Christ lived our life as we should but do not live it. He traveled a journey of obedience even unto death. Now, because of the resurrection he has become life-giving Spirit, being in the position to give life to those who follow him. The Spirit's task in atonement is to form Christ in us and change us into his likeness. The task is to reverse the power of sin in us until death itself is overcome and we can share in the glory of God.

Is God Satisfied?

Most of us are not accustomed to viewing atonement in the context of Christ's representative journey. We are used to thinking of it in a legal framework in which God, the angry judge, requires retribution and satisfaction. We are used to construing the death of Christ as the propitiation of God that makes God willing to show mercy. God is viewed in effect as humankind's enemy, whose justice must be satisfied before he is willing to receive them. The popular view of atonement is that God poured out the fury of his wrath on Jesus Christ, who in bearing this penalty effected an atonement. The theory is that a wrathful Father punished a merciful Son instead of us, with the result that we go free. The logic of it leads inexorably to ideas of a limited atonement, since presumably God does not assault the same person twice.[61]

This is a delicate point for me to discuss. First, it was the view of John Calvin and has been the distinguishing mark of evangelicalism. Inter-Varsity Fellowship in the United Kingdom began as a split from the Student Christian Movement over this very point. It is risky to seem to be calling it into question.[62] Second, a few Scriptures do speak about divine wrath in connection with the death of Christ, so the idea cannot be simply discarded (Rom 3:25). The penal theory may be wrong-headed, yet something like it may be true. It is important to propose a correction, but not an overcorrection. Like Eastern Orthodox theologians, I do not see humanity's relationship with God as *primarily* a legal one or the atonement as *primarily* penal. At the same time I recognize that Christ was in some sense victim as well as victor at the cross. The issue is both subtle and sensitive.[63]

First, by way of correction, a few points should be made to clarify the problem in the popular view of the atonement. For one thing, the theory of penal substitution began its life in apologetics, not exegesis or theology. It originated as a rational explanation of the incarnation. Anselm wanted to explain why God became man *(Cur Deus Homo)*. In his medieval society he approached the atonement as an issue of social propriety. People at that time would have agreed that an offense against divine honor required satisfaction. Anselm's theory presupposed then-current ideas of social obligation and thus could explain how God in Christ could have rendered infinite satisfaction. Later on, Calvin (himself a lawyer) would take the idea in a slightly different direction, claiming that wrath required retribution also. This is what happened on the cross—God's vengeance struck out against Christ *(Institutes* 2.16.1-5).

Of course this creates a very strange impression theologically. It pits the Father against the Son and construes forgiveness as something God finds difficult to give. It makes grace conditional upon penal satisfaction and gives the impression that the Father actually hates sinners and cannot love them until his wrath is appeased. It belies the central point that it was the Father who took the initiative in reconciling the world through Christ.

God was *not* disinclined to be favorable until his wrath was appeased. He is not humanity's enemy; it was love that moved him to send his Son in the first place. Love provided the incarnation and the atonement, not wrath. Our Lord's self-sacrifice bespeaks a gracious God, not an angry God.

Yes indeed, God forgives in a way that takes sin seriously, but he is always ready to forgive and does not have to be persuaded on that score. Remember the elementary truth that the cross reconciles the world to God, not God to the world (2 Cor 5:19). God is the reconciler, not the one requiring reconciliation. God is the subject, not the object, of reconciliation. Love for sinners, not anger, brought Jesus into the world.

God did not reject his beloved Son—Israel rejected him, and the Romans punished him. God, for his part, justified him and raised him from the dead. Christ died as a malefactor and came under the curse of the law at the hands of sinners. His enemies deserved the sentence of death they passed on him. Jesus knew God's heart when he prayed,

"Father, forgive them, for they know not what they do."[64]

It requires courage to challenge traditions that no longer serve. Even the Catechism, having noted that the death of Jesus was not an appeasement of the Father and that Jesus' whole life was atoning, fails to correct these traditions, even though many, both inside and outside the church, need to have them corrected (par. 606-7).

Theological Reconstruction

What does it mean, then, that God abandoned Jesus on the cross? Obviously Jesus was greatly distressed and troubled and did not die calmly. He cried out, "My God, my God, why have you forsaken me?" (Mk 15:34). In some sense he was God-forsaken, though he was the Son of God (Mk 15:39). The Father turned away—something came between them. Jesus cried out to be delivered but entered the darkness instead. Where was his faithful God in all of this?

In order to understand it, we must keep a firm hold on the category of representation. Jesus was the last Adam, who represented the human race in his life journey. He was not the solitary victim of this crucifixion. He lived, died and rose vicariously on our behalf. He trusted God on our behalf, he died in solidarity with us, he arose on our behalf. In his death we all have died (2 Cor 5:14). This means that when wrath was revealed at Calvary, it blazed against sinners in the person of their representative. It blazed against the old humanity represented there. It did not fall on Jesus as third party, not as a victim in isolation, but on Jesus as humanity's representative. God's wrath flashed out against the old Adamic solidarity.

Sin was being judged and punished in Christ, but not after the manner of legal rationality. What we see here is the triumph of love over all enmity and alienation. What we see is a "theodrama" in which God administered the medicine of immortality. At the cross God did not reject the Son. On the contrary, the Father never loved him more than at that moment.[65]

Sin was overcome in the cross when judgment fell and the Son died in our place. He walked the bitter path to death and separation from God. Sinful humankind was delivered up in his being handed over. The decisive point is that, as Barth says, "in his person he has made an end of us as sinners and therefore of sin itself by going to death as the One who took our place. In his person, he delivered up us sinners and sin itself to destruction. He took this present evil world and buried it in his tomb."

The cross was a victory over sin. In cross and resurrection together, God is the victor over sin and death. Christ's death does not merely address guilt—it pierces alienation and overcomes chaos too. It is not simply propitiation but the death of death. Evil is defeated as an enemy of humanity. Calvary is something like a black hole into which is sucked all the power of death and law, wrath and alienation, to be annihilated.

In its wake, the Spirit summons us to enter reconciliation and actualize by faith what is anticipated. God reconciled the world in Christ—God included everybody in it, without even asking. The effectiveness of this reconciliation is not so much opting in as not opting out. In faith we add our yes to God's prior yes.[66] God suffered with Christ as God of the forsaken and godless when he reconciled the world through him. "In the passion of the Son, the Father himself suffers the pains of abandonment. In the death of the Son, death came upon God himself, and the Father suffers the death of his Son in his love for forsaken man."[67]

In the legal framework, the divine wrath has been viewed as vindictive anger and God as vengeful. But wrath is not a dark side of God that frustrates his grace and demands satisfaction. It is an aspect of God's saving righteousness. It is the other side of God's saving action, and it serves grace. Even in wrath, grace is working. Humanity is not destined for wrath but for salvation (1 Thess 5:9). God prefers not to be angry: "I will not execute my fierce anger" (Hos 11:9). He wants to be merciful (Rom 11:32). The cross reflects not God's thirst for retribution but his determination to overcome alienation and enslavement. The means to do this is the participatory journey of Jesus into which the Spirit draws us. Christ's death expressed obedience to the Father which, in representing us, frees us from sin and alienation. As the Risen One he is present with us, making his journey our own. By the Spirit we begin this journey ourselves and experience transformation. Christ did not appease divine anger—his death and resurrection constitute the saving event into which we are being drawn.[68]

The atonement is best understood in a trinitarian framework, in relation to the missions of Son and Spirit. It is realized by the participatory journey of the Son and our insertion into it by the Spirit. By this act this present world order is set aside and the way opened up to new creation. People are called to participate in these events, to immerse themselves in this process.

Jesus Christ entered into solidarity with us and endured all that we endure, including death. He was also raised, justified and glorified. He went through the process we must go through, accomplishing redemption for us. God effected a change in the human situation through this pioneer of our salvation. Drawn into Christ's representative journey, we can be healed. The cross benefits all those who let themselves be linked with his death through baptism. Paul writes concerning himself: "I am now rejoicing in my sufferings for your sake, and in my flesh I am completing what is lacking in Christ's afflictions for the sake of his body" (Col 1:24).[69]

As a trinitarian event, the cross is the work of the Spirit as well as an event transpiring between Father and Son. The Spirit brought Christ to the cross and raised him up afterward. Even at the dread moment of separation, the Spirit was the bond of love uniting the Father and Son. The distance was bridged by the Spirit, and from it came the outpouring of the Spirit on the world. The suffering of the world touched the heart of God, and his compassion poured out to the despised and the ungodly.[70]

There *is* a legal dimension to the atonement, but it should not dominate and eclipse every other dimension. Human guilt is a problem, but mere acquittal was never the goal of the cross. As with Hosea's marriage, God wants our relationship with him restored. Jesus suffered judgment in our place, and the consequences of sin fell on his head. But they fell on him not as third party but as last Adam. In him God was dealing with the old Adamic solidarity. The judgment did not fall on the beloved Son but on our representative and therefore on us. Christ delivered sinful humanity up to a well-deserved destruction.

The participatory model of atonement has a different kind of appeal and rationality from those of the legal theory. It portrays a world in which humanity dies and is raised to life in Christ. It speaks of new creation and of the Spirit who invites us to enter into it by faith.[71]

The work of Jesus can be understood within the history of the Holy Spirit. To do so does not negate but enriches Christology by exalting Christ as the anointed representative of the new humanity. The Spirit enabled the conception of Jesus, the union of the Logos with flesh and the completion of the participatory journey. The incarnation depended on the work of the Spirit and unfolded as a Spirit-empowered representation on behalf of humanity, fulfilling the purpose of creation and healing humanity through a recapitulation of the human journey.

While offering a relational Spirit Christology, I do not intend here to deny truth in the penal substitutionary model of atonement. Grace has to deal with sin, and the law's just condemnation of us must be silenced. Family room cannot altogether displace courtroom in our theological analogies. Still, the amazing thing is that the judge in this case actually loves us and desires our friendship. The two insights can be merged.

This approach also has a practical dimension: while Logos Christology highlights how different we are from Jesus, Spirit Christology underlines how like him we can be. The Father sends us as he sent Jesus, filled with the Spirit. The power that was at work in Jesus is the power at work in us. Having established a beachhead for the kingdom in Christ, Spirit is preparing a people to live in the light of the new order and is planting seeds of hope everywhere for renewal and transformation. Life has appeared in the midst of death, and the Spirit is at work moving the groaning creation toward resurrection.

FOUR

SPIRIT & CHURCH

*T*HE CHURCH MAY BE VIEWED in many different ways: as institution, sacrament, herald, servant, body of Christ, colony and more. Here let us view it from the standpoint of the Spirit. Let us see it as a continuation of the Spirit-anointed event that was Jesus Christ. This is a natural way to regard a community that was created by the Spirit on the day of Pentecost to carry on the kingdom ministry of Jesus and be firstfruits of the new humanity he represented. Spirit was present at the birth of the church as well as at Bethlehem, and the church is dependent on the power of the Spirit just as Jesus was. The church is also an event in the history of the Spirit.

The first act of the risen Lord was to breathe the Spirit on the disciples and send them forth into mission (Jn 20:21-22; Acts 1:8). This alerts us to the fact that the effectiveness of the church is due not to human competency or programming but to the power of God at work. The church rides the wind of God's Spirit like a hawk endlessly and effortlessly circling and gliding in the summer sky. It ever pauses to wait for impulses of power to carry it forward to the nations. What a dynamic and hopeful image to cherish in a day when thinking about the church is often heavy and pessimistic. The main rationale of the church is to actualize all the implications of baptism in the Spirit.[1]

After the resurrection, God's kingdom, which had begun to manifest itself in Jesus himself, would continue to transform the world through the community of empowered disciples. The church is an extension not so much of the incarnation as of the anointing of Jesus. Jesus is the prototype of the church, which now receives its own baptism in the Spirit. Spirit, who maintained Jesus' relationship with the Father and empowered him for mission, now calls the church into that relationship, giving it the power to carry on the mission. There had to be, after Jesus' departure, a colony of heaven, living the life and power and experiencing the freedom of the kingdom. Spirit indwells the church as a perpetual Pentecost and communicates gifts to its members. Spirit ecclesiology focuses not on the quality of the members but on the power of God at work in and through them.[2]

As noted in the last chapter, the representation and participatory journey of Jesus Christ triggered the promised outpouring of the Spirit. Having walked our path to death and been vindicated by God, Jesus poured out the Spirit on all flesh to effect the hope for world transformation. Pentecost completed Good Friday and Easter Sunday by changing history with the transforming power of these events. Christ came to set people free, and now there is a community dwelling in God's love, living freely, embodying the grace of God: Father, Son and Spirit. Now the life-giving Spirit by resurrection, Christ is present in a new way in history, bringing life to the world by the Spirit, who can make his representative journey a reality in people's lives.

The last Adam is forming a new solidarity, enlarging himself as a person. Once confined to Palestine, Jesus has become head of a new international body of Spirit-baptized disciples sharing his risen life. How great are the riches of the glory of this mystery—"Christ in you, the hope of glory" (Col 1:27). The Risen One is working out the participatory journey of atonement in the world through a community that lives by the power of the Spirit.

The danger of subordinating the Spirit to the Son in Christology also exists in ecclesiology. This happens when church is seen as the body of Christ to which the Spirit is added as a helper. The fact is that Christ did not first establish the church and add the Spirit secondarily. The Spirit's role is not a junior role. As Jesus was conceived by the Spirit in Mary and empowered for mission in baptism, so the church is born and empowered by the Spirit. The Spirit who filled Jesus empowers the community of disciples to be the vehicle of God's saving activity. Jesus, who received the Spirit and ministered in power, communicates God's life to the church to carry on the mission. Like Jesus, the church must live not out of its own resources but by the power of the indwelling Spirit, which breathes, strengthens, inspires and guides.

On Easter the narrative shifts its focus from the earthly Jesus to the community of his brothers and sisters who are imbued with the same Spirit. These are the people who indwell his journey and share his living, dying, and rising. "The body of Christ" no longer denotes only the physical existence of Jesus but is a corporate term, referring to the community on its way to Christlikeness. Even the term *Christ* itself can apply to those who participate in the community and share his risen life. As the body has many members, so is it with Christ, for the community is baptized and anointed as he was (1 Cor 12:12-13). Recall how Jesus asked Saul why he was persecuting him in the person of his downtrodden people (Acts 9:4). Christ and his people are tied together. We encounter the Risen One not only in word and sacrament but also when we meet one another. "Where two or three are gathered together in my name, I am there among them" (Mt 18:20).

The Second Vatican Council supplemented a hierarchical under-standing of church expressed by the First Council with the vision of the church as the body of Christ, ordered and sustained by the Spirit. "Rising from the dead, Christ sent his life-giving Spirit upon his disciples and through this Spirit has established his body, the church, as the universal sacrament of salvation" (*Dogmatic Constitution on the Church* par. 48). This was a noble move, though since the council there has been a struggle over how to appropriate this ecclesiology in the local church. The charismatic renewal has helped by introducing priests and laity to a personal experience of the Spirit, but the gap in all our traditions between theory and practice in this regard needs narrowing.[3]

The church is the instrument of Christ, called to carry on his mission in the power of the Spirit. This power is a special kind of power, since he who baptizes us in the Spirit is the Lamb and Servant of God (Jn 1:29, 33). This means paradoxically that though it is the power of creation, it is also the power of suffering love, which does not remove our weakness or eliminate pain. The nature and direction of this power are clarified by the cross, the power of suffering love by which Christ overcame the world. The desire for worldly power is carnal. The Spirit's power comes from the Crucified One, and the reason for seeking it is the desire to be involved in his mission. The church is a dwelling place of God by the Spirit (Eph 2:22). "I will cause breath to enter you, and you shall live" (Ezek 37:5). Only as God breathes on the church is it enabled to carry on Christ's mission.[4]

Although the Spirit is omnipresent and not confined to the church, Spirit's presence in the community is highly significant. For millennia Spirit has longed to breathe into the body of human life more effectively, intensely and redemptively. Pentecost offered the Spirit a unique opportunity to work freely. Here is a community open to God's love, a place where (in principle) there can be a fuller realization of the kingdom, a more decisive presence of God in history. New possibilities have arisen for the Spirit because of the participatory journey of Jesus Christ.

Though present everywhere, Spirit can be more effectively present among those who know the risen Lord, can work there with greater intensity promoting human renewal. The Spirit experienced this freedom in the case of Jesus, but that opportunity was snuffed out in the crisis of his death. With the vindication of the resurrection, however, the movement of world transformation can go forward.

Community is important because God does not want faith to be expressed only in an interior way within the hearts of individual disciples. Human experience itself is social, and faith needs to assume corporate form. It needs to be ecclesial and have public attestation. The Spirit has a vested interest in the church, where men and women confess Jesus Christ and are open to participation in the divine life. The mission of Jesus, bringing hope to humanity and ultimately justice to nations, has been passed on and the power to implement it transferred to the community of disciples.[5]

Community is also central to the purposes of God because it allows the relationality of triune life to be reflected in the created order. This mirroring back gives delight to God and at the same time supplies fulfillment to our own lives as semitranscendent and relational beings. Made in God's image, as differentiated creatures, as male and female, we too delight in community. Stanley Grenz writes, "God intends to bring to pass a reconciled creation in which humans reflect in their relationship to each other and the universe around us the reality of the triune God. God's actions are aimed at establishing the reconciled community of love as the human reflection of the social trinity—the divine nature—which is love."[6]

The Spirit is central for ecclesiology because he is the source of fellowship among humans in history and the bond of love between Father and Son in eternity. Fellowship on earth corresponds in a measure to fellowship in heaven. The Trinity is an open, inviting fellowship, and the Spirit wants the church to be the same, responsive in the same sort of way. God wants to hear from us an echo of the dynamic relations within his own life, anticipating the coming of the kingdom. The church is meant to resemble the triune life by being itself a place of reciprocity and self-giving. The fellowship that we have with one another is related ultimately to our fellowship with Father and Son (1 Jn 1:3). *Fellowship* refers both to divine life and to community life, because the community is meant to reflect the communion of the Trinity, which is the ontological basis of the church.[7]

As Christ himself embodied the new humanity as the last Adam, the church also is meant to embody it and anticipate the future of the world. God purposes a world that receives grace and says yes to love, and this is what the community of disciples does. In some ways church is one social network among others, but it has a higher promise. When the church embodies Easter life, it is capable of becoming a sign of the coming reign of God. It is the human assembly that points to a much larger convocation at the end of time, and the community that anticipates the consummation of God's purposes for the world. The goal of creation was achieved in principle in the resurrection of Jesus. Now it has to take shape in a community that is the firstfruits of the future and the model of what human relationships can be, the sign of God's project for the world.[8]

At Pentecost the church received the Spirit and became the historical continuation of Jesus' anointing as the Christ. The One baptized in water and Spirit now baptizes the disciples. He transferred Spirit to them so that his actions could continue through their agency. The bearer of the Spirit now baptizes others with the Spirit, that there might be a continuation of his testimony in word and deed and a continuation of his prophetic and charismatic ministry.

The church exists for the world, not for itself, by participating in the apostleship of Christ by the power of the Spirit. With the goal of new humanity in sight, God truly delights over his people (Zeph 3:17). The blessings of the kingdom can now flow to the world, and Christ's mighty acts can continue and be enlarged in ever-widening circles through the community at God's disposal. There is a new family on earth, made up of brothers and sisters, among whom Christ is firstborn (Rom 8:29; Heb 2:11). Here the memory of Jesus is kept alive by proclamation, sacrament and mission.[9]

The world begins to become "christomorphic" in the community where love is being perfected (1 Jn 4:12). Such a community is intended to depict what God wants the world to become. At Pentecost a ruptured and broken world began to heal. People from all over the world came together and began to understand one another. A community was formed, full of differences and yet united in its longing for the coming of the kingdom. The conversion of people from many nations foreshadowed the evangelization of the world. Through baptism in the Spirit, the disciples were formed into an agency of the Spirit and a community in which God would work to rescue the world from self-destruction. At Pentecost God began to move the world from alienation to its goal and place in divine life. Michael Welker writes,

"Through the pouring out of the Spirit, God effected a world-encompassing, multilingual, poly-individual testimony to Godself." The church is the sacrament of the presence of Jesus Christ in the world.[10]

Power and Presence

As Jesus was empowered, the church is empowered for its mission by the Spirit. Outward forms are not enough—the power must be at work in us (Eph 3:20; 2 Tim 3:5). The kingdom of God is not just a matter of talk but of power (1 Cor 4:20). Outsiders ought to be able to sense the life-changing presence (1 Cor 14:25). More than churches full of people, God wants (and the world needs) people full of the Spirit.

Let us now take up the issue of power in the church, how Spirit is powerfully present sacramentally and charismatically for the sake of mission. We shall begin with the sacramental, proceed to the charismatic and conclude with transforming mission.[11]

A dualism of spirit and matter has to be confronted here. Moderns perceive Spirit as something ghostly, intangible, impalpable, numinous, lacking concreteness. There is resistance to linking the Spirit to the material. Many of us shy away from physical manifestations of the divine presence and expect intangible, not real-life effects of the Spirit. It is as if the Spirit were a "holy ghost" who does not deal in material reality or transform real worlds. Matter-spirit dualism is, however, not the Bible's view, and it is far from the ancient consensus. There is a physical side of being spiritual. Spirit is not a ghost but the life-giver who moves in and shapes the material realm. We are physical creatures, the Son became incarnate in flesh and blood, and Spirit wants to effect changes in history *concretely*.[12]

It appears that in the early centuries the churches were sacramental and charismatic. The spiritual and the physical flowed together. But the balance has not always been sustained. In the Middle Ages the tendency was to favor sacramental over charismatic, and at the Reformation the sacramental principle itself suffered. Today renewal frequently takes place in nonsacramental contexts, not in the historic churches, which worship God sacramentally. The fire often burns outside the fireplace of the historic institutions. My concern here is to try and recover the two-dimensionality of charism and sacrament original to Christianity.[13]

Let's begin by looking into the sacramental dimension of the Spirit's power and presence. Worship is central because the church delights in what God has done and is doing in history and in its fellowship in relation to the world's future. As firstfruits of new humanity, we worship God on behalf of the world in anticipation of the harvest. We acknowledge God's greatness on behalf of all peoples and press toward the goal of union with God. Responding to the Spirit, we move ever closer to God, shedding preoccupation with self and pursuing the true basis of our human life.

In worship we become assimilated to the humanity of Jesus, mystically and sacramentally, and pursue his journey. To the church Jesus is much more than a historical memory. He is present in the midst of the community as the life-giving Spirit. God summons the church to worship him in Spirit and truth (Jn 4:24; Phil 3:3). Spirit incites us to give God praise as his holy temple (Eph 2:22; 1 Pet 2:5). As he helped the Son to offer himself to the Father, the Spirit helps us come to the Father through the Son, making communion possible.[14]

Material signs foster the relationship between God and creatures. They help us approach the incomprehensible mystery, and they make invisible grace tangible. Sacraments exist simply because we are bodily creatures inhabiting a material world. There is in theory no limit to the number of them. Created reality is richly imbued with sacramental possibilities. The world reflects God's glory; therefore anything can mediate the sacred, where there are eyes to see and ears to hear. Since the Spirit pervades the universe, any event or experience can bring God to mind and mediate his presence. Thus the angel of the Lord appeared to Moses in a burning bush (Acts 7:30), and Elijah heard God speak in wind, earthquake, fire and silence (1 Kings 19:11-12). God speaks in the glory of sunsets and towering peaks. In particular, because humans are made in God's image, we encounter God in other people; we love God when we love them and honor God when we honor them. The sacramental principle operates, let it be noted, not only in liturgy but also in the ordinary experience that grounds it.[15]

The life of many churches needs to be enriched with more signs and symbols. Iconoclasm has impoverished the life of the church and often reduced worship to a cognitive affair. This means that the Spirit is denied certain tools for enrichment. We are impoverished when we have no place for festivals, drama, processions, banners, dance, color, movement, instruments, percussion and incense. There are many notes on the Spirit's keyboard which we often neglect to sound, with the result that God's presence can be hard to access.

Jesus, as the image of the invisible God, is himself the fundamental sacrament (Col 1:15). He reveals the Father into whose presence the Spirit brings us. God has communicated himself and the mystery of his love in Christ. Incarnation is the paramount event of the divine nearness and the fundamental sacrament of our encounter with God. No Christians are really nonsacramentalist in the strict sense, since Jesus is the sacrament we all acknowledge. No one who confesses Christ, the primordial sacrament, and is enriched by the church, the sacrament of Christ, can be called nonsacramentalist. This reveals a unity of the catholic and free churches which should not be forgotten.[16]

The church too is a derived sacrament because, indwelt by the Spirit, it perpetuates the presence of the Lord. Through members of the body, Christ is present in the world by the Spirit. "Where two or three are gathered in my name, I am there among them" (Mt 18:20). Spirit constituted Christ's human body as Word made flesh in Mary and continues to make him effectively present in the church. The Risen Lord lives in the community, releasing his Spirit, drawing people into union with God. Conversions occur when people encounter Christ in members of his body, who become means of grace to them. As he acted through Christ, God continues to act through the words and actions of disciples. If Christ is the sacrament of God, the church is the sacrament of Christ, because it represents him in the world. When people receive grace through members of the body, they experience communion with God. Church and churchly sacraments derive from the basic sacrament, Jesus Christ. The Second Vatican Council calls the church "sacrament of the world" because it exists to brings people into relationship with God (*Dogmatic Constitution on the Church* 1.1).[17]

Ordinarily when we hear the word *sacrament* we think of baptism and the Lord's Supper. But church life is sacramental in more ways than these. God's presence is evoked variously: through singing and prayer, through praise and thanksgiving, through greeting and fellowship, through teaching and instruction, through loving acts and kind service. Reading Scripture in the liturgy is sacramental because it mediates the Word of God. As Vatican II comments, "God himself speaks when the holy Scriptures are read in church" (*Constitution on the Sacred Liturgy* par. 7). For this reason, in some churches (such as the Orthodox) the Bible is given ritual recognition, by being formally carried in and even kissed. As wine is the sign of the blood of Christ, biblical texts enable one to hear God's Word.

Christ is present in the church in many embodied ways. In each of them, the material becomes spiritual and the spiritual is conveyed through material. Among the Quakers silence is sacramental, because they listen for God speaking in stillness. Other Quaker sacraments include the simplicity of the meeting house, sitting together in a circle, singing and praying, waiting and listening. Sacraments are media that transmit the grace of God to bodily creatures, and thank God, there are many of them. By many means of grace Christ pursues his work in us as firstfruits of the new humanity so that he may offer us to the Father.[18]

Let us not impoverish ourselves. Let us not, in reaction to excess, go to the extreme of reducing worship to grim austerity and hyper-spirituality. Human beings are symbol users, and God is a symbol maker. In charismatic circles people are feeling free to recover the richness of dance, clapping, raising hands, percussion, shouting, celebration, processions, banners and the like. We should not put aside means of grace that can enrich our lives. We do ourselves harm when we eliminate arts, drama, color, vestments, pageantry, incense, saints, calendars, lectionary, sculpture. To do so is to threaten the mystery.

Jesus *touched* the leper's skin when he healed him (Mk 1:41). He *touched* the hand of Peter's mother-in-law, and the fever left her (Mt 8:15). Paul laid hands on Timothy's head to communicate the Spirit (1 Tim 4:14; 2 Tim 1:6). Peter and John laid hands on some Samaritans that they might receive the Spirit (Acts 8:17). The physical and the spiritual are not antithetical but cooperative and synergistic. The Spirit is passed from one person to another, from Moses to Joshua, from Elijah to Elisha. God comes to us and deals with us through material signs.[19]

Baptism and Eucharist

The term *sacrament* is normally used to refer to churchly rituals used in worship, and most commonly to baptism and Eucharist. Baptism initiates people into community, and Eucharist renews participation in it. Together they signify initiation and participation, and are properly associated with Christ's commitment in baptism and his willingness to suffer in obedience to God depicted in the Last Supper.

The identity of a community is sustained by ritual as well as word. Sermons touch us on the cognitive level, while ritual moves us on the affective level. Without ritual, traditions wither. Sacraments are material signs and symbols using words and actions, through which God gives life to us by the Spirit. As we open our hearts, we experience being the temple of the living God (2 Cor 6:16).[20]

The effectiveness of the sacraments is bound up with the Spirit and faith. Calvin wrote, "Sacraments fulfill their office only when the Spirit, that inward teacher, comes to them, by whose power alone hearts are penetrated and affections moved and our souls opened for the sacraments to enter in. If the Spirit be lacking, the sacraments can accomplish nothing more in our minds than the splendor of the sun shining upon blind eyes or a voice sounding in deaf ears" (*Institutes* 4.19.9). Faith is also important. Vatican II states,

> In order that the sacred liturgy may produce its full effect, it is necessary that the faithful come to it with proper dispositions, that their thoughts match their words, and that they cooperate with divine grace lest they receive it in vain. Pastors of souls must therefore realise that, when the liturgy is celebrated, more is required than the mere observance of the laws governing valid and licit celebration. It is their duty also to ensure that the faithful take part knowingly, actively, and fruitfully. (*Constitution on the Sacred Liturgy* par. 11)

Baptism and Eucharist are the two central sacraments that have been present from the beginning. Others were introduced gradually but were conceived in relation to these originals. For example, the sacrament of confirmation (receiving the Spirit through the laying on of hands) and reconciliation (repentance through confession) are related to baptism, while anointing the sick, marriage and ordination to holy orders are related to Eucharist.

Baptism is the act in which the Spirit initiates individuals into the fellowship of the body of Christ (1 Cor 12:13). As Jesus when baptized in water received the Spirit, so he would baptize us in water and in Spirit. Born of water and Spirit, we become members of his mystical body and receive the forgiveness of sins. Jesus says, in the long ending of Mark, "The one who believes and is baptized will be saved; but the one who does not believe will be condemned" (Mk 16:16). At Pentecost, Peter called the people to be baptized and receive the gift of the Spirit in the context of their water baptism (Acts 2:38). Through the sign of water, people are baptized into solidarity with Christ and put on Christ (Gal 3:26). They receive the washing of regeneration and renewal of the Spirit (Tit 3:5-6). Baptism is the moment when the Spirit is imparted and when people open themselves to gifts of the Spirit. Baptism is an expression of the obedience of faith and the moment when God gives the Spirit. In experience the Spirit may be manifested before baptism, as with Cornelius, but water remains the public sign of the Spirit's coming (Acts 10:44-48).[21]

The Spirit is normally given with water in response to faith. This makes baptism a sacrament and means of grace. Proper initiation is water baptism coupled with Spirit baptism. Earlier encounters with the Spirit call for a fresh infusion in water baptism, and later encounters should be viewed as occasions of release of the potentials of grace bestowed in the sacrament. One does not begin life in the Spirit more than once, but one may be filled with the Spirit many times in terms of awareness and appropriation.[22]

At baptism there ought to be an invocation of the Spirit. We find a nice example of this in the order for baptism of the Armenian Apostolic Orthodox Church: "We therefore pray thee, O Lord, send thy Holy Spirit into this water and sanctify it as thou didst sanctify the river Jordan by descending thereinto and prefiguring thereby this font of baptism for the regeneration of all men."

As a member of the free church tradition, I am not used to thinking of baptism this way. Baptists seldom make the link between water and Spirit baptism, but see water baptism as human response only. A sharp line is often drawn between baptism in water and in Spirit. The former is viewed not as a sacrament but as a response to what God has done in Christ, the true sacrament. Baptism and Eucharist are demythologized as events of grace and portrayed as events of response. For Karl Barth, baptism in the Spirit is conversion, and water baptism is the first step in following Jesus. In such thinking baptism is witness to a human decision and not an occasion of receiving the Spirit. A number of scholars agree that water baptism plays no essential role in initiation; thus a wedge is driven between water and Spirit.[23]

This does not seem to square with a number of Scriptures that connect the coming of the Spirit more closely with water baptism, and it is certainly out of keeping with the tradition of one and a half millennia of church history with regard to the sacramental character of baptism. Most Christians historically have held that God acts in baptism to bestow grace. As Tertullian said, "The act of baptism is carnal, in that we are plunged in water, but the effect is spiritual, in that we are freed from sins" (*On Baptism* 7). As the Spirit came upon Jesus as he came up out of the water, so water and Spirit baptism are associated. This is the impression conveyed by sayings such as Peter's: "Baptism . . . saves you" (1 Pet 3:21). Scripture seems thus to support the catholic position—as Luther says, God's blessings are poured out on candidates for baptism. The breaking of this link seems to have been the result of Zwingli's dualism of matter and spirit, which led many Protestants into antisacramentalism.[24]

At first baptism was administered to converts, not to infants. In baptism people renounced their sins and received anointing for ministry. Baptists today continue the practice and defer baptism of children until riper years, whereas catholic traditions (Roman Catholic, Orthodox, Anglican, Lutheran, Reformed, Methodist) opt for infant baptism, in which parents along with the congregation promise to raise the child in the faith and provide for her or his spiritual formation. Confirmation later completes baptism by adding the dimension of faith (*Catechism of the Catholic Church* par. 1225). This makes a certain sense. In religion, as other areas of life, parents take responsibility for children as they grow up. Naturally they want them to be part of the faith community and to be nourished by the means of grace. To deprive a child of this blessing, they reason, would place them outside the community and might even propel them in the wrong direction.

The danger of baptizing infants is that the action might be regarded as magical and the importance of faith be lost sight of. We must not rely on a ritual to save us in the absence of a call to serious discipleship. The danger of insisting on believers' baptism, on the other hand, is that we might regard the human decision so highly that we forget God's enabling grace. What about the mentally handicapped? Can God not work grace in the young and weak? Can the Spirit not anoint them? It also places the children of believers in an awkward position ecclesially.

As a Baptist, I opt for the dedication of infants and water baptism later, as a practice that can preserve the elements we all wish to protect (anointing, dedication, renunciation, responsibility). On the other hand, infant baptism followed by real confirmation could have the same result. Each community will have to decide in its own setting which danger is greater and what it should do. Whatever we decide (and I am not taking a position), the relationship between water baptism and Spirit baptism should be kept. One might think of the Spirit as truly present in infant baptism, with the effectiveness of it unfolding gradually as the child grows in faith over the years. For all of us, however, baptism points to a lifetime of following Jesus, however performed and whoever the candidates. All the baptized are called to live in newness of life (Rom 6:4).

As regards the Eucharist, it commemorates Jesus' self-surrender to God. He commanded it to continue so that the charism of self-giving would be perpetuated in the church down through history. Christ promised to be present in the meal ("this is my body") so that believers might experience his presence and commit themselves to his mission when they partake of it. His own charism was deposited, as it were, in the Eucharist, where Christ is present in the elements as the One who surrendered himself to the Father.[25]

In the Eucharist we receive Jesus in the form of bread and wine and share thereby in his death and resurrection. He makes himself known to us in the breaking of bread (Lk 24:35). The supper is our supernatural food and drink (1 Cor 10:4). It puts us in touch with the bread that came down from heaven (Jn 6:35). Therefore we invoke the Spirit upon the bread and wine, that they might become the vehicles of his body and blood. This is captured in many prayers of consecration: "We ask you to send your Holy Spirit upon the offering of your holy church. Gather into one all who share in these sacred mysteries, filling them with the Holy Spirit and confirming their faith in the truth." And it is prayed: "Recalling his death, proclaiming his resurrection, and looking for his coming again in glory, we offer you, Father, this bread and this cup. Send your Holy Spirit upon us and upon these gifts, that all who eat and drink at this table may be one body and one people, a living sacrifice in Jesus Christ, our Lord."

The effectiveness of the sacrament is not due to any magic surrounding what happens to the elements; rather, it is due to the power of the Spirit in the action itself. There must be a coming of the Spirit upon the sacrament and the people. Consider this Ethiopic eucharistic prayer: "We beseech thee to send thy Holy Spirit upon this oblation of the church, that in joining them together, thou mayest grant that it be to them for holiness and for filling them with the Holy Spirit, and for strengthening of faith in truth, that they may glorify and praise thee through thy Son our saviour Jesus Christ."[26]

As bodily creatures, we need embodied expressions such as baptism and Eucharist to make inward grace visible and tangible. Worship is rich when it makes use of material media. Without them it can be thin, abstract, notional. Symbols help believers apprehend the invisible things of God and serve as channels of grace.[27] God acts in the sacraments in the context of the response of faith. They are neither magical actions nor mere symbols of human response. In the sacraments God offers grace that is effective when people receive it. The sacraments do not work automatically but derive their effectiveness from the presence of the Spirit in relation to faith.

Misunderstanding about this may be due not just to prejudice but also to the focus in Western Catholicism on the transformation, even transubstantiation, of the elements of the Eucharist. The situation is better in the Eastern churches, where a change in the elements is less emphasized. Stress is placed instead on participants' encountering the presence of Christ. In the prayer of invocation, clergy stand before the altar with arms outstretched, imploring the Spirit to descend on the gifts, while a deacon fans the air, depicting the movement of the Spirit; the elements are also displayed after the service. In other words, the Eastern Church has a more dynamic understanding of Eucharist than the Roman tradition. "The transformation of the elements is not the central issue for the Orthodox believer. For him, the central event of eucharist is the descent, appearance, and divine presence of the resurrected Christ."[28]

By invoking Spirit at Eucharist, we understand that the effectiveness of the sacrament is due not to any magical operation but to the coming of Spirit in response to prayer. Because effectiveness is not automatic, participants' preparation for their response cannot be neglected. Grace, when offered, must be received in faith by a genuine response. If not, the sacrament fails and the ritual is empty.[29]

The sacramental principle, along with other beliefs of the church, such as the possibility of signs and wonders, has suffered from modernity, which leaves little room for the activity of God. In the modern view, what is real is what can be scientifically established. This mindset looks for physical causation and disregards divine action. It is materialistic in outlook and exalts reason while discounting revelation and tradition. When influenced by modernity, religion is powerless in both its sacramental and its charismatic dimensions. Modernity does not expect God to be present or to move in power in either realm.[30]

Let us not tolerate skepticism in regard to God's presence in the sacraments or the charisms. Spirit is not opposed to material media and signs. The Spirit speaks through human voices, feeds us with bread, washes us in water. Worship is weakened when the sacramental is lost. There is loss of mystery, liturgical beauty and traditional practices. Such neglect not only represents a break with the historic churches but also brings a self-impoverishment that accelerates secularization.[31]

The sacramental principle has been widely acknowledged in the historic churches. The sacraments ought to be viewed as means of grace and not reduced to mere ordinances. They are both events in which God moves and acts of obedience. One should not repudiate sacraments because they have been abused, for to do so impoverishes the church. They are God-given and embodied means of grace. Sacraments are events in which the Spirit comes and we respond.[32] My own sense is that the more we experience the love of the Father in movements of renewal in the church, the more we will reject the rationalistic repudiation of sacraments, and the more we will thirst for the concrete manifestations of the Spirit found in the historic liturgies.

The Catechism concludes:

In this sacramental dispensation of Christ's mystery, the Holy Spirit acts in the same way as at other times in the economy of salvation: he prepares the church to encounter her Lord; he recalls and makes Christ manifest in the faith of the assembly. By his transforming power, he makes the mystery of Christ present here and now. Finally the Spirit of communion unites the church to the life and mission of Christ.

Charismatic Presence

As well as receiving sacraments from the Spirit, we need to cultivate openness to the gifts of the Spirit. The Spirit is present beyond liturgy in a wider circle. There is a flowing that manifests itself as power to bear witness, heal the sick, prophesy, praise God enthusiastically, perform miracles and more. There is a liberty to celebrate, an ability to dream and see visions, a release of Easter life. There are impulses of power in the move of the Spirit to transform and commission disciples to become instruments of the mission.

The longer ending of Mark captures the early view of these matters: "Signs will accompany those who believe: by using my name they will cast out demons; they will speak in new tongues; they will pick up snakes in their hands, and if they drink any deadly thing, it will not hurt them; they will lay their hands on the sick, and they will recover" (16:17-18). Hebrews says something similar: "It [salvation] was declared at first through the Lord, and it was attested to us by those who heard him, while God added his testimony by signs and wonders and various miracles, and by gifts of the Holy Spirit, distributed according to his will" (Heb 2:3-4). Paul confirms it: "The weapons of our warfare are not merely human, but they have divine power to destroy strongholds" (2 Cor 10:4).[33]

The Scriptures describe a rich effusion of gifts upon the church and do not indicate that they will be withdrawn before the parousia. Paul writes, "In every way you have been enriched in him, in speech and knowledge of every kind—just as the testimony of Christ has been strengthened among you—so that you are not lacking in any spiritual gift as you wait for the revealing of our Lord Jesus Christ" (1 Cor 1:5-7). For this reason Paul urges the Corinthians, "Pursue love and strive for the spiritual gifts, and especially that you may prophesy" (1 Cor 14:1). Paul expects gifts to operate widely in the churches. He tells us not to quench the Spirit by despising any of them (1 Thess 5:19-20). Paul would have agreed with Moses (I think) in his reply to Joshua: "Are you jealous for my sake? Would that all the LORD's people were prophets, and that the LORD would put his spirit on them" (Num 11:29).[34]

The term *gift* or *charism* has a spectrum of biblical meanings. It may refer to the gift of salvation (Rom 6:23), some benefit communicated through one's life (Rom 1:11) or a specific ability such as speaking in other tongues (1 Cor 13:1). The word is related etymologically to grace *(charis)* and points to the gracious workings of God. Gifts are divine actions that build up the community and advance its mission. They demonstrate the power of the Spirit, who is at work in the church. They are manifestations of the Spirit's presence (1 Cor 12:7). Spirit works not only noetically, creating an awareness of the work of Jesus, but ontically as well, releasing supernatural, life-giving powers. Gift-giving is an aspect of the work of the Creator Spirit who energizes history until God's goals are realized.[35]

It is a false dichotomy to split the charisms that flow from liturgical actions from charisms that flow free of institutional structures. God gives benefits through sacraments administered by ordained clergy as well as in other ways. Indeed they are interrelated. Gifts of leadership are charismatic as well as prophecy and healing. Paul said to the elders of Ephesus, "The Holy Spirit has made you overseers, to shepherd the church of God" (Acts 20:28). Leadership is a gift of the Spirit and a part of the larger charismatic structure of the congregation. Through leaders, persons may meet Jesus and experience the Spirit. Leadership is especially needed when the Spirit is flowing freely in the church, to protect it from the abuses of freedom. Revivals are messy and create considerable disorder. At times when the power is being poured out, we should pray for the Spirit to rest on our leaders that they be able to rule us well, for the good of the body. The need of wise pastoral oversight is even greater when the Spirit is breaking through than at ordinary times.[36]

Yet the circle of gifting is wider than liturgy and institutional leadership. The church and its leaders belong to the Spirit—the Spirit does not belong to them. They are subject to the Spirit, who is not under their control. The church is under the reign of the Spirit, not the reverse. The Spirit is called the Spirit of Jesus, not the Spirit of the church. Any church that denies the Spirit freedom stands in danger of becoming a lifeless and self-glorifying church. Paul does call us to be concerned that things be done decently and in order (1 Cor 14:40). But he is not advocating an order that quenches the Spirit. He is commending an order in which prophecy and tongues, revelation and knowledge are flowing, not an order that clamps down on such things. Paul is asking for order in the midst of a charismatic meeting, an order that does not rule out freedom and surprises.[37]

God gives us leaders, but clericalism must not be allowed to snuff out freedom. The community is blessed with gifts in every member. Some are exceptional like prophecy; others are everyday like generosity. Each is given to serve the community; all of them are intended to be conduits through which God's love can flow down. There are all kinds of gifts, not only for a select few but for everyone. The church is a charismatic community with all sorts of giftings, including but surpassing ordained leadership. God delights in both form and freedom. There is value both in the freely charismatic and in the regular activities of the Spirit in the ordered community. In this balance we avoid anarchy on the one hand and bland uniformity on the other.[38]

The charismatic dimension crops up in Old Testament narratives where the Spirit comes upon persons, giving them abilities for delivering the people. We see it in the inspiration of the prophets and in the promise that prophecy will become a universal gift. The Old Testament looks forward to the day when there will be an outpouring of the Spirit, not just on leaders but on people at large, even the disenfranchised (slaves, women, young people). All will be able to prophesy and see visions.[39]

The charismatic dimension was prominent in Jesus' ministry as he inaugurated the kingdom with words of authority and deeds of power. He challenged the rule of Satan and brought the kingdom of God near in a saving wholeness. The miracles and healings of Jesus were not incidental to his mission but concrete evidences of God's reign of love. His signs announced the end of Satan's reign and the coming transformation of the world: a new phase of history is beginning that will culminate in new creation.[40]

This pattern continued after the resurrection in the mission of the church. Paul's preaching was not in words of human wisdom but with a demonstration of the Spirit and power (1 Cor 2:4-5). He described his mission as being "by word and deed, by the power of signs and wonders, by the power of the Spirit" (Rom 15:18-19). The author to Hebrews spoke of how God was bearing witness by signs and wonders, miracles and gifts of the Spirit (Heb 2:4). It seems implied that this would be the pattern of the Christian mission until the coming of Christ. While it is true that the ministry of the apostles was foundational and unrepeatable, their signs and wonders were directed to human needs that persist to this day. Why would the relevance of the kingdom to these needs vary? Why would the sick not always need prayer and the possessed deliverance? Spirit has not gone into retirement, or the power of the kingdom into recession.

Some doubt this, contending that charismatic life was not meant to persist after the age of the apostles. But it is hard to make the case for their view biblically. God's kingdom has arrived in the power of the Spirit, and the impression is given that it will be so on into the future. Spiritual gifts are not linked to the apostles narrowly but broadly to kingdom ministries. The promise of the Spirit was for the first generation and also for their children (Acts 2:39). Gifts belong to all the latter days of salvation history, not just to a short time. The ideal is for every congregation to be well equipped with gifts (1 Cor 1:4-9). Every evangelist should proclaim the gospel powerfully in word *and deed*. The theory in the writings of B. B. Warfield that certain gifts have ceased, for example, is more easily explained in terms of his polemic against the Catholic Church and his apologetic agenda vis-à-vis miracles in the period of the Enlightenment rather than in terms of biblical data.

Sadly, the cessationist mindset becomes self-fulfilling. Failing to take seriously what the Bible sets forth as possibilities, people come under the influence of secular modernity by the back door. It leads to an experiential deficit that prevents people from entering into full Spirit reality.[41]

Spirit was not so much a creedal issue for the early church as a fact of their experience. His coming made a difference to their lives, outwardly and empirically. It had powerful and palpable effects. The love of God burned in their hearts, people spoke God's word with boldness, they prophesied and saw visions, they healed the sick. The Spirit was not a theory but altered real-life situations. People were awake to the powers of life, and spiritual gifts were basic to church life—gifts for building up the community and gifts for empowering mission.[42]

Joel's prophecy was fulfilled at Pentecost, and the new epoch began which is the watershed in salvation history. At baptism Jesus entered the new age as the anointed representative of humanity. It culminated on the cross, where Jesus went through a baptism of suffering (Lk 12:49-50; 22:42). Now raised to life, Jesus can baptize his disciples in the Spirit as it was prophesied that he would do (Lk 3:15-16; Jn 1:33). Salvation history has been lifted onto a new plane, and global mission begins. The Pentecost event parallels the baptism of Jesus—the disciples were baptized and empowered for mission, as Jesus had been in the Jordan. At Pentecost a transference of power and anointing took place from Jesus to the disciples. Like Jesus, they were clothed in power and equipped for mission directed by the Spirit.[43]

The New Dimension

The charismatic dimension has implications for worship and ministry.

Beyond sacramental occasions of the Spirit are celebration and giving room for inspired speech and action. Spirit comes in liturgy but also freely in possibilities we need to treasure and cultivate. Be careful not to close down the freedom of the Spirit or refuse any gift designed to enrich life and mission. Let us consider three of them which the churches need to recover.[44]

Paul considered prophecy the most important gift in a congregation (1 Cor 14:1). It is called "revelation" because God speaks through someone, giving a word needed at that moment (1 Cor 14:30). Prophetic words are inspired words designed to upbuild, encourage and console (14:3). The picture Paul paints for us is that of a people waiting on God and listening to the Spirit. The potential can be glimpsed in the fact that world missions began by means of prophecy. The church in Antioch was fasting, praying and listening to its prophets when the call came to commission Paul and Barnabas as missionaries (Acts 13:1-4). Prophecy is one way the Spirit leads God's people forward in mission.

It is wrong for churches to suppress this gift. The community that silences its prophets is in danger of becoming a Spiritless place. Outwardly things may run smoothly, but inwardly the Spirit is rebuked. Prophecy is a charism that belongs to church life and should not be a rare occurrence. Like tongues, it arises from encountering God and from listening. Teaching is of crucial importance, but the prophets must also be heard. A climate of listening must be fostered among God's people.[45]

Prophetic utterances can vary greatly in quality. Our hearing is far from perfect. Human elements enter into the word of God. Inspiration does not eliminate this factor. Therefore prophecies are not self-authenticating but must be tested. There can be false or trivial prophecies. There must be testing. As Paul said, when one speaks, others need to weigh what is being said, because prophets are subject to the congregation and are not exalted over it (1 Cor 14:29). The *Didache* reveals that by the year A.D. 100, the need of criteria for measuring claims to prophecy was already felt.[46]

Nevertheless, the fear of false prophecy must not prevent us from listening to God. Paul's principle holds: "Do not quench the Spirit. Do not despise the words of prophets, but test everything; hold fast to what is good" (1 Thess 5:19-21). Let us ask with Zedekiah: "Is there any word from the LORD?" (Jer 37:17). To his credit, the king asked for the Lord's word, even though the answer did not please him. We must make room in our liturgies for the word of the Lord.

Healing the sick was a prominent activity of Jesus, and it deserves a place in the ministry of today's church. The long ending of Mark reads, "They [the disciples] will lay hands on the sick, and they will recover" (16:18). The gospel is about healing in the broad sense and even envisages a wholly renewed universe. God cares about the healing of individuals, communities, nations and the cosmos. Spirit gives gifts of healing which speak eloquently of God's care for the whole person (1 Cor 12:9, 28). Healings signify the dawn of God's reign and point to the day when the eyes of the blind will be opened (Is 35:5-6). Even apart from the gospel imperative, sickness is a major human concern, and simply for the sake of building bridges to people, churches ought to signal God's concern about it.

Healing prayer does not imply a negative view of medical science. The powers of healing are at work in the creation. Our bodies, when damaged, immediately begin to heal themselves. What medicine can learn about God's healing which is built into creation is all to the good. Skill in medicine is a creational charism. Prayer for healing simply means that we place problems of physical bodies before the Father and ask for help. It is not that we worship health or demand to be free from suffering. On the contrary, we accept our frail and mortal life. There is "a time to be born, and a time to die" (Eccles 3:2). We live and we die unto the Lord, accepting whatever comes from his hand (Rom 14:8). Humanity was made for resurrection, and healing is at most a temporary stop-gap. Nevertheless, in times of crisis and trauma God invites us to lay our concerns humbly before him.[47]

James mentions the use of oil in the context of praying for the sick (Jas 5:14). This unction is not only for persons at the point of death but for the sick at large (*Constitution on the Liturgy* par. 73). When we anoint the sick, God makes himself present tangibly and sacramentally. Gestures and symbols are important along with the use of language. As bodily creatures, we respond to such actions and are helped to reach out to God for blessing.

As we open ourselves to prayers for healing, let us be careful not to trespass on the divine freedom. God is free to grant healings, whether few or many, whether usual or unusual, as he chooses. Those that are granted point to the coming kingdom but do not replace the need for complete renewal. Not until resurrection will sickness and death be removed completely. How many signs will be given depends entirely on God's will. We know that God wants to relieve suffering but that he has other concerns as well to think about. For example, God maintains the stability and regularity of the universe and may have reasons for not interfering too often in the natural order. Raising the dead has happened, but not very often. In addition there are factors related to issues of soul making and character formation. When we pray for healing, we simply ask: Lord, here are our needs; give us what you please.[48]

Though there are exorcisms in the Gospels and teaching about spiritual warfare in the Epistles, intellectual and practical recognition of this dimension is often missing in Christian communities today. Jesus thought it important to deliver people from Satan's grasp by the Spirit. Jesus sent the apostles to preach and cast out demons also (Mt 10:7-8). He said, "If it is by the Spirit of God that I cast out demons, then the kingdom of God has come to you" (Mt 12:28). Exorcisms reveal the presence of God confronting evil and bondage. Jesus may have spoken of such matters in the language of his time, but that does not mean he was not wrestling with dark and powerful realities, whatever they are called. Then and now, Satan is engaged in ruining human lives, and Jesus is intent on winning victories over him. John says, "The Son of God was revealed . . . to destroy the works of the devil" (1 Jn 3:8).

Without falling into superstition, let us not make the mistake of minimizing the titanic struggle between God's kingdom and the powers of evil. God's sovereignty is not uncontested in this world, and his kingdom does not come without a fight. There are people who need to be delivered from Satan's power, and the church is responsible for ministering deliverance.

Spiritual warfare needs to be taken seriously in many areas. Even churches can become entrapped and need setting free. Such deficiencies often lie deeper than that which can be observed. Communities come under the control of traditions and doctrinal strongholds and can be incapable of extricating themselves. It is notorious how spirits of bitterness and conflict dozens of years old can continue to dominate congregations. Even denominationally, we cannot save ourselves but must cry out to God to save us.

A false dichotomy should not be created by distinguishing too sharply between gifts natural and supernatural. Spirit is active in creation as well as redemption and can activate natural potentials already present. Intuition, for example, is a natural faculty, developed more in some than others; healing is a process going on all the time in our bodies; possession is a condition known to psychology. Spiritual gifts are not necessarily discontinuous with natural possibilities. Spirit supplies natural gifts like artistry and creativity, and it would be strange if all this were bypassed in spiritual gifting. Gifts of the Spirit can animate natural capacities and may not be foreign to nature as created by God.[49]

Openness to the Spirit

How charismatic life is restored in the churches is mysterious. On the one hand, the level of God's manifest presence itself varies, and the degree to which there are signs, wonders and anointing is not constant. God is free to be present as he wills, on a spectrum from ordinary to extraordinary ways. It is simply not under our control. When the power falls, it is marvelous in our eyes. On the other hand, openness is a human variable. Response runs the gamut from unbelief to unrestricted surrender (Mk 6:5; Acts 4:29-30). The best-case scenario is God's manifested presence coupled with unrestricted human openness. The worst case is the withdrawal of God coupled with human indifference.

History witnesses to revivals of Spirit when God rends the heavens and comes down. At such times people fall under the power, sinners are converted, the sick are healed, and history is changed. Let us ask God to disturb our tranquillity so that he may surprise, refresh, empower us. Let congregations be transformed to flow with celebration and hope. Lord, grant us a fresh anointing, a renewing of our baptism and a release of its latent potentials. We desperately need a demonstration of the Spirit with power for the mission to go forward. Over and above the evidence that God raised up Jesus, evidence is needed of people having been set free. Nietzsche's Zarathustra taunts the church: "They would have to sing better songs to make me believe in their Redeemer." Though these are the words of a bitter and lonely philosopher, they make a valid point. Are there not many forms of faith today called Christian that leave people captive and do not set them free?[50]

Mark records that Jesus could not do any miracles in Nazareth because of unbelief (Mk 6:5). Limited expectations dishonor and diminish God's freedom to act. Where there is no confidence in God's saving power, the church declines (Ps 78:22). Therefore, let God's people be open to the power of the Spirit without restriction. Let us not allow tradition to control our reading of the Bible in ways that silence its message. Let us not restrict what God is wanting to give us.

Many today suffer worldview impediment. Though we may believe intellectually that God can move in power, something inside of us says this is not going to happen, prayer is an illusion, the sick must only go to doctors. This may be coupled with a fear of change. We have our comfort zones and may prefer the orderliness of an unrenewed church to the disorderliness of renewal. There are reasons for not wanting the Spirit to move. We do not want to look ridiculous. We may not want to exchange Sunday-morning religion for real discipleship. We may not want to run the risk of opposition, which usually comes when the world discovers that the church is serious about mission. May the Lord shake us loose and allow us to see the possibilities of new creation.[51]

Jürgen Moltmann puts a finger on the issue:

The essential impediment to the charismatic experience of our potentialities for living is to be found in our passive sins, not our active ones. For the hindrance is not our despairing attempt to be ourselves, but our despairing attempt not to be ourselves, so that out of fear of life and fear of death we fall short of what our lives could be. The charismata of the Spirit are present wherever faith in God drives out the fears of life and wherever the hope of resurrection overcomes the fear of death.[52]

Our responsibility is to be open. Regardless of whether this is a time of revival, we belong to a community baptized in the Holy Spirit. God has given us the power to be witnesses, and it is essential to be open to the Spirit. In particular, we need to be open to the full range of spiritual gifts, not a select number.

The problem becomes visible when we think of gifts as falling along a spectrum from *A* to *Z*. Let *A* to *P* refer to gifts we are comfortable with (such as teaching and administration) and *R* to *Z* represent gifts we are hesitant about (like prophecy and healing). Whereas the early Christians were open to the full spectrum of gifts, often we are not. Our communities hardly recognize certain gifts as real possibilities. The result is, because we are not open to them, that these charisms are not operative. Limited expectation results in an experiential deficit. Gifts *R* to *Z* are impeded from operating in communities that do not acknowledge them as real options. We need to allow the gifts to be rekindled among us as we raise the level of our expectation and allow God to decide what should happen. Openness does not mean knowing the outcome—for example, whether miracles will be few or many. It just means openness.[53]

We need to ensure, of course, that our openness is not undiscerning. Under the guise of charism, there can be undocumented claims, irresponsible prophecies, elitism, charismania. There can be inspired utterances that contradict the word of Scripture and refuse to be subject to the discernment of the community. There can be a love of power that is not the power of love and sound mindedness (2 Tim 1:7). There can be lust after the theology of glory, which looks for victory, prosperity and success but repudiates the cross and the power that works through love.

There are risks in any call for openness. But fear of making mistakes and seeing counterfeit charisms must not close down faith in us. How tragic it would be if focusing on dangers closed us to the Spirit. It is a fundamental principle that God must be free to act when and where and how he pleases.[54]

Office and Charism

Given the promise and the peril, the need of office alongside charism is evident. The two are positively disposed to one another. Charism needs office the way a delicate plant needs a solid pot to hold it. Church is community *and* institution—the former being the goal of the latter, the latter holding the promise of the former. Freedom needs order, and order needs freedom in the church. We need neither a supercharged church without discipline nor a lifeless church without Spirit. Renewal needs wise oversight to protect it from abuse. It needs leaders who encourage and supervise the ministries of the laity. Such leaders benefit the body when they are visionary and create room for the Spirit.

At the same time, leaders can impede renewal if they are unduly cautious. Rigidity can set in when a certain kind of order is preferred to the disorder of the divine presence and when the word is preferred to the Spirit. Leaders are sometimes nervous about Spirit, which may explain why revivals usually break out in communities less hampered by office. The way of the institution may make it necessary for God to work at the fringes, with the people others look down on, because they are open. God's strategy may be to stir the fire outside the mainline churches where people are more open to it, with a view to moving it back into those churches later, after the fruit is tested and those who are slow to receive are softened.[55]

Paul experienced the problem of maintaining order where freedom was operating. He exercised his own authority as an apostle and commended various offices of teaching and oversight, while exhorting the people to evaluate what they were hearing.[56] It was and is a delicate balance. Leaders are important to the community, yet community must not be too tightly controlled. Leaders should not be trying to control everything but foster life and discern gifts of those under their care. Ideally there should be a harmonious synergism of gift and office, a dialectic of charism and institution, for the Spirit is given not only to officeholders but to the whole congregation. Laity should respect leaders, but everyone should also listen to prophets and honor gifts of faith. The work of officeholders is to foster the charisms of the community and harmonize them for the common good.[57]

Renewal in the Spirit promises enrichment for the churches. True, mistakes have been made and divisions created in the course of renewal. It is not always a happy situation. Misunderstandings happen owing to historical circumstance, and separated ecclesial communities are formed. Nevertheless, the goal is unity and empowerment. The goal is not to divide but to bless the church. God grant, in the not too distant future, that renewal will be integrated into mainline churches and result in the revitalization of Christianity as a world movement.[58]

Transforming Mission

What has been said about the church as the continuation of Jesus' anointing and the Spirit as present in sacramental and charismatic ways all has to do with mission. God did not pour the Spirit out for us to exult in it as a private benefit. The purpose was (and is) to empower witnesses to God's kingdom (Acts 1:8). God justifies and saves individuals only to give them a vocation in the service of the kingdom. He awakens a knowledge of the truth in people in order to conscript them into the service of mission. God wants a community that, like Jesus, gets caught up in the transformation of the world. The church is the provisional representation of God's call to humanity, and like Jesus it exists for the world and nonmembers of the church.[59]

Vocation is so important—and so neglected. We are saved not just for our own benefit but to become disciples of Jesus who bear witness to and embody the coming kingdom. We have been brought into the representative journey of Jesus in order to live in ways that contrast to worldly ways. Otherwise the salt loses its savor, and we become conformed to the world (Rom 12:2). Christians are called to live the life of beatitude, the life that anticipates and prefigures new creation (Mt 5:3-10). When we forget this, the spiritual life becomes empty and its point is lost. It leads to the very unreality of so much Christian living. Though Jesus gave us a vocation, multitudes live as though they had none. Believers are often frustrated because they belong to churches that are not clear about mission. Normally they would discover their vocations within the fruit-bearing activities of the community. But if a congregation has forgotten its own vocation to be a continuation of Jesus' anointing, its members become confused and may be sucked back into worldly patterns for want of vision and structures of accountability.

A major hindrance to mission is the lack of interest in discipleship on the part of many Christians. No one is naturally disposed to join Jesus in the business of confronting the powers of evil or in the costly action of embodying the new order. It is hard to market a mission that goes beyond appealing for faith and advocates practicing the way of Jesus in the world. It is almost impossible unless the church keeps the vision alive and before us.[60]

The Spirit comes in power through sacrament and charism to enable the church to participate in God's mission of mending creation and making all things new. The church is placed at the disposal of the Spirit and commissioned to serve the kingdom in the world. The Spirit is present in order that the world might be touched by divine grace. We have been called out of darkness into marvelous light to declare God's mighty deeds (1 Pet 2:9). The challenge facing the church is not theory but practice—not so much showing that Christianity is intellectually plausible as enacting the gospel in recognizable signs of the kingdom.[61]

Mission is a Spirit event—it is God's mission, not ours. It is not a duty following the work of Christ but is itself God's work. Pentecost was an act of God that initiated the new age, which is to be the sphere of God's new actions. It was a historical turning point and the beginning of the end-time harvest. Indeed, mission is a sign of the end. "This good news of the kingdom will be proclaimed throughout the world, . . . and then the end will come" (Mt 24:14). Spirit is the power behind mission, and the church is an instrument of it, not its initiator. The church can participate in God's mission only if it has the power of Pentecost (Lk 24:49).

Mission is not human effort responding to a commandment. It is not even obedience to the Great Commission. It is natural and spontaneous. Only after the Spirit fell did the disciples speak (Acts 2:4). The Spirit creates a witnessing church. "It is not you who speak, but the Spirit of your Father speaking through you" (Mt 10:20). Spreading the gospel is dependent not on human wisdom and strength but on a demonstration of Spirit and power (1 Cor 2:4-5). Mission is not something we do to expand the size of the church; it is something God does to gather and bring justice to the nations. The Spirit is not the sustainer of the church but the driving power of its mission. The main thing for us to do is place ourselves at the Spirit's disposal.[62]

The goal is world transformation. "See, I am making all things new" (Rev 21:5). The church, filled with the Spirit, is agent of God's coming kingdom and sacrament for the world. God touches the world when the church speaks the truth, proclaims good news, performs Jesus-actions, identifies with pain, builds community, shares and forgives.[63] The mission is holistic and has broad parameters. Spiritual ecstasy is not meant to be an end in itself—the goal is transformation. The purpose of the outpouring of the Spirit is to bring the kingdom near and change real-life situations. Mission is an activity that initiates people into the kingdom and promotes the reality of the new order.[64]

In early texts the Spirit clothes judges like Gideon and Sampson with power to rescue people from oppression. In Isaiah's prophecy, Spirit commissions the servant to bring justice and mercy to nations. He wants to restore community, transform life and instill hope. In Joel's prophecy, Spirit acts on behalf of the weak and powerless, giving the disenfranchised a voice. The theme of liberation is central in Jesus' ministry. He rejects charismatic actions done in his name if they do not promote the will of God (Mt 7:21). For Paul too, the purpose of spiritual gifts, including spectacular ones, is fostering deeds of love (1 Cor 13:1-3). Gifts are like a pipe down which love is to flow. Spirit is about renewing life and creating community in order to benefit people. The Spirit becomes tangible in the deeds of love that function like sacraments in the world.

The power of the Spirit is given to help the church become a servant who follows the sacrificial path of Jesus. The believers have said yes to Christ's representative journey on behalf of humankind, and God's strategy now is to create out of them a new community marked by deeds of love and caring that anticipate the coming kingdom. We look not only for the salvation of souls but for the redemption of creation. Our goal is not to triumph in world politics but to live the life of beatitude, in which blessings of the age are prefigured in this world. Discontented with existing realities, we put our hope in the God who raises the dead. We say: Come, Lord, send your power, make us whole. We love your kingdom—we want to see more of it.[65]

The Spirit can throw a wonderful party. He can set our hearts on fire and fill our mouths with songs of praise. But the goal remains the gathering of the nations and the transformation of creation. Sacramental and charismatic grace is wonderful, full of awe and delight, but still the goal is the formation of compassionate, truthful, tender creatures. Spirit is longing for more redeemed human beings like Mary, mother of Jesus, who wait patiently at his cross, full of love for him and for the world.

We need renewal not because we are bored but because a powerless church cannot become a mighty army. Disciples who are discouraged and enjoy no intimacy with God will not be able to follow Jesus in costly ways. Not until they know God as their Father, as Jesus knew him, and taste God's kindness. To become kind and loving, we must know God's love and kindness. We need grace to help others in their infirmities. The Spirit awakens us to life to enable us to liberate others.[66]

Spirit may be mysterious, but we are not left in the dark about his goals. The Spirit is not a mystical presence beyond any comprehension. Yes, Spirit is invisible and beyond our control, but that does not mean he is incomprehensible. Spirit wants God's will done on earth as in heaven—justice, mercy and love. This is demanding, but it is not mysterious. If we are open to the Spirit, we must also be open to the goals of the Spirit. "If we live by the Spirit, let us also be guided by the Spirit" (Gal 5:25). Spirit brings us into intimacy with God, not to foster mystical rapture as an end in itself but to sensitize us to the will of God. Spirit wants us to follow Jesus and embody the kingdom in our lives and relationships.[67]

Empowered Mission

We are called to holistic mission in the power of God. Our own baptism in the Spirit is a prolongation of Jesus' baptism, and our mission is an extension of his mission. Jesus is looking for laborers to enter the vineyard and carry it forward (Mt 9:37). This involves proclaiming the gospel, healing the sick and caring for needs. We cannot love our neighbors without caring for their needs. We cannot teach converts to observe all of Christ's teachings without attending to human needs. After Pentecost, human situations were transformed when the Spirit came in power (Acts 2:43-45; 4:32-35). It will be always so.[68]

Because mission is holistic, it must be empowered—it simply cannot be carried out by our human wisdom and strength alone. Actions have to be initiated and empowered by the Spirit. The Shepherd has to go on ahead of us. There is a partnership in which the Spirit is the leading player and we are junior partners and instruments. It is God's mission, and we are being caught up in it. The Spirit bears witness, and you also (Jn 15:26-27). When the New Testament describes the disciples as ordinary, uneducated people, afraid and often lacking understanding, is it not telling us that participation in mission does not depend on being talented and well educated (Acts 4:13)? Does it not prove that any success they enjoyed was not due to them but to God? If there was greatness in the disciples, surely it was not their ability but their openness to the Spirit. It was baptism in the Spirit that enabled them to give testimony to Jesus Christ. This reminder can help us deal with our own feelings of inadequacy in the face of the task. What a relief to know God uses weak people! This underscores how crucial it is to maintain a good relationship with the Spirit.

The shape of empowered mission is not arrived at ideologically or even pragmatically. In mission we ask not just "Is this action good and necessary?" We also ask, "Where is God leading? Is this God's undertaking?" There are no rules and regulations for mission, because Spirit leadership is central. Mission is not social work but deeds directed and empowered by the Spirit. Through the gifting of the whole congregation, the church is enabled to express its missionary character as it speaks the Word and ministers in the power of God (1 Pet 4:10-11). Apostles and evangelists plant churches, accompanied by signs and wonders; prophets speak the word of God to specific situations; those with the gift of faith point the way forward. The Spirit motivates and equips the church to move in mission.[69]

The world did not set the agenda for Jesus. People could not predict what he would do next, because he had no plan but sought what the Father wanted. He did not operate from a program. Need alone did not constitute the divine call. He waited for God's urging and the Spirit's guiding. In the same way, the church should not go where God is not leading or become involved just because the world tells us to. There is no formula or doctrine of the church's role in society. The church lives out its witness in concrete historical situations, waiting for God to lead. There is a role for thinking about what to do next, but this thinking should be always done in the context of waiting on God.

Prayer is evidence of dependency on God. In prayer we envisage a new future, and we protest the world order as it is. We stand against darkness and invoke God's light. Using weapons of the Spirit, we pull down strongholds and join the uprising against the present disorder. Prayer shows that we belong to a different order of reality which defies the powers of evil and anticipates the kingdoms of this world becoming the kingdom of Christ (Rev 11:15). History belongs to intercessors, because history belongs to God.[70]

Mission is holistic because sin is more than personal infraction. Sin affects the structures of the world, and we oppose sin in all its manifestations, including our own complicity in what is wrong. Conversion points, then, not only to individual change but beyond to the coming transformation of the world. Since we are creatures in society and in a world, God wants to renew both us and our created context. If God did not intend that, he would be tackling only half the problem. Social sanctification and cosmic renewal are ultimately part of God's plan. This can begin to happen as the church injects values of God's kingdom into the public square and improves the climate for them. As salt and light, the church is a catalyst for righteousness in society. Many benefits exist in society because of Jesus Christ. The church can be a means by which God's kingdom gets its foothold in the world.[71]

At the same time, there is a certain powerlessness in the messianic way of bringing justice. The servant of the Lord does not cry in the street and does not quench the dimly burning wick (Is 42:2-3). He has authority, but it is the authority of one who suffers and one who is politically powerless. In the temptations Jesus rejected worldly ways of power and chose the path of suffering love. His hope for worldly change was based on the presence of new community. This approach need not lead to disengagement for fear of accommodation. Instead we choose a different sort of engagement. The nonviolent messianic community penetrates the social order in its own fashion.[72]

A mission whose goal is the transformation of the world is stupendous. A powerless church can hardly consider it. It presupposes the anointing and empowerment of Spirit. May the Spirit quicken in us a fresh vision, so that we see ourselves as a continuation of Jesus' anointing, are enriched with the entire charismatic structure and remember the transforming mission of Jesus.

God has broken into history—the new age has begun. We wait for the consummation of history and hope for the glory of God. We are neither optimistic or pessimistic about the world, but wait in hope, serving the Lord. As the church echoes trinitarian relations, it models the coming kingdom and prefigures the destiny of humanity.

FIVE

SPIRIT &
UNION

WHEN WE LOOK AT salvation from the standpoint of the Spirit, we view it in relational, affective terms. Every religion on earth has its idea about the goal of life. Martin Luther's experience of salvation as justification has skewed the Christian understanding somewhat toward legal terms. Emphasis has been placed on the sinner's change of status, from guilty to not guilty, rather than on personal union with God. While Luther caught an aspect of the truth, a more relational model is required. Spirit is leading us to union—to transforming, personal, intimate relationship with the triune God. "This is eternal life, that they may know you, the only true God, and Jesus Christ whom you have sent" (Jn 17:3). Jesus adds, "That the love with which you have loved me may be in them, and I in them" (v. 26). As the psalmist says, "Lord, you have been our dwelling place in all generations" (Ps 90:1).

Let us explore salvation now as the beatific vision, as the embrace of God. Bernard of Clairvaux was eloquent on this theme. He writes in a sermon on the Song of Songs, "If the Father kisses the Son and the Son receives the kiss, it is appropriate to think of the Holy Spirit as the kiss" ("Holy Spirit: Kiss of the Mouth," sermon 8). Salvation is directed toward the loving embrace of God.[1]

Obviously salvation is multifaceted and has many dimensions—conversion, new birth, justification and sanctification—but the goal is surely glorification and union with God. Luther fixed on something very important—the removal of our condemnation. But this is but a facet of salvation, part of a much larger scenario. Salvation is the Spirit, who indwells us, drawing us toward participation in the life of the triune God. The goal is union with God at the marriage supper of the Lamb. Thus Jesus prays, "Father, I desire that those also, whom you have given me, may be with me where I am, to see my glory, which you have given me because you loved me before the foundation of the world" (Jn 17:24).

This image of salvation is captured in the parable of the prodigal, whose father longs for him to return to his bosom. It is a picture of God, who is a relationality of love, working to bring lost humanity into loving union with himself in the fellowship of Father, Son and Spirit. God intends to elevate humanity to life with God, and this is what we are beginning to experience on earth. We are destined to find our true selves in God, in whom we live and move and have our being. Christ dwells in our hearts by faith, and Spirit sweeps us up into the love of God. Walking in the Spirit, we become ever better acquainted with the love that surpasses knowledge and are filled with the divine fullness (Eph 3:16-19). The Spirit summons us to a transforming friendship with God that leads to sharing in the triune life. Thanks to the grace of Christ and the love of God, the Spirit dwells in us and unites us to the corporate triune fellowship (2 Cor 13:13)—and this divine work characterizes the last days before the new creation.[2]

To think of salvation in this way is to recover what early theologians called *theosis*. This category invites us to think of the goal of salvation as participation in the divine nature, in a way that preserves distinctions proper to Creator and creature without losing sight of their union. Paul calls this sharing the glory of God: "Since we are justified by faith, we have peace with God . . . [and] access to this grace in which we stand; and we boast in our hope of sharing the glory of God" (Rom 5:1-2).[3]

The Reformation made justification the focus in the polemical situation it faced. Rome had lost sight of the truth, and Luther's achievement was to have recovered it. Today the Catholic Church admits Luther's insight. But acquittal before God is only the beginning, not the end of salvation. After being justified, we enter the process of being conformed to Christ and anticipate sharing God's glory in the new community and new creation. This has been the emphasis of Orthodoxy: our identity is found in relationship with God. The goal is immersion in the richness of the divine life. Theosis is the source of what C. S. Lewis calls the inconsolable longing in us. Ecstasy awaits us. We are not just being pardoned but are being transformed and divinized. Christ is being formed in us (Gal 4:19).[4]

Peter gives it classic expression: Christians are becoming "participants of the divine nature" (2 Pet 1:4).[5] The destiny of the community is to be embraced in triune life as its final condition. This lies behind what Paul says when he claims that love (not faith or hope) abides forever. Though faith will be replaced by sight and hope by fulfillment, love is everlasting and is never surpassed. By faith we take hold of grace and by hope we wait patiently for it, but love is the very nature of God and therefore the environment of eternity. Love characterizes life in the age to come. We will sit down at table in the kingdom and occupy the place prepared for us (Jn 14:3; Rev 19:7). Second Peter 1:4 is not an isolated thought or throwaway line but enunciates a fundamental biblical teaching—what Paul speaks of as being united to Christ and John speaks of as a mutual indwelling in God. Union with God is not peripheral to salvation but the goal. Hope for it is kindled in our hearts by the Spirit.[6]

Pope John Paul II writes, "Man is called to a fullness of life which far exceeds the dimensions of earthly existence, because it consists in sharing the life of God." If we appreciated the prospect of union with God more, we would not think to complain as much about the arduousness of the journey. We are strangers and exiles in the world, but in the end we are going home to be enfolded in trinitarian life.[7]

Note that in the flow of this book I am choosing to treat the salvation of individuals after the doctrine of the church. This is not due to a devaluation of the personal aspects of salvation. Remember, the shepherd leaves the ninety and nine to look for one single lost sheep. God loves individuals and numbers the very hairs on each one's head. Every individual is precious to God. No, I place the personal after the corporate in view of the fact that individuals are shaped in communities. One becomes a person in relationship with other persons, not otherwise. John Donne was right to say no man is an island, because the self is a delicate flower that requires a social context in order to flourish. A child raised by wolves would not become a person, though the potential to become one is there. Similarly, one becomes a Christian by coming into contact with the church—by hearing the good news, encountering the presence of God in the people or in some other way. If there were no church, there would be no Christians either. Church is the sacrament of God which brings his presence near.[8]

Union with God

The purpose of life is a transforming friendship and union with God. United to Christ in his participatory journey, we are on the path to share in God's life through death and resurrection. The living flame of love is preparing souls for union with love. Jesus speaks of this oneness: "The glory that you have given me I have given them, so that they may be one, as we are one, I in them and you in me, that they may become completely one, so that the world may know that you have sent me and have loved them even as you have loved me" (Jn 17:22-23).[9]

Union with God is a state of intimacy, and sexual imagery may be used for it. Paul says that the love of male and female points to the mystery of Christ's love for us (Eph 5:31). The reason we should reject prostitution is that we are one with the Lord (1 Cor 6:15-19). Salvation itself aims at a wedding (Rev 19:9). The new Jerusalem, coming down out of heaven, is prepared as a bride for her husband (Rev 21:2). The angel says to John, "Come, I will show you the bride, the wife of the

Lamb" (Rev 21:9). This strong imagery links salvation to the fulfillment of our deep desires as gendered creatures. Picking up on it, spiritual writers such as John of the Cross comment at length on the Song of Songs. They see salvation as a mystical loving union in which, without losing identity, one experiences interpersonal union and communion with God (*Philokalia* 2.216). It is beautifully expressed by Bernard of Clairvaux:

Jesus, the very thought of thee
With sweetness fills my breast;
But sweeter far thy face to see,
And in thy presence rest.

The Eucharist prefigures the wedding banquet. Breaking bread and drinking wine are tangible signs of our future feast with Christ (Lk 14:15). For this reason Communion should be a celebration, not a sad memorial. Orthodox liturgy captures the spirit of celebration implicit in the sacrament: "Let us rejoice and exult and give him glory, for the marriage of the Lamb has come, and his bride has made herself ready."[10] This is really what atonement means. The term *atonement,* which is used only once in the King James Version of the New Testament, is an old expression meaning "at-one-ment" and is usually translated "reconciliation" (Rom 5:11). It speaks of unity between God and humanity. Owing to its association in theology with theories of the work of Christ, it has lost some of its original relational content. Actually the word *atonement* speaks to us of the loving relationality into which the Spirit is drawing people. Spirit is bringing us into intimacy with the Father through the Son, who is sharing his divine sonship with us.

Spirit calls us to become children of God in and alongside the Son and to join in his self-surrender to the Father. Always the object of the Father's love, the Son has always reciprocated it in the Spirit. God invites creatures to participate in this divine dance of loving communion. God has not left us outside the circle of his life. We are invited inside the Trinity as joint heirs together with Christ. By the Spirit we cry "Abba" together with the Son, as we are drawn into the divine filial relationship and begin to participate in God's life. Union with God is the unimaginable fulfillment of creaturely life, and the Spirit is effecting it in us. This is what the church fathers meant when they said, "God became man, that man might become God" (Irenaeus *Against Heresies* 3.19.1; Athanasius *On the Incarnation* 2.54).[11]

We worship the God who descended to the depths of our fallen condition and opened a path of ascent to union. The purpose of our creation was fellowship with God, to be children of God with the Son. God sent forth the Son to make this possible and the Spirit to share the experience of sonship with us (Gal 4:4-7). As a result of the hypostatic union of two natures in Christ, our human nature has been restored and made capable of participation in God.

What we call union (theosis or divinization) is not pantheism—there is no absorption of the person in God. By the grace of God and *as creatures* we participate in him. United to Christ without becoming Christ, we are also united to God without becoming God. It is a personal union in which the distinction between Creator and creature is maintained. We enter the dance of the Trinity not as equals but as adopted partners. When Peter says we participate in the divine nature, he is indicating not ontological union but union in resurrected bodies. This is a personal union, not an ontological union. It does not deny the distinction between God and creature or make God the only reality. As the Persons of the Trinity dwell in and with one another, so we, created in the image of God, dwell in and with God, sharing the life of the Trinity and experiencing movements of love passing between the Persons.[12]

As we clarify our own thinking in this regard, let us not jump to conclusions about what Eastern religions may intend when they speak of absorption into the infinite or the divine. Even Hinduism, which sounds monistic and nondualistic, speaks dialectically. It is not always clear that nonduality is meant. Sankara, who understands God to be beyond conceptual reach and salvation as union, can sound rather Christian at times. We need to be clear about what we intend and patient to hear what others wish to say. It may be that when we celebrate union with God as the goal of salvation, we have something in common not only with the Eastern churches but also with non-Christian Eastern religions. There may be more commonality than we thought in this area. Believing in the prevenient grace of God as we do, we would find this cause for thankfulness, because it could open up more fruitful dialogue and enhance our witness among the peoples of India.[13]

Union with God begins on earth and is not reserved entirely for the future. We experience it when we are caught up in the life of God (while remaining ourselves) in prayer. Praying with the help of the Spirit, we begin to participate in the triune life, standing before the Father, in union with Christ, through the Spirit. Or, as Paul says, "It is no longer I who live, but it is Christ who lives in me" (Gal 2:20). Believers, in Christ by the Spirit, are beginning to participate in God and experience the love pouring from the Father to the Son. Washed by waves of delight, we return love with the Son, waiting in the presence of God, and Spirit intercedes within us. In this life we are beginning to experience union with God. We are coming into the fullness of God (Col 2:9-10).[14]

Union with God is not limited to spirits. The creation does not disappear or nature go into oblivion. The goal is new creation, a transfigured universe where righteousness and peace dwell. It is a new Jerusalem that we hope for, where resurrected saints inhabit the cosmos set free from its groaning (Rom 8:23). The goal of union is not a one-dimensional union of spirits but a multidimensional consummation of creaturely existence in God.[15]

Justification and Theosis

Union with God was not the central category for the Reformers. As a monk Luther feared God's judgment and sought acquittal in Jesus Christ. Since then Protestants have made justification a principal article of faith. This means that the legal dimension has dominated our thinking about salvation.[16] Being forgiven and acquitted is no doubt important. Justification is a moment in salvation, but not necessarily the central motif. Since we have been forgiven, our eyes are on the goal of union with the love of God. Christian experience is more than a feeling of relief at having evaded divine retribution. Justification is a step along the road of salvation, but it points forward to transformation and union. It is not the principal article of all Christian doctrine, as Luther claimed. It captures a truth—the truth of God's unmerited favor—but it cannot be the model of salvation as a whole. Being saved is more like falling in love with God.[17]

The fact is that legal thinking and the doctrine of justification are not as prominent in the Bible as we have made them. God is not primarily an angry judge needing satisfaction but a passionate lover seeking at-one-ment. Justification is a Pauline concept in Romans and Galatians, but it plays a smaller role even in his epistles than it did for the Reformation. Even in those epistles it features in a debate over Gentiles and the Jewish law. Luther's rediscovery of justification was important for himself and for sixteenth-century reforms, but it is not as central for us, and not even for an astute interpretation of Paul's theology. Unlike Luther, the apostle did not have a guilty conscience. As a Jew, he considered himself blameless before the law (Phil 3:6). Justification for him had less to do with a guilty conscience than with the new age inaugurated by the resurrection of Jesus.[18]

God's righteousness for Paul is not a threat requiring appeasement. In Greco-Roman thought, justice was a strict norm against which one is judged innocent or guilty. But in Hebrew thought, *righteousness* is a term indicating God's saving activity. God is "righteous" because he sustains creation and enables it to flourish. The righteous God goes the second mile to heal broken relationships. We are justified by faith when we surrender to God's saving righteousness, which assures us of final vindication. In justifying sinners God is not engaging in fantasies but declaring that they have been incorporated into the victory of Jesus Christ. For Paul, justification tells us how God accepts Gentiles. God accepts them the same way he accepts Jews—by grace through faith. By electing Israel, God intended to bless Gentiles, and he is doing so by the saving action of righteousness in Jesus Christ. Salvation, then, is more than relief at not being condemned; it sweeps us up into the love of God for participation in the divine nature.[19]

The key thing is that salvation involves transformation. It is not cheap grace, based on bare assent to propositions, or merely a change of status. Romans 5 with its doctrine of justification is followed by Romans 6 with its promise of union. It is not just a matter of balancing two ideas; it is a matter of never conceiving of the former without its goal in the latter. For the justified person is baptized into the death and resurrection of Jesus Christ. If there is no newness of life, if there is no union with Christ, if there is no coming out from under the dominion of sin, there is no salvation.[20]

Awakening to Love

If salvation is union, conversion is awakening to love. The Father longs for the return of his sons and daughters. He cries, "Sleeper, awake! Rise from the dead, and Christ will shine on you" (Eph 5:14). He wants us to come to ourselves and awaken to love, to remember our destiny and return home with Jesus, the true prodigal. The Spirit is wooing human beings to come into their proper destiny and come home to God's love. Let them not reject God's purpose for them but acknowledge their sins and believe the good news (Mk 1:15; Lk 7:30).[21]

Love woos—it does not compel. Conversion is not coerced.

We are saved by grace through faith; a response is involved. Genesis records that Abram "believed the LORD, and the LORD reckoned it to him as righteousness" (Gen 15:6). Faith pleases God, and he rewards those who seek him (Heb 11:6). God took the initiative, but Abram responded. Pleased by his response, God made him a partner in the work of redemption.

God convicts and moves us toward intimacy. His Word is powerful, but there must be a response to it. God does not overpower but saves those who yield to his persuasion. God lays hold, but sinners must also consent to be laid hold of. They must let God renew them. Like Cain, prey to the power of sin, we are reminded of our freedom. Cain was free in the face of sin to repudiate it. "Its desire is for you, but you must master it" (Gen 4:7).[22]

We are not in a position to give God much that he needs. But there is one thing he wants from us that nobody else can give. And if we do not give it, he will not receive it. I refer to our personal love. God can have our love only if we decide to give it. God made us to love him, and the key issue is what we decide to do with that freedom. God empowers but does not overpower. Grace works mightily but does not override. God is a loving parent, not a tyrant. One can be saved only by grace, but grace saves no one who does not respond.[23]

God acts in history in concurrence with temporal givens and finite agents. It is possible to cooperate with God and work in line with God's purposes or to refuse. Whether large or small, the human factor is taken into account.[24] Even Jesus' miracles could not compel faith in people with no openness. Even witnessing a miracle does not force a person to interpret it as a divine sign. It might be attributed to Satan or ignored altogether (Mk 3:22). Signs and wonders are ambiguous in the absence of openness (Jn 2:23). This is because it is love's way not to overpower but to be gentle and persuade. God gave human beings freedom, and he respects it. Grace is offered but must be accepted.[25]

Spirit may draw, but people must consent. The Spirit helps us, but we are also coworkers with God (2 Cor 6:1; Phil 1:19). We work out our salvation, while God is at work in us (Phil 2:12-13). In conversion there is an interplay of grace and assent. Heaven rejoices when someone turns to God, because it is never a foregone conclusion. Conversion is not predestined but arises from free response. Therefore the angels delight when sinners respond to grace. The father did not stop the prodigal from leaving home and did not compel him to return. In his leaving and his returning, his liberty was respected.

The heavenly Father deals with us as sons and daughters (Heb 12:7). A good parent does not try to control his children but teaches them how to use their freedom properly. A parent has authority over children but should not wield it as a tyrant. Parents lay out a possible future but do not and cannot make their child choose it. They lay guidelines down but cannot determine the outcome. God is not all-determining, and God's grace is not irresistible. He lets the prodigal go and rejoices when he returns. This philosophy is reflected in Jesus' word to Jerusalem: "I would have gathered you, but you were not willing" (see Mt 23:37). He offered himself to them but became the stone that the builders rejected (Mt 21:42).

We are invited to the feast—but will we come? The Son has taken a redemptive journey—but will we participate in it? Grace initiates, but we have to respond. Spirit prepares the sinner to be disposed for relationship, but the outcome is not assured. People may resist God's overtures. Stephen lamented, "You are forever opposing the Holy Spirit" (Acts 7:51). God wants to hear the yes he heard from Mary and from Mary's son. He rejoices in Peter's yes and mourns over Judas's no. Grace draws but does not compel. God works within us, but we may stifle the invitation and shut ourselves off. As Paul said, "By the grace of God I am what I am, and his grace toward me has not been in vain. On the contrary, I worked harder than any of them—though it was not I, but the grace of God that is with me" (1 Cor 15:10).

From Mary we learn to respond to God's initiative. The Spirit showered grace on her because she was open. So the Spirit came upon her and the power of the Most High overshadowed her (Lk 1:35). Mary responded by faith to God's grace. She listened to the promptings of the Spirit; therefore she is blessed among women (Lk 1:42).[26]

Depravity and Responsibility

Some theologians do not think sinners are able to respond to God. How can they do so if they are dead in sins? (Eph 2:1). The only way they can respond is by being re-created first. They must be regenerated and effectually called before they can say yes to God. Some take *sola gratia* to mean that conversion is an act of divine monergism—God does it all. Augustine came to this conclusion in reaction to Pelagius, and Luther followed him in concluding that sinners are so completely captive to sin that they cannot even call out for divine help. Persons are not able to believe, he said, because of the bondage of the will. They are not free to love God unless their will is replaced. Sinners have to be reprogrammed to respond. But this is not so much salvation by grace "through faith" as it is salvation without faith. Sinners are compelled to have faith by irresistible grace, which programs it. In this view it is not so much that sinners are drowning as that they are dead and unable to cry for help. Sinners cannot respond positively to God because they are unconscious of any divine initiative.[27]

There is no pure freedom, and sin is indeed a problem of the will. But this does not require irresistible grace and does not cancel human responsibility. Paul has it right: "Wretched man that I am! Who will rescue me . . . ? Thanks be to God through Jesus Christ our Lord!" (Rom 7:24-25). Sin is indeed powerful, but sinners are able to respond to grace. In the parable of the wedding feast, when the invited guests refuse to attend, the king tells the servants to invite everybody to come who wants to (Mt 22:3, 9). Obviously these people are thought of as capable of responding. In the parable of the pearl, the merchant is not dead but an agent actively searching. Indeed, he seeks the pearl with energy until he finds it. In another parable God is looking for receptive hearts as the fertile soil in which to plant his word. For Paul the grace of God was not in vain because he responded to it (1 Cor 15:10). The Galatians are asked how they received the Spirit; the answer is that they received it by faith (Gal 3:2).[28]

What does it mean, then, that sinners are dead in sins? It does not mean they are corpses. For Paul goes on to say elsewhere that sinners are walking according to the prince of darkness (Eph 2:2) and can exercise faith and be made alive by Christ (Eph 2:8). Their deadness is not an inability to believe but an inability to merit God's favor. Paul makes this explicit: "You were . . . raised with him through faith in the power of God" (Col 2:12). The Colossians' faith, expressed in baptism, was the vehicle of receiving the new life. Paul does not say to the Philippian jailer, "Be saved and then believe"; he says, "Believe on the Lord Jesus, and you will be saved" (Acts 16:31). Scripture everywhere assumes our ability to call on God and everywhere holds us responsible on account of it. We are influenced by God, by environment, by nature and more. Many factors affect our culpability, but in the last analysis we are accountable.

Our accountability is part of what it means to be made in the image of God. We are structured in such a way as to be able to respond to him. This is fundamental to human dignity and has not been destroyed by sin. God invites us to turn to God because we *can* turn. Otherwise he would be mocking us. His invitations are addressed to everyone. Jesus does not say, "Come unto me—if you are elect." He says, "Whosoever will may come." There is an ember of the image of God still in us, and the Spirit blows upon it. People have capacity for the faith God looks for. The Spirit woos us but does not impose on us.

Eastern Orthodoxy has always rejected any doctrine of grace that denies freedom, because freedom is essential to the image of God in us. We require grace to enter into fellowship with God, but we have a part to play. Salvation requires the operation of both grace and the human will.[29]

The Greek fathers before Augustine took this view. Faced with fatalism in the pagan world, they defended human freedom. As I noted earlier, it was Augustine who introduced the notion that sinners cannot respond, and Luther extended it in *Bondage of the Will*. He argued, for example, that because God foreknows everything, everything happens by necessity, including any human responses. Fortunately the Lutheran confessions and Luther's disciple Philipp Melanchthon did not accept this extreme doctrine.[30] The Council of Trent spoke of prevenient grace, which assists sinners to conversion if they assent and cooperate with it. Without grace one cannot move toward faith, but with it, one can do so (6.5). Grace is not irresistible. God initiates salvation, but it does not take hold apart from our response. God's grace is like a river sweeping objects ahead of it, but sinners can still cling to the banks to avoid being swept along.[31]

Sinners recapitulate Adam's decision and identify with the fallen Adamic solidarity. Thus they are responsible agents. Jesus invites sinners to repudiate Adam and to emulate his own obedience, identifying with the new humanity. The capacity to make the choice indeed arises out of and is made possible by an encounter with grace, but without salvation being forced on anyone. Salvation is a gift to be received. Creatures are not left to themselves, but God does not override their choices; God values the relative autonomy he gave to humankind, despite the risks that accompany it.[32]

Apart from grace there cannot be faith, but faith is authentically a human response and act of cooperation. Faith does not make grace unnecessary, and grace does not make faith automatic. Grace is powerful but may be frustrated by refusal. Faith is gift and human act. Even in the ministry of Jesus, grace could be accepted or rejected. At the same time, our liberty needs to be sanctified. The will is grievously affected by sin and needs to mature in holiness. We need to grow in our freedom because we do not yet desire the good as we ought to. Liberty needs to be trained and directed toward goodness (Tit 2:12).[33]

Though God does not normally overpower people, I do not deny that it sometimes seems that he does. God brought a lot of power to bear on Saul on the road to Damascus, such that he fell down before it. It was a strong call. At the same time there was a response even here, for Paul says that God's grace was not "in vain," that "I was not disobedient" and that "Christ Jesus . . . judged me faithful" (1 Cor 15:10; Acts 26:19; 1 Tim 1:12).

More striking was the Gadarene, who was in no position to ask for grace until he was delivered of the legion of demons. There are people in this world who are incapable of giving a response to God, such as the severely mentally challenged. We must not be doctrinaire about what God is free to do in such situations to magnify his grace. He is not obliged to respect our freedom, even if he usually does so.

What I want to focus on is God's desire to be loved in a nonprogrammed way. He asks us, "Do you love me?" Our whole life is our answer to that question. At every point in the journey is an opportunity to say yes or no. God treats us as significant agents—that is why the human response is integral to conversion. The proof of this is hell: the only reason for it is the fact that God honors our freedom that much. He refuses to override a no even though he would dearly love to.

Event of the Spirit

Spirit is Lord and giver of life, in creation and new creation. Spirit gives us creaturely vitality and resurrection newness. Spirit indwelling is a mark of a Christian (Rom 8:9). New life is sharing in the Spirit (Phil 2:1; Heb 6:4). Created spirit is touched by uncreated Spirit, who introduces it to the living God. "The true aim of the Christian life is the acquisition of the Holy Spirit" (St. Seraphim of Sarov). Let us continue to view salvation as Spirit event.[34]

We have been baptized into the death and resurrection of Christ. Our baptism in the Spirit links us to the Lord's journey and anoints us for his ministry. "God . . . has anointed us, by putting his seal on us and giving us his Spirit in our hearts as a first installment" (2 Cor 1:21-22). In effect, as Jesus became Christ by being anointed by the Spirit, so it is with us. It sounds odd, but Paul's words imply that we have been anointed as "little Christs" alongside Jesus. This makes plain what the purpose of anointing is: not to excite religious affections as ends in themselves but to empower people to follow Jesus on his path. "As the Father has sent me, so I send you" (Jn 20:21). We are anointed as disciples of Jesus. Spirit stirs a passion for God in us with the purpose of our following Jesus and becoming like him.

The Spirit fires the affections, warms the heart and makes the face shine. But "spiritual delicacies," as John of the Cross calls them, are not given for excitement value but for fruitfulness. The purpose is to fire us up in the service of God. Augustine writes, "If it pleases you to clap and shout for joy when you hear God's love for you declared, it is well and good! But, if it excites you to praise his love in this way, I hope you will be just as excited when I say that love must be a force that is at work in your heart, leading you to serve one another" (*Homilies on the First Epistle of John* 10).

Conversion is an event of the life-giving Spirit (2 Cor 3:6). It is living water within, springing up to eternal life (Jn 4:10, 14; 7:37-39). The Risen Lord breathed on the apostles and said, "Receive the Holy Spirit" (Jn 20:22). This was reminiscent of God's breathing life into Adam's nostrils and of the breath blowing over the valley of dead bones. Jesus came that we might have life (Jn 10:10). To this end he gives the Spirit to us. Paul's conversion is described in terms of his being filled with the Spirit (Acts 9:17). Cornelius and his circle are said to have been saved when the Spirit fell and they spoke in tongues and extolled God (Acts 10:44, 46). The promised Spirit of the end times is being poured out, and people are being introduced to the age of messianic salvation.[35]

Spirit comes in the proclamation of the Word. More than a cognitive issue, this creates a power encounter. Paul says, "Our message . . . came to you not in word only, but in power and in the Holy Spirit and with full conviction" (1 Thess 1:5). In the same vein, he speaks of what Christ accomplished through him in his mission to the Gentiles: "by word and deed, by the power of signs and wonders, by the power of the Spirit of God" (Rom 15:18-19). The impact was more than a result of impressive human wisdom. The Spirit removed veils (2 Cor 3:16-18). There were demonstrations of Spirit and power (1 Cor 2:4-5). It was power ministry: "For this I toil and struggle with all the energy that he powerfully inspires within me" (Col 1:29). The power of the word (likely a word of prophecy) serves as a sword in the Spirit's hands (Eph 6:17). The word in power can penetrate the heart (Heb 4:12-13); it can lay its secrets bare (1 Cor 14:24-25). The grace of God, though resistible, is a mighty river, seeking to carry sinners along with it.[36]

Peter instructed converts to be baptized in order to receive the gift of Spirit (Acts 2:38). Paul asked some at Ephesus whether they had received the Spirit when converted. Hearing that they had not, he baptized them in the name of Jesus and laid hands on them that the Spirit might come. In the context of water baptism, the Spirit fell, and they spoke in tongues and prophesied (Acts 19:6). Paul asked the Galatians about their experience of the Spirit too, whether they had received the Spirit and seen any miracles (Gal 3:2, 4). The force of these texts is that being Christian is bound up with having a relationship with the Spirit. Believers are expected to have a transforming encounter with the Spirit, which greatly affects their lives.

One can see the importance of a vital encounter with God in relation to religious certainty. Reason plays a role—there are evidences in support of faith. But in the last analysis, it is a matter of the heart. Faith stands not thanks to words of human wisdom, but by God's power. Reason can create a climate for faith but not take a person over the threshold. Experiencing God has to be part of the package. To be a real Christian is to be alive in the Spirit in a life-transforming manner.

Therefore spirituality is a vital part of our witness. Each believer should focus on the power of God at work in his or her life and expect God to make him or her an instrument of the kingdom. As the Spirit leads the church into mission, he leads each believer too. We need to be sensitive to divine appointments day by day. We should live with the expectancy that God will channel love through us. Spirit does not promise feeling states of constant victory and exhilaration, but to be present with gifts when needed for mission.

It seems to me that most of us are not all that clear about salvation as a Spirit event. I say that because of the language we normally use for conversion. It is more common to hear people speak of converts "receiving Christ" than of receiving the Spirit, though the New Testament speaks otherwise. How many references actually speak of receiving Christ? We appeal to Revelation 3:20, where Christ knocks in the hope of being welcomed, but the context makes it clear that here he is knocking on the door of a congregation, not an individual. Colossians 2:6 speaks of receiving Christ but uses language for receiving and transmitting tradition, not mystical reception. More promising is John's Gospel, which says that though Jesus was not accepted by Israel, he can be received by us. Even better is John 14:23, where Father and Son are said to make their home in those who love Jesus. So there is a slim basis for talking about receiving Christ, but the language of receiving the Spirit is much more common in Scripture. The fact is that we welcome Christ when we receive his Spirit.

It is not wrong to speak of "receiving Christ," but why do we prefer it over more scriptural language? The New Testament speaks of confessing Christ and receiving Spirit. Why do we shy away from speaking of conversion as a Spirit event? Perhaps the reason is that we do not want to reduce conversion to an experience, which can wax and wane. Also, we may be a little fearful of religious affections and prefer to keep things on the cognitive plane, at the level of assent to propositional truth. These are valid concerns. My appeal, however, is that we not lose sight of the experiential side. Peter speaks of joy unspeakable and full of glory (1 Pet 1:8). Becoming a Christian is being caught up in the sublime love of God, and that is what gave the first disciples power to spreading the gospel. God had transformed their lives, and they could not but speak (Acts 4:20).[37]

Our attachment to "new birth" language sends the same message. We are not comfortable with thinking of conversion as Spirit event. We like to ask not whether someone has received the Spirit, but whether she has been "born again." Again, this is legitimate but unbalanced. When the Fourth Gospel speaks of the new birth, it recalls God's breathing life into Adam, and new birth is a metaphor for Spirit salvation (Jn 3:5). Peter speaks of being born again to a living hope (1 Pet 1:3). Nevertheless, the imagery of new birth is fairly infrequently used compared with language of receiving the Spirit.

Besides using talk of the new birth to eclipse salvation as reception of the Spirit, the *way* we use such language is misleading. First, we disregard the use of the term for the regeneration of the whole cosmos and make it a private, individual matter (see Mt 19:28). We disregard Scripture's new creation imagery. Second, the dimension of baptism is usually dropped when we refer to it. Third, we use it to refer to an experience and play down the transformation of life implied by it. Fourth, we forget that *you* is plural in John 3:7 and that being born again refers to participating in community. The main point, though, is that we avoid biblical language for conversion as Spirit event and prefer other language.[38]

Christ took the representative journey on behalf of all human beings, and now the Spirit is drawing people into it, making the mission of the representative existentially effective by pouring the love of God into our hearts (Rom 5:5). Spirit is poured out on us richly (Tit 3:6), anointing and sealing us (2 Cor 1:21; Eph 1:13). We are no longer natural but spiritual men and women (1 Cor 2:14). We have been adopted into a filial relationship with the Father, as Jesus was in the Jordan (Rom 8:18; Gal 4:6). As he trusted his Father, experienced sonship and received the Spirit, so we, having endorsed Jesus' representative journey, are on our way to becoming sons and daughters alongside the Son.

Corporately we are the temple of the Spirit (1 Cor 6:19), and personally we are indwelt by the Spirit, which unites us to Christ and leads us to intimacy with God. Not an obscure mystical relationship, our union leads us into familiarity with God's heart. It is an intimacy that does not eclipse concerns about mission but creates a longing for the kingdom and God's will to be done on earth.[39]

Spirit was not primarily an intellectual belief for early Christians but a dynamic fact of experience. Although the Spirit points to Christ and glorifies him, Spirit does not stay in the background as a junior assistant. The Spirit is creating new realities and making people instruments of the ongoing process of mission. Christianity is not a religion of intellectual reflection with little affective impact. We proclaim the presence of the kingdom in the power of the Spirit.[40]

Receiving and Actualizing

Conversion, then, is a Spirit event, associated with faith and baptism. Peter told people to be baptized with water in order to receive the gift of the Spirit (Acts 2:38). Jesus spoke of being born of water and Spirit (Jn 3:5). He instructed the disciples to baptize in the name of

Father, Son and Spirit (Mt 28:19). By this action believers are baptized
into the body of Christ (1 Cor 12:13). There is a renewing Spirit bath
and a washing of water by the word (Tit 3:6; Eph 5:27).

Baptism appears to be the occasion when the Spirit comes. There
is not a dichotomy between water baptism and Spirit baptism. In the
sacrament of water baptism, God blesses those who respond to his
Word. More than symbol or act of obedience, the act has a spiritual
effect. In baptism a person reaches out and God gives the Spirit. This
does not imply that the Spirit was absent before, for clearly he was
working preveniently and in the hearing of the Word. It is not so much
that the Spirit is tied to water as that baptism is part of a conversion
complex in which the Spirit is received. The connection is not rigid.
People are converted and then seek baptism. Cornelius was dramatically converted and filled with the Spirit before water baptism (Acts
10:44-48). Nevertheless, water and Spirit baptism are associated, and
an encounter with the Spirit should be expected with the sacrament.[41]

Baptism ought also to be an occasion of charismatic experiences.
When the Ephesians were baptized in water, they spoke in tongues
and prophesied (Acts 19:5-6). Similarly with Cornelius: when the Spirit
fell, he and his family were heard speaking in tongues and extolling
God (Acts 10:46). When the dove descended on Jesus, a voice spoke
from heaven. Baptism and conversion are Spirit events, and charisms
express themselves when the giver of the gifts is present. The baptized
should be led to expect to experience stirrings of the Spirit. When we
neglect the charismatic dimension of baptism, the debt will have to
be made up later. The major cause of the thirst for a second blessing
or Spirit baptism today is the earlier neglect of baptism and confirmation as charismatic events.[42]

Infant baptism is an ancient practice and for that reason deserves
our respect, though the meaning of baptism is clearer when the
candidate is a convert who confesses Christ and receives the Spirit.
Perhaps it is best to say regarding infant baptism that while grace
is present, the fullness awaits actualization in conscious experience
at a later time. One could view infant baptism as prospective of
blessings to be realized in the future. After all, baptism is prospective for everyone, even adult converts, and its blessings are realized

over a lifetime, not all at once.

Baptism in the Spirit, which is sacramentally symbolized in water baptism, gets worked out over a lifetime, whether it begins in infancy or later life. For all of us, it is God who takes us from our mother's womb (Ps 71:6). Renewal is not accomplished suddenly but progressively—"from glory to glory" (see 2 Cor 3:18). Everyone has a certain capacity to appreciate music, but it may have to grow and be nourished. Similarly, it takes time to learn how to ride the wind of the Spirit and to appropriate all of the rich promise of baptism.

What about second blessings? Some experience dimensions of Pentecost early, some later in the Christian life. Though every Christian is washed, sanctified and justified in the name of the Lord Jesus Christ and in the Spirit of God, few realize all that is entailed by it experientially all at once. None of the baptized completely realize the full implications in terms of grace and freedom, holiness and power, that are promised. Hilary of Poitiers spoke of God's gifts coming on us like gentle rain, bearing fruit little by little. Grace is received at baptism but not completely actualized in experience. Our initial experience of grace can open up to wider spaces of the Spirit. For some it opens up to power for worship and witness; others are freed to delight and rest in God. I myself, for example, am scholarly in orientation and need to grow in the ability to rejoice and celebrate. I need the Spirit to set me free in relation to certain potentials of my baptism. There is variety in the way God works in people, and there are different dimensions of the Spirit that may lie dormant and need to be actualized.

Simeon the New Theologian (b. 949) believed that Christians normally receive full possession of the Spirit later in life. Though the Spirit is truly present in every baptized person, the gift unfolds and enters our conscious awareness later, when it is rekindled. There are different reasons for this. It may be because we achieve a greater openness or a more complete self-emptying. It may be due to a change of social setting. It can be difficult to appropriate blessings in church contexts where the manifestations of the Spirit are treated skeptically or where certain gifts are thought to be withdrawn. Since the power dimension of the Spirit is obscured today in many churches, it is inevitable that many will not come into contact with it until something changes in their situation. The second-blessing doctrine is fallout from much bad teaching and bad practice in the church. If the power dimension is overlooked (as it often is), the deficit will have to be made up later.[43]

The rhythm of actualization varies from person to person. One's initiation may be dramatic or undramatic. Unforeseen turns in the road may appear at any time. It is normal to experience moments of renewal and release of Spirit. The gift of God may have to be fanned into flame (2 Tim 1:6). There always needs to be growth in our relationship with the Spirit. So there is always subsequence, always more.

Western culture favors rational and scientific knowledge and downplays the capacity for religious affections. This is what makes so many Western churches spiritless. It is natural for us, culturally speaking, to quench the Spirit. In our culture it is OK to shout in praise of a home-run hitter at a baseball game, but not acceptable to make a joyful noise to the Lord in church. As far as conscious experience of the Spirit goes, reality often goes unrealized. It is hard for the Spirit to break through and set us free. It is hard for us to dance in the presence of God, to expect signs and wonders.[44]

Because the power dimension of the Spirit has been most neglected, subsequent encounters are most often charismatic in nature. The power for effective witness comes better late than never. One could use the metaphor of baptism to refer to it, or one might prefer to reserve the term for initiation. The latter has the advantage of not giving the impression that some Christians and not others are Spirit-baptized.

The term is not the issue. Whatever we call it, it is important that the full package of baptismal blessing be quickened in us, however it may do so. The pentecostal reality is much more important than the terminology. It may be best to speak of spiritual breakthroughs as actualizations of our initiation. They address the problem that conversion is too often unempowering and not experientially life-changing. In such cases it is usually not the second blessing that is abnormal, but the deficient initiation.[45]

Initiation is the beginning, not the ending. We enter the realm of the Spirit by faith and baptism, but its reality surfaces over time in varying patterns. Our baptism in the Spirit is continually being renewed and realized. It has a sacramental expression in water baptism, but the experiential reality enters our consciousness in a variety of ways over time. There can be and is very often a temporal gap between initiation and the flowering of what was signified by it. The delay may be due to our unwillingness to trust God and yield up areas of our life. It is not easy to surrender to God, but the Spirit is urging us to do so over a lifetime.

I warn against assuming that those with what appears to be a formal faith are not Christian. One can be baptized and not yet have entered deeply into Christ. It is best to assume that baptized people are God's children, because they bear the sign of Christ, and to urge them to enter a fuller experience of their inheritance.

Luke sometimes writes as if conversion and Spirit baptism are separated in time. For example, he describes a second pentecostal event in the lives of the disciples (Acts 4:31). He tells how the Samaritans accepted the word of God and received the Spirit a few days later (Acts 8:14-15). He shows that Paul's conversion took three days to complete. Such passages, however, do not imply a doctrine of subsequence—their concern is for experience and reality. I take the meaning to be this: if for any reason the Spirit is not present in power in one's life, the situation should be rectified. God gives the Spirit in power, and it is important that we receive it and walk in it.

The issue is not terminology, and the question is not *when* but *whether* one has encountered the Spirit in experience. To paraphrase Jesus, what does it profit a man if he receives initiation without power? Reality, not terminology, is the issue. Whether we call it Spirit baptism or do not is unimportant compared with the problem of Christians who are experientially deficient, who do not know the Spirit's power. We must know God experientially, not just cognitively. We need to be empowered for mission, freed from fear, able to speak, full of praises. We need a breakthrough in the realm of the Spirit, an awakening to the presence and power of God. There may need to be a release of the Spirit, a flowering of grace in experience, an openness to the full range of the gifts.

On this point Pentecostals excel. They face up to the necessity of fuller actualization and do something about it. They confront the problem of subnormal appropriation and seek a breakthrough. One might say that they are good at jump-starting an initiation that had become stalled for whatever reason. They do it by empowered liturgies in which the reality of the Spirit is palpable, and they supply a social setting in which countless believers have been enabled to break through barriers. We can quibble with their theology, but no group knows better how to confront the problem of nonrealization.

Renewal is an actualization of our baptism, which issues in a greater openness to the Spirit. The Spirit, who is already present in the believer, becomes present in a new way. God becomes more real: there is a greater sense of his presence, an increase in power to bear witness, a greater openness to and manifestation of gifts. What was previously intellectual becomes experiential. The indwelling of the Spirit is experienced in a conscious way (Gal 5:25; Eph 3:16-17). We experience enlightenment, taste the heavenly gift and the goodness of the word of God, and discover powers of the age to come (Heb 6:4-5).

It is analogous to what happens in a marriage. It would be nice for a bride and bridegroom to experience rapturous union from the beginning of their marriage and sustain it always. But this is not essential, and in fact it usually fails to happen. Relationships can sag for a time and be revitalized later. In the same way, there are many factors that impede Easter life. God knows that and calls us to come higher up and deeper in. God is not much worried about the precise order of stages of Christian experience. The order varies in any case. God's concern is practical—not when but whether a person has been filled with the Spirit. Tom Smail rightly exhorts us, "By whatever name—receive!"

A longing to enter a more conscious relationship with the Spirit is not a selfish desire, because euphoria is not the goal. The goal is vocation and mission. We need the power of the Spirit to be disciples of Jesus Christ. We are chosen not to privilege but to service, to be God's partners in the mending of creation. For this we need an abundant supply of power and spiritual gifting. The goal is not experience as such, but power for mission and fruit-bearing. For the sake of vocation to mission, there must be God's reality in us. Faith must not be just theory nor its basis just historical reality. The miracle of encountering God cannot be replaced by anything else.

The sacrament of receiving and rekindling the gift is often the laying on of hands. In his ministry, Jesus often touched sick people (Lk 5:13). They in turn reached out to touch him (Mk 5:28). Peter and John laid hands on people too, and they received the Spirit (Acts 8:17). Paul speaks of Timothy's gift that was in him through prophecy and the laying on of hands (1 Tim 4:14). He also speaks of the gift passed on through the laying on of his own hands (2 Tim 1:6). Those who desire greater spiritual fullness should ask for prayer and the laying on of hands from those who are filled.

The Significance of Glossolalia

The gift of speaking in tongues is related to renewal but suffers from polemics. Some exaggerate its importance by claiming it as sole initial evidence of Spirit filling, while others, in reaction, refuse to take it seriously. Ironically, by being exaggerated the gift has actually been diminished.[46]

Let me begin by saying that it is not necessary to speak in tongues. There is no law of tongues in the New Testament. Peter did not say that converts would speak in tongues, and the converts on the day of Pentecost did not speak in tongues so far as we can tell (see Acts 2:37). The point is that there are more ways than one to evidence the Spirit's presence. Peter, quoting Joel, hails prophetic speech, for example, as a key manifestation (Acts 2:17). Knowing what to say in the face of accusation is a sign of the Spirit (Mk 13:11). Giving away possessions and giving one's body up in martyrdom are evidence (1 Cor 13:3). It is best to say that speaking in tongues is normal rather than normative. The apostles spoke in tongues when they were filled with the Spirit, but this may not be the pattern for everybody always. We might say that tongues is normal but not the norm.[47]

However, speaking in tongues is a noble and edifying gift. "Those who speak in a tongue do not speak to other people but to God; for nobody understand them, since they are speaking mysteries in the

Spirit" (1 Cor 14:2). They build themselves up by means of it (1 Cor 14:4). In this context tongues does not seem to be an intelligible language but a way of responding to the inexpressibility of God, a way of crying to God from the depths and expressing the too-deep-for-words sighings of the heart. Tongues is prayer without concepts, prayer at a deep, noncognitive level. We surrender to God when we pray in tongues and give control even of our speech over to him. Prayer in tongues is perhaps to prayer what abstract art is to painting.[48]

Our love of rationality resists it. As educated persons, we do not want to say anything excessive or ill-considered. We want be in control and keep things safe and familiar. We do not even like mysteries very much; we want theology to be as rational as possible. Academics in particular are trained to guard their speech, so as not to blurt out something they are not sure they want to say. It can be hard for them to yield to tongues. The gift places us in unfamiliar territory and requires us to be childlike in prayer. But this may be why tongues is important. It is a means God uses to challenge strategies of control. It is a humble but also a humbling gift to which we should be open.[49]

The Spirit is given in baptism and is realized in experience throughout life. Believers whose experience runs dry and who are unaware of charisms should seek renewal. Renewal will not remove our human weakness; it does not guarantee a perpetual high, but it will help us live for God. Each receives the Spirit in the shape of a particular charisma, which establishes the way we serve the Lord. "Each has a particular gift from God" (1 Cor 7:7). Like DNA and fingerprints, it is uniquely ours. It is the gifting we need to be fruitful Christians. So let us not try to be what we are not, but allow the uniquely shaped gift that God has made us come to expression.

From Image to Likeness

The Spirit awakens us to love and unites us to the Son to set us free and make us like him. Paul writes, "Those whom he foreknew he also predestined to be conformed to the image of his Son, in order that he might be the firstborn within a large family" (Rom 8:29). God is forming a new community to prefigure the coming kingdom. Spirit is the power by which sin's hold is broken and we are enabled to love God and neighbor more selflessly. Conformity to Christ is the goal of our walking and growing in relationship with the Spirit. This is also the purpose of God for the human race—to bring it into conformity with Jesus Christ, God's true covenant partner.

Our potential and future are glimpsed in the risen Christ. God has made us covenant partners in him and does not abandon us to our sins. As God's true partner, Jesus arrived at the goal ahead of time as our representative and opened the way for us to follow through participation in his journey. Yet it takes time for this liberation to work itself through. Spirit baptism needs to issue not only in power for mission as Luke says, but also in holiness and conformity to Christ as Paul emphasizes.[50]

Genesis says that humanity was created in the *image* and *likeness* of God (1:26-27). Though the terms are synonymous in the text, Eastern Orthodoxy has discerned a distinction between them, between a created image and an acquired likeness. The one term speaks of a created given, the other of a potential future. It lets us view Spirit as moving humans from created image to Christlikeness. It lets us think of human beings as presently not in their final state but unfinished, needing to grow toward maturity and perfection. We do not now possess both aspects of the image of God; likeness is to be realized only in the future in communion with God, when our relationship with God and our fellows is complete.[51]

Created in the image of God, we are destined to be changed into the likeness of Christ, sharing glory in the new creation. The goal is for creatures who reflect God's nature as agents to acquire Christ's likeness in loving fellowship with God and neighbor. Paul even paints a picture of how it happens. Gazing at the glory of the Lord, we are changed into his likeness little by little. In effect, we gradually become what we behold (2 Cor 3:18).[52]

Image is inherent, but likeness is to be acquired. The same Spirit who directed the process of creation to issue in image bearers now is taking the process toward likeness. Humans now represent God in the creaturely realm, having dominion over the earth, but their character can develop into either similarity or dissimilarity with God's.

They may tend toward union with God or veer away from it.

The distinction of image and likeness allows one to differentiate our present condition as imaging God from our future condition as reflecting Christ. We possess the image but not yet the likeness, the latter being a potential that requires us to cooperate with Spirit. The notion meshes with developmental views of humanity and yields insights for theodicy. Certain evils may not be the result of the fall into sin but may exist because they are instrumental to the task of soul making.[53]

Stressing image as a created given also allows one to recognize human dignity after the Fall. Sin damaged humans and threatened our likeness to God, but it did not destroy the sinner's identity as image bearer. The Fall did not result in a radical loss of dignity or freedom. Orthodoxy's recognition of the distinction between image and likeness explains in part why the doctrine of original sin did not take hold in Orthodox circles as strongly as it did in the West.

Conformity to Christ in the presence of God is the goal of human life. Spirit is moving us from earthly to heavenly life, from "bios" to "zoë," as C. S. Lewis put it. The fall of Adam complicated this but cannot frustrate the realization of God's purpose, because as Paul says, "where sin increased, grace abounded all the more" (Rom 5:20).

Conformity to Christ issues in a certain mode of life. Accepted in the Beloved, we too are chosen and gifted, in the midst of our weaknesses, to take up Jesus' journey and become gifts to the world. In giving we receive, pressed down and running over. We experience the joy of giving and are multiplied like loaves. We pray, "Make me an instrument of your peace." We realize the fulfillment of our human destiny in the give-and-take of relationships.[54]

A Dynamic Process

Growing in likeness to Christ, like walking in the Spirit, is a dynamic and gradual process. It is also an area in which our initiation in the Spirit needs to bear fruit over time. A newborn baby is ready to grow as soon as it emerges. Its senses come to life, its eyes open to the light. The child begins to breathe air and feel the warmth of its mother. But just as growth to physical maturity is a process that takes a long time, so is growing into Christlikeness. It does not happen at once. It takes time to be made free from sin on every level where we are held captive. It is painful to be separated from the bias to self and be prodded to follow the Man of Sorrows. It takes time for conversion to be made complete and for the Spirit to lead us into deeper love for God and neighbor. It takes time for our baptismal initiation to work itself out in a holy life.

But we have this confidence: "Even though our outer nature is wasting away, our inner nature is being renewed day by day" (2 Cor 4:16). We believe with Paul that Christ is being formed in us, like a baby in the womb (Gal 4:19). We sing,

O Jesus Christ, grow thou in me
And all things else recede;
My heart be daily nearer thee,
From sin be daily freed.

When we say yes to God, Spirit births Christ in us and transformation begins. Baptized into Christ, we are washed, sanctified, justified in the name of Jesus and by the Spirit (1 Cor 6:11). Rooted and grounded in love, we begin the journey toward conformity. Dying and rising with him, we move toward sonship and Christlikeness by grace through faith.[55]

The Christian life is an outworking of cooperation with the grace of God. Paul worked harder than any other apostle, "though it was not I, but the grace of God that is with me," he said (1 Cor 15:10). He fought the fight, he ran the race, he kept the faith (2 Tim 4:6). Having received life from the Spirit, believers now conduct earthly life in the steps of the Spirit in accordance with the gospel (Gal 5:25). Renewed moral life is fruit of our communion with Christ in the Spirit. Through obedience to God's will, we concretize our union with Christ as vessels of God's grace. We are up against an arduous struggle with the darkness and brokenness in us. What the flesh desires is opposed to what the Spirit wants for us (Gal 5:17). The works of the flesh are antithetical to its fruit (Gal 5:19-21). We need a cleansing from every defilement of body and spirit (2 Cor 7:1). We have to put on Christ and be clothed with him (Rom 13:14). The path to likeness is a long, gradual journey.[56]

Though the struggle is real, holiness and happiness go together. There is a cost to nondiscipleship. Refusing to be a disciple of Christ and refusing to grow into his likeness is a great loss as well as a wasted opportunity to become what God made us to be. To refuse to be renewed is to refuse abundant life in this age and in the age to come. To refuse to be conformed to Christ's likeness is to forfeit the goal for which we were made. It also wounds God's heart and grieves the Spirit, who longs to see us changed (Eph 4:30).

The Direction

The direction of conformity to Christ is not spelled out in laws and detailed commandments but indicated in a more general way. It is summed up in terms of "the mind of Christ" (Phil 2:5). His journey is becoming our journey as we are caught up in participation by the Spirit, who is completing atonement by effecting transformation in us. In union with Christ, God's love floods our being by the Spirit (Rom 5:5). It is not so much a matter of an imitation of Christ as our being the locale for the realization and radiation of his love through the Spirit. Fruit begins to grow on our branches, and though we cannot cause it, we must want and allow it to grow.

The destined likeness has become visible in the Son, who revealed the Father and our goal by his incarnation. On the one hand, Jesus is the stamp of God's nature and the radiance of his glory (Heb 1:3). The fullness of the Godhead dwells bodily in him (Col 1:19; 2:9). Thus he reveals the Father. On the other hand, he is the new Adam in whom the true human likeness can be seen. It is measured by Christ's action: "You know the generous act of our Lord Jesus Christ, that though he was rich, yet for your sakes he became poor, so that by his poverty you might become rich" (2 Cor 8:9). John adds, "We know love by this, that he laid down his life for us—and we ought to lay down our lives for one another" (1 Jn 3:16). The goal of redemption consists of being conformed to this new image of humanity, achieved by the Son in the Spirit and appropriated by us through the Spirit.

When the Son took flesh, he bestowed a fullness of grace upon our human nature, delivering it from sin and death. Humanity in principle was raised with Christ and glorified together with him. When we are converted, we are pointed in the direction of union with God and likeness with Christ through participation in his vicarious humanity by faith. We enter into covenantal partnership with God and, secure in his acceptance, begin to live in newness of life and bear fruit. Faith frees God to work out in us the kind of life he has always longed for the creature.

Jesus sums up the goal as being to love God with all our heart and our neighbor as ourselves. This is exactly what he himself did. It is a path of giving without self-seeking, of embracing the unlovely. Paul sums it up in what is virtually a hymn to Christ: "Love is patient; love is kind; love is not envious or boastful or arrogant or rude. It does not insist on its own way; it is not irritable or resentful; it does not rejoice in wrongdoing, but rejoices in the truth. It bears all things, believes all things, hopes all things, endures all things. Love never ends" (1 Cor 13:4-8).

Conformity to Christ also involves entering into the sufferings that result from worldly resistance and hostility. The path is to pursue love in a fallen world. More than Christlike, it is Fatherlike, since the Son reveals the Father. The goal is not only to become like Christ but also to become like the Father: to become compassionate like he is, to love as he loves, to give as he gives without expecting anything in return, to welcome sinners as he welcomes them, to love even enemies. Freely we have received, freely we may give.[57]

The likeness of Jesus is different from the likenesses of him that are fashioned by culture. Societies create totems, gods that represent what people value most. In North American society Jesus is often and easily transformed from one who gives his life for the kingdom to one who symbolizes success and power. The focus must be kept clear on the Jesus of revelation, not the Christ of culture. Spirit points us to Jesus of Nazareth and is creating in us a lively expectation of the new order of God's kingdom.

Jeremiah bought a field in order to identify with the restoration of Jerusalem that would come after the time of judgment. By analogy, the Christian life is proleptic of new creation. Our lives ought to be full of gestures that prefigure God's coming kingdom the way Jesus' life did.

Obviously we arrive at death in a state of unfinished conformity to

Christ. What happens then? Is the shortfall in Christlikeness miraculously made up, or is there opportunity after death for further sanctification and maturation? The Catholic tradition has taught the latter, and it makes some sense. Since in this life renewal comes not by instant metamorphosis but by gradual transformation, perhaps conformity to Christ continues after death as a journey. If life is a process of education, perhaps there is a training school above. Catholic theology calls this purgatory. It affords the possibility of progressive sanctification after death before entry to heaven. The Catechism says, "All who die in God's grace and friendship, but still imperfectly purified, are assured of eternal salvation but after death undergo purification, to achieve the holiness necessary to enter the joy of heaven" (par. 1030).

John Wesley once reflected that he thought that some would need to mature in paradise while awaiting the last day. A person like Job, for example, who had responded to God in life but lacked Bible and sacraments, would meet Christ at death and need time to grow in him. The pre-Christian believers of the Old Testament would be found in the same position. They began to respond on earth but would need opportunity to grow in grace. Realistically, how different is it with Christians?[58]

The Spiritual Journey
St. John of the Cross likened the Christian journey toward union with God to the ascent of Mount Carmel. He pictures it as an arduous path and a narrow way. The refiner's fire both delights and wounds; our relationship with the Spirit is not all sweetness and light. It is bittersweet, because we share in cross and resurrection. The cross is not only a past event but also a present factor in experience. "We ourselves, who have the first fruits of the Spirit, groan inwardly while we wait for adoption, the redemption of our bodies" (Rom 8:23). When enslaved people glimpse freedom, their chains really begin to hurt. When we are given hope, we feel even worse about tears not wiped away and brokenness unhealed.

At conversion (though not only then) we experience the sweet presence of God with indescribable joy (1 Pet 1:8). After a period of restless searching, God gives us peace and happiness. But we soon learn that there is dying as well as rising. There comes at intervals the dark night of the soul, when God seems to withdraw his presence—times when we are cast upon him and cry out to him in anguish. Jesus, who knew God's fatherly presence all his life, died crying, "My God, my God, why have you forsaken me?" Those who identify with Jesus must expect to taste both the experience of presence and the experience of Godforsakenness.[59]

The purpose of troubling experiences—so far as we can discern it—is to wean us from our idea of a God who always pampers us and to bring us to God as he really is, our rock and fortress. We are deprived of the pleasures of Christian experience in order to move to greater heights. We can be guilty of lust for spiritual things as well as material. We can lust for pleasures of the soul and not really desire virtue. We can be gluttonous for spiritual sweets and delicacies. We must be weaned from this and not shy away from the dark night. God is not always near and intimate. God pursues good purposes in the silence and aridity of the night too. The wilderness experience of withdrawal from spiritual sweetness is essential for maturing. Let us not flee from it—God has a deep work to do in our lives. Is garbage not taken out weekly, rather than only once? Is it a pleasant duty? The cup of discipleship must be drunk to the bitter end. Let us not shrink back and refuse to let God transform us. If renewal stops with spiritual delicacies, it will not fulfill its purpose.[60]

Are Christians the only ones God is renewing? No, as John says: "Everyone who loves is born of God and knows God" (1 Jn 4:7). Nothing is said here about a profession of faith. John simply says that if someone is truly loving, grace is at work, even if anonymously, in that person's heart. The prevenient and sanctifying grace of God is at work in the world beyond the church, and we should be sensitive to its fruits. As Peter says, "In every nation anyone who fears [God] and does what is right is acceptable to him" (Acts 10:35). Conversely, John also says that unloving persons are not born of God, whatever creed they profess. People cannot be walking in darkness while walking in fellowship with God, regardless of what they say (1 Jn 1:6). Godliness and holiness as well as doctrine are criteria for truth and reality in religion.[61]

From Corruption to Incorruption

The goal of salvation is union with Christ in divine glory. The process of conformity that begins on earth will be completed in the new creation, when the dead are raised incorruptible and life is renewed in totality. The gap separating this world from the next is a wide one that cannot be bridged save by God's own action. Spirit is preparing us for the great leap to consummation, when life really begins. It will be a totally new situation. Sin and death will be no more. Creation will be set free from its bondage to decay and obtain the glorious liberty of the children of God (Rom 8:21). There will be a new heaven and new earth in which God will dwell with mortals (Rev 21:1). The nations will be his peoples, and he will be their God forever (Rev 21:3). God will be fully present and known. Humanity will reach the goal of union with God, and there will be a perfected community, where love reigns in all relationships. Then we will share in the glory of God, in the divine sphere of life.

What Jesus prays will come true: "Father, I desire that those also, whom you have given me, may be with me where I am, to see my glory, which you have given me because you loved me before the foundation of the world" (Jn 17:24). The goal of union, communion and participation will be realized—"the love with which you have loved me may be in them, and I in them" (Jn 17:26). Hendrikus Berkhof comments, "When God has lifted his human creature out of this provisional and alienated form of life and brought him home into his very presence, then, at last, life really begins."[62]

What we have inherited from Adam is not so much guilt (which we bring on ourselves) as corruption and death. Therefore what we need from Christ is not so much acquittal as resurrection. Indeed we are saved by his life (Rom 5:10). Life triumphs over death in the resurrection and brings immortality to light (2 Tim 1:10). Those who share in his sufferings will share in his glory as well (Rom 8:16-17). They will be like him and see him as he is (1 Jn 3:1-2). Life will be given to our mortal bodies by the Spirit, who will transform the body of our humiliation to conform it to the body of his glory (Rom 8:9-11; Phil 3:21).

Let me reiterate: union with God is not pantheism—creatures never cease to be creatures. This is not ontological unification. Instead we are to be caught up into the relationship of triune love. Our nature will be restored by resurrection and made capable of participating in the divine life. Conformed to Christ, we will share the glory of God and enter the fellowship of Father, Son and Spirit (1 Jn 1:3).

Death is the moment of our return to God. It is the end of the journey and the culmination of our yes. It is the opening up of the eternal life we have already begun to live in union with Christ. Death is not defeat, then, but the final yes and the moment of fulfillment. God calls us to our final rest, which is his own everlasting embrace. Henri Nouwen says, "For the beloved sons and daughters of God, dying is the gateway to the complete experience of being the beloved. For those who know they are chosen, blessed, and broken to be given, dying is the way to becoming pure gift."[63]

God is supremely beautiful and dwells in unapproachable light (1 Tim 6:16). This light has shone in the face of Jesus Christ, who descended into the abyss of brokenness, divesting himself of all comeliness. Christ is now raised and transfigured, and by faith we glimpse the glory of God. As we wait for his parousia, Spirit fosters in us an anticipation for the coming glory, making us long for the day when Christ will hand the kingdom over to the Father (1 Cor 15:28). Through the Spirit we wait for the hope of righteousness (Gal 5:5), when the Spirit brings creation home to its Maker. Let us tell the world not so much to flee the wrath of God as to enter the journey that leads to the Father's house, where we will know the true God and Jesus Christ whom he sent and be flooded with love everlasting.[64]

The goal is a sabbath rest of unbroken communion. "Let us therefore make every effort to enter that rest" (Heb 4:11). As the temple of God, as community and individuals, let us tend the flame that burns on the altar (1 Cor 3:16; 6:19). The Spirit indwells us with a view to the eternal dwelling of God with humanity (Rev 21:3). There is no temple in the new Jerusalem, because the Lord is there (Rev 21:22). As we await the consummation, let us then cultivate friendship with God and meditate on life in union with God. Let us hold fast to the mystery that is "Christ in you, the hope of glory" (Col 1:27). Let us open ourselves completely to the Spirit and ask for the realization of God's gift in us. Let us actualize our baptism in every possible way: in love and holiness, in power and freedom. God is with us and in us. Therefore let us live in his presence and bathe in his love. Let us grow into union with God, yoked together with others in the community and eagerly awaiting the marriage supper of the Lamb.

How lovely is your dwelling place,
    O LORD of hosts!
My soul longs, indeed it faints
    for the courts of the LORD;
my heart and my flesh sing for joy
    to the living God. (Ps 84:1-2)

Here is the answer to our scattered confusion, to the "muchness and manyness" that afflict us moderns. We must not forget that there is a sanctuary within us to which we ought always retire. "Eternity is within our hearts, pressing upon our time-torn lives, warming us with intimations of an astounding destiny, calling us home unto Itself."[65]

SIX

SPIRIT &
UNIVERSALITY

I N THIS CHAPTER WE come to the issue of access to the grace of God
in Jesus Christ and the light that Spirit casts on it. We know that God,
lover of humanity, desires all to be saved (1 Tim 2:4). His embrace is
wide and open to a lost and ungodly race. If only what Jesus'
opponents said were true: "Look, the world has gone after him!" (Jn
12:19). God woos sinners—if only they would come. Jesus said, "I,
when I am lifted up from the earth, will draw all people to myself"
(Jn 12:32).

The biblical hope for the world is that "the LORD will become king
over all the earth; on that day the LORD will be one and his name one"
(Zech 14:9). Isaiah predicts,

> On this mountain the LORD of hosts will make for all peoples
> a feast of rich food, a feast of well-aged wines,

of rich food filled with marrow, of well-aged wines strained clear.
And he will destroy on this mountain
the shroud that is cast over all peoples,
the sheet that is spread over all nations;
he will swallow up death forever. (Is 25:6)
There is a universality in the gospel—Jesus came to bring justice to
the nations (Is 42:1). The psalmist writes,
May God be gracious to us and bless us
and make his face to shine upon us,
that your way may be known upon earth,
your saving power among all nations.
Let the peoples praise you, O God;
let all the peoples praise you. (Ps 67:1-2)
But how is the voice of God heard outside communities where Christ
is named? If anyone failed to hear about God's love, would God's
heart not be broken? Theology has not found it easy to handle biblical
universality. It has tended to place so much emphasis on the uniqueness of the work of Christ that it has often left the impression that
most members of the human race are without hope of salvation. Many
people think that unless persons become Christians and church
members, they are going to hell through no fault of their own, and
there is no remedy. Even though such a notion does little justice to
God's desire that all receive his love and be saved, it has been the
accepted reasoning for centuries. Even today what I call restrictivist
thinking holds sway in large parts of the church, though less now than
before.

Though wrathful against sin and rebellion, God still does not want
to exercise wrath:
My heart recoils within me;
my compassion grows warm and tender.
I will not execute my fierce anger. (Hos 11:8-10)
The Incarnate Word was filled with grace and truth, not just with truth
(Jn 1:14). Truth by itself can be heartless and cruel. It can shrivel up
and harden and be used to crush others. But God's truth is full of
grace, soft and tender.

Counting against restrictivism is not only God's nature as Father and the universality of the atonement of Christ but also the ever-present Spirit, who can foster transforming friendships with God anywhere and everywhere.[1] Spirit is present in the farthest reaches of this wonderful, ambiguous world. The Lord and giver of life broods over the depths of creation and renews the face of the land. The Spirit is present everywhere, both transcending and enfolding all that is, present and at work in the vast range of happenings in the universe.

The Spirit meets people not only in religious spheres but everywhere—in the natural world, in the give-and-take of relationships, in the systems that structure human life. No nook or cranny is untouched by the finger of God. His warm breath streams toward humanity with energy and life.

In a profusion of images, Hildegard of Bingen depicts Spirit in marvelous ways: as the life of creatures, as a burning fire that sparks, ignites, inflames and kindles our hearts; as a guide in the fog, a balm for wounds, a shining serenity and an overflowing fountain that spreads to all sides. Spirit is life, movement, color, radiance and a stillness that restores, bringing withered sticks and souls alive with the sap of life. The Spirit purifies, absolves, strengthens, heals, gathers the perplexed, seeks the lost, pours the juice of contrition into hardened hearts and plays music in the soul, melodies of praise and joy. The Spirit awakens mighty hope, blowing winds of renewal everywhere in creation.[2]

The cosmic breadth of Spirit activities can help us conceptualize the universality of God's grace. The Creator's love for the world, central to the Christian message, is implemented by the Spirit. He is "the hope of all the ends of the earth and of the farthest seas" (Ps 65:5). He is the reconciler of the whole world (2 Cor 5:19). A rainbow of mercy encircles his throne (Rev 4:2-3). God's mercies fail not; his generosity is inexhaustible. Let no one limit his liberality or begrudge its extent (Mt 20:15). God is always reaching out to sinners by the Spirit. There is no general revelation or natural knowledge of God that is not at the same time gracious revelation and a potentially saving knowledge. All revealing and reaching out are rooted in God's grace and are aimed at bringing sinners home.[3]

Access to grace is less of a problem for theology when we consider it from the standpoint of the Spirit, because whereas Jesus bespeaks particularity, Spirit bespeaks universality. The incarnation occurred in a thin slice of land in Palestine, but its implications touch the farthest star. Spirit helps theology break free of attitudes that diminish grace and create hopelessness. Slogans valid at one time can become invalid in another. A narrow outlook is now communicated by this ancient saying: "There is no salvation outside the church."[4] Originally this was a warning against apostasy and was not intended as a statement on access to grace. Whatever it used to mean, however, it now conveys the sense that great masses of people live and die without any hope. It has come to mean that there is no salvation outside Christianity.

Many today are struggling with that tradition. It may have been influential in the past, but today many both inside and outside the church are skeptical. They find it hard to believe that the God and Father of our Lord Jesus Christ, who seeks a single lost sheep out of a hundred, would be that severe in his dealings with us. It is not only the influence of modern culture that fosters this sort of skepticism. Many believers have developed a sense that the God revealed in Jesus has not been well served theologically in this matter and that a better explanation must be possible.[5]

Recognizing the cosmic breadth of Spirit activities can help us understand the divine universality, since God's breath is everywhere, reaching out and touching people. The bond of love of the Trinity is the power of God in the world, ceaselessly pouring out love and creating hope. The Spirit has a thousand ways of passing by and gracing people. We can abound in hope for people through the power of the Spirit, who inspires hope in us, not only for our future but also for the future of the world and for the ungodly whom God would justify (Rom 15:13). Christ's work is complete and for all—"one man's act of righteousness leads to justification and life for all" (Rom 5:18). There is no way around it—we must hope that God's gift of salvation is being applied to people everywhere. If so, how else than by the universal presence and activity of Spirit?

The Bible is a book of hope. God declares through the Seer, "I am making all things new" (Rev 21:5). God is setting creation free from bondage and giving it the liberty of the children of God (Rom 8:21). God will lift humanity up into union and make his dwelling with us. Chaos will be overcome, together with all that ruins and destroys. The new Jerusalem, the bride of Christ, will descend from heaven and surpass every aspiration. Astonishingly, even nations that persecuted the church will be present in the new city, not destroyed but redeemed. Christ will rule over them, and the treasures of civilizations will be brought in.

A river flows through the middle of this city, and the tree of life heals the nations, probably from the very wounds they suffered by resisting God so long. The curse is lifted, and the sword barring access to Paradise is removed. The Spirit and the bride urge all to come and join the dance. Their words are not "Come, Lord Jesus," as we might expect; instead they are inviting sinners to drink God's living water (Rev 22:17). What an all-embracing vision of God's love for humanity and for creation![6]

Questions of access to salvation and religious pluralism can be approached profitably from the perspective of the future. God has a purpose for the nations. We should not take our cue from the present, where God's purposes are relatively unrealized, but from the future. Israel may be rejecting Christ now, but God has plans to be merciful toward both Jews and Gentiles (Rom 11:32). The nations will be gathered—Assyria and Egypt alongside Israel will constitute the people of God in that day (Is 19:25). At the moment religions are locked in competition and coexistence, in dialogue and apologetics, but it will not always be so. We anticipate the day when the rulers of earth bring their honor and glory into the new Jerusalem (Rev 21:24, 26).

The Christian message is good news, not just for the well-behaved and pious, not just for Jews and Christians, not just for the elect few; it is good news for the world, for all sinners without discrimination, for all the hopeless, the forgotten, the marginalized. The last Adam represented humanity, and God is saving the whole world through him. God longs for the return of his lost sons and daughters and wants his house to be full of guests (Lk 14:23). When some refuse to attend the banquet, the king in the parable orders his servants to go and invite everyone they can find (Mt 22:8-9).

Let us not forget to hope: love "bears all things, believes all things, hopes all things, endures all things" (1 Cor 13:7). In regard to those outside the church, let us be patient and long-suffering, not judgmental. God's love suffers long—let us hope against hope and never give up. Love knows no hopeless cases.

Let us not be too sure who will be justified and who condemned. No one is automatically barred from heaven. We leave all people to the mercy of God. We are good news people—negativity does not become us. Neal Punt says that negativity "detracts from the positive, world-embracing, and thrilling good news of what God in Christ has done for humanity."[7]

Two Errors to Avoid

There are two errors to avoid when we think of the gospel's universality: one is to say dogmatically that all will be saved, and the other is to say that only a few will be. The first error, called universalism, is widespread in mainline churches; the other, called restrictivism, plagues traditionalists.[8] Universalism is perhaps less of a threat, because a number of biblical texts indicate plainly that persons are free to accept or reject salvation. Although certain texts taken in isolation could imply universal salvation, the warnings that occur in the same books must influence their interpretation. Though God is able to save all people and would even like to, Scripture does not encourage us to think that everyone will accept his love or that God will use his superior power to overcome all rejection. The scope of redemption is universal, but Scripture suggests that one can be finally impenitent and be excluded from the kingdom (Rev 21:8, 27).[9]

The fact that God does not override the possibility of human refusal is attributable to the value he places on freedom. God wants humans to love him freely and accepts the risk that some will refuse. God values the give-and-take of creation too highly to override it. Having established a significant universe, he does not cancel its significance. God accepted risk when he made human beings capable of rejecting love and placing themselves outside grace.[10]

At the same time, let us not place inordinate emphasis on self-damnation. Jesus preached good news and did not come to condemn the world (Jn 3:18). He was not a hellfire preacher, though he spoke of hell. Our emphasis, like his, should be on God's extravagant love of human beings, not on God's anger (see Tit 3:4).[11]

Restrictivism is the more widespread error when it comes to salvation, especially among evangelicals. The term denotes a doctrine that non-Christians will all be damned, whether they hear the gospel or not. If the ark of salvation should not reach them, it's too bad—they will drown. Access to salvation is limited to those who hear and accept the gospel message. Since only a minority have had the good fortune to have been born in the right place at the right time to hear and accept the gospel, heaven will be lightly populated while hell will brim with souls. The majority will have no way to avoid hell. I wonder if the Corinthians were not anxious about this in relation to their ancestors, so that they invented a baptism for the dead (1 Cor 15:29).[12]

It is hard to defend restrictivism. According to the idea of double predestination, God passes over some and offers them no mercy. "By the decree of God, for the manifestation of his glory, some men and angels are predestined unto everlasting life, and others foreordained to everlasting death" (Westminster Confession 3.3). In this view God is not troubled by the sparse harvest of salvation or the unfairness of salvific arrangements. God approves of things exactly as they are, having decided whom to sovereignly love and whom to sovereignly hate. Since God ordains everything, it follows if the unevangelized did not hear the gospel, they simply were not meant to hear it. This gives the fear of God new meaning and his justice a new twist. But what a dreadful potentate God is and what an awful justice he displays, according to this theory.[13]

Restrictivism is too heavy a burden for most people. It is hard to believe that the divine plan would leave so many without hope. Would the Shepherd who leaves the ninety and nine to search for one lost sheep devise so restrictive and heartless a plan? Is there no understanding that would do more justice to God's love for the nations?

In reply, restrictivists ask, Are you guided by Scripture or driven by a desire for universality that really stems from your culture and your feelings of pity rather than the Word of God? This is always a good question to ask theologians on both sides of any issue, and the reader will have to judge whether a sound biblical and theological case can be made for wider hope.

Universality and Particularity

There is a tension inherent in the Christian faith between universality and particularity, a tension between the belief that God loves the whole world (universality) and the belief that Jesus is the only way to God (particularity). It challenges skills of theological interpretation to explain how they both can be true. Does God love the whole world or not? God may desire all to be saved, but it is hard to see how they possibly can be. How can a large number meet the requirement of believing in the gospel? It would seem that they cannot. If hearing the gospel clearly is required for salvation, it would seem that God does not want all to be saved. This is not a problem invented by skeptics, though they like to use it against us. It is primarily a challenge to theological interpretation, to explain how it proposes to correlate universality and particularity.

I believe it would help us if we recognized the twin, interdependent missions of Son and Spirit. It reduces tension between universality and particularity and fosters a sense that they are complementary rather than contradictory. The two poles turn out to be both-and, not either-or.

Here is the scenario. Christ, the only mediator, sustains particularity, while Spirit, the presence of God everywhere, safeguards universality. Christ represents particularity by being the only mediator between God and humanity (1 Tim 2:5-6), while Spirit upholds universality because no soul is beyond the sphere of the Spirit's operations. Spirit is not confined to the church but is present everywhere, giving life and creating community. Hovering over the waters of creation, Spirit is present also in the search for meaning and the struggle against sin and death. Because inspiration is ubiquitous and works everywhere in unseen ways, Spirit is in a position to offer grace to every person. Because Spirit works everywhere in advance of the church's mission, preparing the way for Christ, God's will can be truly and credibly universal.[14]

The life-giving Spirit, breathed out by the Father, works in the world and in all of history. The Spirit renews the face of the ground, gives life to every creature and bestows insight. The texts that speak of this include those picturing the Wisdom of God, which is associated with the Spirit. We read in Proverbs,

Does not wisdom call,
    and does not understanding raise her voice?
On the heights, beside the way,
    at the crossroads she takes her stand;
beside the gates in front of the town,
    at the entrance of the portals she cries out:
"To you, O people, I call,
    and my cry is to all that live." (8:1-4)

God's wisdom is present in creation, and God calls out to all people everywhere by means of it. Beyond Torah and special revelation, wisdom speaks within human experience itself. We are summoned to pay heed to the order of the world and to observe the wisdom displayed in the structure of things. God speaks even where Christ is not yet named—God does not leave himself without witness (Acts 14:17).

Proverbs goes on,

When there were no depths I was brought forth,
    when there were no springs abounding with water. . . .
    I was beside [the LORD], like a master worker;
and I was daily his delight,
    rejoicing before him always,
rejoicing in his inhabited world
    and delighting in the human race. (Prov 8:24, 30-31)

The world is not chaos but meaningful and good. The Spirit hovers over it and calls us to consider our place in the world and to choose good rather than evil. Love God, do what is right, do not follow paths that lead to death: such truths do not belong only to civic righteousness and common grace but have a larger meaning. They reflect the divine concern for every person and show that no one is far from God's presence. God "is not far from each one of us" (Acts 17:27).

God's Spirit and wisdom are at work everywhere—their actions pervaded history from the beginning and continue to do so. John V. Taylor calls Spirit the "go-between God" because he ceaselessly fosters relationship, within the Trinity and also between God and humanity. If history is thought of as a stage play, Spirit is its director, touching the world and directing the economy of salvation by subtle influences. He spreads his gifts generously, even to people outside the church and in the wider world. Martin Buber, for example, was not a Christian but was surely gifted by God. Acknowledgment of these universal operations grounds mission in the activity of the Spirit at the heart of creation and maintains universality. It lets us avoid narrow perspectives and be hopeful about people who have not yet acknowledged Jesus as Lord.[15]

Grace is extant not only in Christian contexts but in every place where the Spirit is. There is grace in general revelation and special revelation, and both are fulfilled in Jesus Christ. God reaches out to sinners in a multiplicity of ways, thanks to the prevenience of the Spirit. God loves sinners, and the Spirit works in them that they may ultimately become obedient to Jesus Christ. Granted, such a goal can take much time to achieve. Yet instead of saying there is no salvation outside the church, let us simply say there is no salvation outside grace, or only finally outside Christ.

The tension between universality and particularity is eased when we do justice to the twin mission of Son and Spirit. The truth of the incarnation does not eclipse truth about the Spirit, who was at work in the world before Christ and is present now where Christ is not named. The mission of the Son is not a threat to the mission of the Spirit, or vice versa. On the one hand, the Son's mission presupposes the Spirit's—Jesus was conceived and empowered by the Spirit. On the other hand, the mission of the Spirit is oriented to the goals of incarnation. The Spirit's mission is to bring history to completion and fulfillment in Christ. Thus the double mission of Son and Spirit can provide the perspective we need to handle the tension of universality and particularity.[16]

God's empowered presence graces the world, giving life and hope. It is the source of movement in the world and is present wherever reality reaches out to God. Spirit is not an esoteric "ghost" but an empirical power that breaks forth in perceptible ways. This is the power that called forth life from nonlife and the power drawing humanity to God. The Spirit struggles against the evil that pulls us downward and strives to bring creation to completion in God (Augustine *Confessions* 13.7.8).

Spirit works ceaselessly to persuade human beings to trust and open themselves up to love. Those with eyes to see can discern the Spirit's activity in human culture and religion, as God everywhere draws people to friendship. People can search for him and find him because "he is not far from each one of us" (Acts 17:27). People can shut themselves off from God and refuse the call, but they may also respond to the One who rewards those who diligently seek him (Heb 11:6).[17]

The Spirit's work is not limited to Jews and Christians. God is truly "the Savior of all people, especially of those who believe" (1 Tim 4:10). Peter says, "God shows no partiality, but in every nation anyone who fears him and does what is right is acceptable to him" (Acts 10:34-35). These words suggest that faith is more than assent to theological propositions. It involves a relationship of trust in God which manifests itself in godly living.

There are believers who do not belong to any church. Jesus has sheep that do not belong to this fold: "I must bring them also, and they will listen to my voice. So there will be one flock, one shepherd" (Jn 10:16). Humanity was made to live in fellowship with God, and Spirit everywhere woos sinners to come home.

The incarnation should not be viewed as a negation of universality but as the fulfillment of what Spirit had been doing all along. The birth of Jesus by the Spirit was the climax of a universal set of operations. Hovering over Mary, Spirit was engaged in new creation. The incarnation marked a new stage in Spirit's universal operations. Spirit, everywhere at work in the whole of history, was now at work in Jesus to make him the head of a new humanity. Throughout history the Spirit has been seeking to create such an impression of God's true self in human beings and hear the response to God that would delight his heart. This is what happened in Jesus by the Spirit. The invisible became visible, and a yes was heard on behalf of the race. Jesus became the receptacle of God's self-communication, and in him God received complete acceptance. Therefore the Spirit filled Jesus without measure and opened up the possibility for us to share this fullness. The floodgates of grace were opened for the world.[18]

"And the Son"
The term *filioque* ("and from the Son") was introduced into the Nicene Creed by the Western church, so that the third article reads, "I believe in the Holy Spirit, the Lord and giver of life, who proceeds from the Father *and the Son [filioque]*." The Western church acted unilaterally by inserting this term without heeding protests from the East, and this resulted in the first great division of the church. Making this insertion represented a misuse of power. But there is another aspect of the issue to consider.

The idea of adding *filioque* was not perverse theologically. The risen Lord did and does pour out the Spirit on the church. But the phrase in the creed can lead to a possible misunderstanding. It can threaten our understanding of the Spirit's universality. It might suggest to the worshiper that Spirit is not the gift of the Father to creation universally but a gift confined to the sphere of the Son and even the sphere of the church. It could give the impression that the Spirit is not present in the whole world but limited to Christian territories. Though it need not, the *filioque* might threaten the principle of universality— the truth that the Spirit is universally present, implementing the universal salvific will of Father and Son. One could say that the *filioque* promotes Christomonism.[19]

In my view the phrase diminishes the role of the Spirit and gives the impression that he has no mission of his own. It does not encourage us to contemplate the broad range of his operations in the universe. It tends to restrict Spirit to the churchly domain and deny his presence among people outside. It does not encourage us to view the divine mission as being prior to and geographically larger than the Son's. It could seem to limit Spirit to having a noetic function in relation to Christ, as if the Spirit fostered faith in him and nothing more. It undercuts the idea that Spirit can be active where the Son is not named and supports the restrictive reading of the axiom "Outside the church, no salvation."

My principal objections to the *filioque* are not related to its actual meaning. First, inserting it was an abuse of power. The Roman jurisdiction had no right to alter an ecumenical creed without consulting the larger church. Second, the insertion fostered a theology of restrictiveness. The original wording upheld the freedom of the Spirit to operate everywhere and did not suggest his confinement.

Greek Orthodox bishop Kallistos Ware writes, "Many Orthodox feel that, as a result of the filioque, the Spirit in Western thought has become subordinated to the Son—if not in theory, then in practice. The West pays insufficient attention to the work of the Spirit in the world, in the church, in the daily life of each man."[20] The creed was better before this term was added to it, because it recognized Spirit as the power permeating the cosmos and energizing all of history. The mission of the Spirit is not subordinate to the Son's but equal and complementary. The *filioque* was introduced into the creed in an irregular way and adversely affects our understanding of salvation.[21]

The Catechism of the Catholic Church concedes that the opinion of the Eastern churches is as valid as its own on the theology of this point (par. 248) but does not take the step of retracting the clause or its earlier condemnation of the East at Lyon (in 1274). Surely it would be healing to the divided church and liberating to its vision of salvation if the *filioque* were withdrawn. Yves Congar comments, "The Roman Catholic Church could . . . suppress the filioque in the creed, into which it was introduced in a canonically irregular way. That would be an ecumenical action of humility and solidarity which, if it was welcomed as genuine by the Orthodox church, could create a new situation favourable to the re-establishment of full communion."[22] Amen!

The Larger Framework

Viewing the Son's incarnation as an event in the history of the Spirit lets us consider particularity in the context of universality. The mystery of God was uniquely and unsurpassably revealed in Jesus (particularity), but this happened with the aid of the Spirit, who had always been working in creation and in history before that time (universality). God sent his Son in "the fullness of time" to a world being prepared by the

Spirit (Gal 4:4). What God was aiming to reveal in Jesus was long in preparation, and Jesus came as fulfillment to a process in which the Spirit had been a central player.

Spirit gives us a clue to the universality of God's plan, as the searching and gathering love of God preparing the world for redemption. This allows us to see the offer of grace as something as broad as history itself. Jesus did not represent the first offering of God's grace—rather, the offer reached its culmination and high point in him. The offer was so intense and world-changing through his participatory atonement that the Spirit could then come in pentecostal power.

Creation and redemption, then, are continuous, not discontinuous. Creation is not a work lacking in grace but the gift of divine love. Marcion saw no grace in creation and no continuity between creation and redemption. He even identified the God of creation as a different deity. Though this view was condemned, today's neo-Marcionites make a similar distinction when they deny that creation is a work of grace and that God is reaching out to people everywhere.[23]

The issue is hope and whether we are entitled to have it. Salvation can be a universal possibility if we recognize the universal, loving activities of the Spirit. God has always wanted friendship and reconciliation with sinners. What Jesus made explicit and implemented has always been true. There is a stream of redemptive revelation. We read in Hebrews, "Long ago God spoke to our ancestors in many and various ways by the prophets, but in these last days he has spoken to us by a Son" (1:1-2). It has always been possible to cast oneself on the mercy of God, even when one's theology is conceptually incomplete. God is a Person, and people can receive the gift of his love without knowing exactly who the giver is or how much it cost. This is the way that holy pagans like Enoch, Melchizedek and Job were saved.[24]

Zwingli grasped the significance of this point: "There has not lived a single good man, there has not been a single pious heart or believing soul from the beginning of the world to the end, which you will not see in the presence of God."[25] This hope leads us to recognize moves of the Spirit everywhere in the world. The hope is also expressed by Vatican II: "Those also can attain to everlasting salvation who through no fault of their own do not know the gospel of Christ or his church, yet sincerely seek God and, moved by grace, strive by their deeds to do his will as it is known to them through the dictates of conscience" (*Church* par. 16).

"Prevenient grace" is the term Wesley used to refer to universal, gracious operations of the Spirit. In his context the issue was how sinners could exercise faith without it being a contribution to salvation. His answer was that grace comes before (prevenient to) the response, before any human movement toward God. It enables sinners to respond to the Spirit, who draws them to the light without forcing them.[26] Wesley also used the category at times in his thinking about the issue we are concerned with here, universality. Spirit precedes evangelization, not only empowering witnesses to preach and heal but also present already in all the places where they go. For Wesley this understanding eased the problem of the fate of the unevangelized and enabled him to say that people would be judged by the light they have and by their response to it.

God wants a relationship with sinners, and if we accept the category of prevenient grace, we acknowledge that God offers himself to creatures. Spirit speaks to everyone in the depths of their being, urging them not to close themselves off from God but to open themselves up. Because of Spirit, everyone has the possibility of encountering him—even those who have not heard of Christ may establish a relationship with God through prevenient grace.[27]

Karl Rahner defends prevenient grace and the universality of the Spirit's operations in somewhat different language. He sees God presenting himself to every human being, as was his intention when he created humans. It flows from his purpose in creation, not from some obligation to humankind. God wants everyone to have the possibility of salvation. This does not spell universalism, because one can either open or close oneself to the offer. It simply gives everyone the opportunity of encountering God on the basis of grace and shows that his salvific will is genuinely universal. If one is open to the divine mystery, a relationship begins. Its development toward union with God follows, whether it takes a short while or a long time.[28]

Reformed theology recognizes universal operations of the Spirit in its category of common grace. The significance of such grace is diminished, however, by the use of the term *common* rather than *special*. In the Reformed view, common grace is a gift of God to sinners, but a gift that helps them only in nonsalvific ways. Common grace helps people behave better than they would if left to themselves. The notion seems to have arisen to explain why sinners do not seem as depraved as the Reformed system of doctrine says they should be. Speaking of common grace is a way of admitting that human depravity is less than total without revising the doctrine. Calling grace "common" is odd, but at least it recognizes that the Spirit is at work in the whole world.[29]

God's presence fills the world and touches every heart. Spirit should not be restricted to one segment of history or one sphere of reality. The Spirit flourishes everywhere, beyond the boundaries of church. The Spirit's ministry is global, not only domestic, and ontic, not only noetic. Spirit can be encountered in the entire range of experience, having always been present in the whole world, even in the groaning creation, preparing it for new birth (Rom 8:23). World history is coextensive with salvation history. Recall that God reminded Judah, "Are you not like the Ethiopians to me?" (Amos 9:7). Remember that Jesus has other sheep than those of this fold, and he will bring them too (Jn 10:16).[30]

Spirit in Other Religions?

Does prevenient grace bear fruit in the religious life and traditions of humankind? If the Spirit is gracing the world, does he grace it in the area of religions? Does God's offer ever get thematized in the myth, doctrine or ritual of non-Christian religions?

The first hurdle we have surmounted in this chapter was restrictivism. We could have stopped there. The main thing is to be able to have hope for the otherwise hopeless. But this other issue, the role of religions in the providence of God, cannot be easily sidestepped. People demand to know if theology can grant the possibility of the Spirit's being at work in other faiths.

A positive answer seems possible.[31] If the Spirit gives life to creation and offers grace to every creature, one would expect him to be present and make himself felt (at least occasionally) in the religious dimension of cultural life. Why would the Spirit be working everywhere else but not here? God is reaching out to all nations and does not leave himself without witness (Acts 14:17). Would this witness not crop up sometimes in the religious realm? It seemed to do so for Cornelius, a non-Christian whose moral and spiritual life before conversion is highly praised in Scripture (Acts 10:2). Evidently the Spirit had been at work in his life and faith prior to his conversion. People search for God in religions; are we to say that they never encounter God in religion, in spite of the inadequacies and distortions that are to be found in every religious worldview?[32]

Revelation goes out to the world and comes to expression in the course of human history. This is what has been called general revelation. As the artist is revealed in her work, God the Creator is revealed in the beauty and order of the world over the course of its unfolding. God is drawing the nations, and religions supply occasions when people can respond to him. God communicates with all his creatures, and they are able to relate to him. Paul made this plain at Athens, when he connected Greek worship with the knowledge of the true God (Acts 17:22-31). Of course the Athenians' theology was distorted and incomplete. But it did contain certain insights into God's purpose.

Because truths are embedded in various religious traditions, we ought to seek redemptive bridges to other traditions and inquire if God's word has been heard by their adherents. We ought to look at other traditions with empathic understanding—and at our own religion with a critical eye. If we did so, we might be enriched and be moved to do our theology less in the "Christian ghetto" and more globally.[33]

Let us be more consistent. In the past we have listened to non-Christian voices, such as Plato and Aristotle, because we thought they had truth to offer. We thought that we might learn from them, and indeed we did. We did comparative theology using insights from classical Greece. The result was not always beneficial, but we did it. Why stop there? Maybe there are others to whom some truth has been given. It does not diminish faith in Christ to inquire but shows our openness to learn more truth as we wait for the parousia. Theology should not be done in narrow, constricted spaces but should interact with other religious philosophies in the hope of mutual enrichment. A further advantage is that in such dialogue, opportunities arise for proclaiming Christ as God revealed and incarnate in a human life.

Let us appreciate the spirit of Irenaeus, who said, "There is but one and the same God who, from the beginning to the end by various dispensations, comes to the rescue of humankind" (*Against Heresies* 3.12.13). Openness to others does not imply that they have heard God's voice accurately and know only truth with no admixture of error. All of us make mistakes in our theologies, because God's ways are not coercive and because the truth can be suppressed by un-righteousness. But we should not prejudge such things. Spirit is present everywhere, and God's truth may have penetrated any given religion and culture at some point. We should be eager to find out. What an opening for mission it would supply![34]

We have to say both yes and no to other religions. On the one hand, we should accept any spiritual depth and truth in them. On the other hand, we must reject darkness and error and at the very least see other faiths as insufficient apart from fulfillment in Christ. The key is to hold fast to two truths: the universal operations of grace and the uniqueness of its manifestation in Jesus Christ.

I see this flexible attitude in Acts: in Peter's openness to pagans (10:35), in Paul's generous spirit at Lystra (14:17) and in the Athens apologetic (17:22-31). The Bible sounds many different chords. If the book of Romans sounds a pessimistic note, St. Luke sounds a hopeful one. He gives the impression that aspects of religion can be brought to fulfillment in Christ. It goes along with his extending Jesus' gene-alogy all the way back to Adam, showing that Jesus is the fulfill-ment of God's dealings with humanity. Grace has never been absent from history but has always been preparing for the coming of Christ (Lk 3:38). Jesus is the culmination of all God's providential dealings, not just in the case of Israel.[35]

Reasonable though this possibility sounds, it has not often been entertained by theology. The Christian tradition has seldom been this positive toward other traditions, and Protestant theology in particular has been reluctant to grant that the Spirit is in any positive way active in the religious life of humanity.[36] Among the reasons is fear lest the uniqueness of Christ's incarnation be jeopardized if the Spirit were thought to be active outside gospel and church. It might blur the distinction between true and false religion and lead to all kinds of assimilation and syncretism.[37]

Nevertheless, it would be strange if the Spirit excused himself from the very arena of culture where people search for meaning. If God is reaching out to sinners, it is hard to comprehend why he would not do so in the sphere of religion. There is some indication of this in Scripture. Although the Bible condemns error and evil in non-Jewish or non-Christian religions, it also sometimes looks favorably on adherents of such religions.

Abram's encounter with Melchizedek, for example, reveals God at work in Canaanite culture. The patriarch accepted the blessing of Melchizedek, a pagan priest, and paid tithes to him. Abram seems convinced that they were both worshiping the one and only God and to have realized that his own calling did not make God a private possession. The encounter showed him that while he was to be a source of blessing for the nations, God was also at work among them (Gen 14:17-24). Soon after that, Abram met King Abimelech, who surprised him by displaying more piety and uprightness than he himself had (Gen 20).

Similarly in the New Testament, as noted earlier, Cornelius is depicted as a devout man in whose religious life God was already at work and to whose prayers God attended before he heard the gospel (Acts 10:1-8). Such people are in effect believers of other dispensations who await messianic salvation. They are servants destined to become sons and daughters, as Wesley put it.[38]

Religion is an important segment of culture, and God is in touch with it. It is central to human life, because we were made for fellowship with God and our hearts are restless until we find him. People look to religion for answers to deep questions. God is at work drawing them. Spirit, who is at work everywhere, is at work in the history of religions, and religions play a part in the history of grace, as the Spirit moves the world toward the kingdom. The world is being prepared for the gospel as redemptive bridges are built in human cultures. No wonder we find saintly people and signs of truth in world religions. They may provide a window of opportunity for the Spirit to engage sinners, without diminishing the importance of Jesus, the fulfillment of all such aspirations.[39]

Vatican II asks us not to reject anything that is true and holy in other religions. It speaks of seeds of the Word of God which reflect rays of his light. It urges us to look for ways in which people may be responding to his urgings (*Declaration on the Relationship of the Church to Non-Christian Religions* par. 2). John Taylor writes, "The eternal Spirit has been at work in all ages and all cultures making men aware and evoking their response, and always the one to whom he was pointing and bearing witness was the Logos, the Lamb slain before the foundation of the world."[40] John Paul II speaks similarly about the Christian attitude to other religions and refers to Spirit in this connection. In an early encyclical (*Redemptor Hominis,* 1979) he spoke of the presence of Spirit in non-Christian religions.

Though Jesus is not named in other faiths, Spirit is present and may be experienced. God can speak to people's hearts through the Spirit. "The Holy Spirit in a manner known only to God offers to every man the possibility of being associated with the paschal mystery." Regardless of time and place, it is possible for anyone to receive God's offer of grace because of the Spirit, who is active everywhere.[41]

Many readers are moved by the story C. S. Lewis tells in *The Last Battle,* the final volume of the Chronicles of Narnia. A pagan soldier named Emeth learns to his surprise that Aslan regards his worship of Tash as having been directed to him. Emeth says,

> I fell at his feet and thought, Surely this is the hour of death, for the Lion (who is worthy of all honour) will know that I have served Tash all my days and not him. Nevertheless, it is better to see the Lion and die than to be the Tisroc of the world and live and not to have seen him. But the Glorious One bent down his golden head and touched my forehead with his tongue and said, Son, thou art welcome. But I said, Alas, Lord, I am no son of Thine but the servant of Tash. He answered, Child, all the service thou hast done to Tash, I account as service done to me. Then by reason of my great desire

for wisdom and understanding, I overcame my fear and questioned the Glorious One and said, Lord, is it then true, as the Ape said, that thou and Tash are one? The Lion growled so that the earth shook (but his wrath was not against me) and said, It is false. Not because he and I are one, but because we are opposites, I take to me the services which thou hast done to him, for I and he are of such different kinds that no service which is vile can be done to me, and none which is not vile can be done to him. Therefore if any man swear by Tash and keep his oath for oath's sake, it is by me that he has truly sworn, though he know it not, and it is I who reward him. And if any man do a cruelty in my name, then though he say the name Aslan, it is Tash whom he serves and by Tash his deed is accepted. Dost thou understand, Child? I said, Lord, thou knowest how much I understand. But I said also (for the truth constrained me), Yet I have been seeking Tash all my days. Beloved, said the Glorious One, unless thy desire had been for me thou wouldst not have sought so long and so truly. For all find what they truly seek.[42]

As is clear from this excerpt, Lewis understood God to be at work in the religious life of humanity.

Because of the Spirit's ubiquitous inspiration, we do well to be open to people of other faiths. We should watch for whatever Spirit may be teaching and doing among them. This posture creates the possibility of a dialogical relationship. We can enter into the faith of others and acknowledge truths and values found there. These are our fellow human beings, seeking truth as we are. God is reaching out, and people are responding. So let us watch for points of contact and bridges of communication. God reveals himself to all nations in creation and in history. There is nothing to fear from interreligious dialogue. It is a privilege and an opportunity to speak with others about what concerns them most. Without in any way being hesitant about making known the claims of Christ, we should listen and learn from the insights of others. Believing in the finality of Christ does not require us to be arrogant in our claims or closed to grace at work in other people.

In the Middle Ages theologians reflected on how grace might be accessible to those outside the church. In grappling with it, they spoke about a "desire" *(votum)* for God and the sacraments. Just as prior to the birth of Jesus, when belief in God was sufficient for salvation, so now, they surmised, people can express the desire for Christ by trusting in God. Under certain circumstances, an implicit desire for salvation, involving faith and love, would be sufficient. God would accept such a disposition and regard it as a movement in the direction of Christ. This mode of teaching was picked up by Vatican II.[43]

One can avoid the one-sided Christic view by referring to the Holy Spirit, who renders effective the mission of Christ and makes God's reign present everywhere. There are elements of grace found in other religious traditions, and one hopes they may mediate God's presence for people.[44]

This is not a trivial issue. It is an urgent matter, since over the centuries the majority of humanity has existed without hearing the gospel. The theory assumes that God, who chooses humanity to be saved and who sent his Son to die on behalf of them all, knows (like Aslan) how to recognize inclinations toward him when they are present. Such desire for God does not give people everything they will ultimately need—it is a weak initiation and lacks the nurturing context of church. But it allows a decision to turn from self-centeredness and to give oneself to God and neighbor. It involves a kind of dying to self and rising to life. It is not in any way an achievement of which one may be proud, but is a work of grace. It involves the sense of being gifted and enriched by God.[45]

At the same time, let me say that we should not glorify religion or overlook error. Though most religions contain some truth, they also contain much that is dark and oppressive. We know that from our own experience of Christianity, in whose history sin has often tragically manifested itself. As we listen for the Spirit in other religions, we must be prepared to encounter error and abuse. John Paul II, despite his positive regard of other faiths, has issued criticisms of Buddhism (concerning its disdain for the world and detachment) and of Islam (for portraying God as majestic but not gracious). And, of course, however many positive elements are found, non-Christian religions lack the knowledge of God's reconciling act in Jesus Christ.[46]

It would certainly not be wise to regard religions as such as vehicles of grace. Rahner goes too far with his category of "lawful" religion. He goes beyond admitting, as I do, the possibility of the Spirit's speaking to people of other faiths to say that religions are valid as temporary means of salvation before evangelization. It is one thing to be attentive to the Spirit at work in a religious context and to be thankful if a religion helps inculcate holiness and virtue. It is another thing to claim that other religions are vehicles of grace and salvation. What Buddhism offers (Nirvana) is not the same as what Christianity offers (union with God). Views of the proper goal of life differ from one religion to another. Buddhism does not point to Christ, and Christianity is not interested in dharma. One can be sensitive to the Spirit among people of other faiths without minimizing real and crucial differences between them.[47]

It is possible on the basis of the particularity of Christ to propose a global theology. God has not left himself without witness anywhere, though he has revealed himself definitively in one particular human life. Moral and spiritual worth can be found in other faiths, yet God's revelation in Christ is of surpassing value, normative in relation to general revelation and universal in significance. Jesus is the incarnation of God, but the Spirit also sustains human relationships with God broadly. On this basis, we expect the Spirit to be drawing humanity into the range of Christ's saving work everywhere.[48]

Spirit, present in the whole world and at work among all peoples, is at work in the sphere of religious life, so that religious experience may play a preparatory role for the coming of Christ. Spirit is at work in advance of mission, preparing the way for Jesus. This modest proposal claims only that God is everywhere at work, even in the religious sphere, and may be speaking to people with ears to hear. We do not claim to know how the Spirit works among non-Christians, but only that he is active. This gives us hope and opens us to charitable relationships with those of other faiths.[49]

In regard to the question of revelation in other religions, we must walk very prudently. On the one hand, God's decisive self-revelation took place only in Jesus Christ. There is no other deity revealed in other religions. The one God is the triune God. On the other hand,

God is not our property and possession but is active throughout creation and history. The history of Israel, for example, led to the coming of Jesus. Here God was at work apart from Jesus Christ but leading up to him. By analogy with Israel, we watch for anticipations in other faiths to be fulfilled in Christ. We do not affirm the possibility of God's revealing himself outside Christianity begrudgingly—we welcome it! Not only does such a possibility suggest bridges in other cultures to enhance mission, but it also allows us to hear the word of God from others and deepens our own understanding of revelation.[50]

The Criterion

If we listen for the Spirit's voice in the midst of the ambiguity of religions, the issue of discernment becomes key. Just as we ask where God is at work in the world providentially, so we ask where the Spirit is moving in the realms of human experience. The issue of a criterion is urgent: how do we judge such matters?

The need for a canon or measuring stick is evident. It was evident at the 1992 World Council of Churches meeting in Canberra, Australia. In the name of a global perspective, a Korean theologian attributed to the Spirit a range of pagan beliefs and practices. A similar thing happened at the 1994 "Re-imaging" conference in Minneapolis, where the goddess was invoked and historic theology was trashed in the name of Spirit.

Many such problems continue to arise. What are we supposed to make of the Hindu god that is said to drink milk? Was God not in the events surrounding the collapse of communism and of apartheid? Is the power being experienced in the "Toronto Blessing" from God, or is it fraudulent? We need a criterion for discerning the movings of the Spirit.

There are things in the world that cannot be attributed to God. God reigns over the world, but warfare and resistance are also real. God is not the only power there is, and God does not control everything unilaterally. There is a struggle between good and evil in history, and divine victory waits for the future. Though present everywhere, Spirit is not identical with everything, and certainly is not related to that which deceives and destroys. Powers hostile to truth and threatening to life must be discerned and resisted.

In the 1930s, for example, many intelligent Americans and Europeans were fooled when they visited Berlin and Moscow; the same thing happened in China in the 1960s. These naive visitors experienced a spirit of renewal and returned home enthusiastic for regimes that later proved to be oppressive, even murderous. They thought they had glimpsed new possibilities for human life, but they were sadly and dangerously duped and deluded.

The apostle John warns us not to believe every spirit, because there are false prophets and false Christs (1 Jn 4:1). Paul speaks of Satan's being disguised as an angel of light (2 Cor 11:14). He writes, "Our struggle is not against enemies of blood and flesh, but against the rulers, against the authorities, against the cosmic powers of this present darkness, against the spiritual forces of evil in the heavenly places" (Eph 6:12). Open as we should be to the Spirit in the world, we must test everything, holding fast to what is good and abstaining from every form of evil (1 Thess 5:21).[51]

How do we recognize the Spirit at work in the world beyond the church? The answer again is found in the double mission of Son and Spirit and the link between them. Truth incarnate is the criterion for testing spirits. The question to ask is christological (1 Jn 4:2-3). Spirit is in agreement with the Son and agrees with what he said and did. The Paraclete, Jesus tells us, brings to our remembrance what he said; he does not speak on his own but says what he hears. "He will take what is mine and declare it to you" (Jn 16:13-14; see also 14:26). Thus Spirit points to the criterion of incarnate wisdom. What the Spirit says and does cannot be opposed to revelation in Christ, because Spirit is bound to the Word of God. The reciprocity is clear—Spirit births the Son in Mary's womb, and the Son identifies the ways of the Spirit. To identify prevenience, we look for the fruit of the Spirit and for the way of Jesus Christ.

The gospel story helps us discern movements of the Spirit. From this narrative we learn the pattern of God's ways. So wherever we see traces of Jesus in the world and people opening up to his ideals, we know we are in the presence of Spirit. Wherever, for example, we find self-sacrificing love, care about community, longings for justice, wherever people love one another, care for the sick, make peace not war, wherever there is beauty and concord, generosity and forgiveness, the cup of cold water, we know the Spirit of Jesus is present. Other spirits do not promote broken and contrite hearts. Such things tell us where the brothers and sisters of Jesus indwelt by the Spirit are.

Jesus uses this criterion himself for recognizing his sheep: "I was hungry and you gave me food, I was thirsty and you gave me something to drink" (Mt 25:35). Why does he consider these his sheep? Simply because they are just like the children of the merciful Father. Obviously they belong to the kingdom, because their faith is manifest in their actions. They are doing the works of the kingdom by the grace of God. These are not actions that Satan would be promoting (Mk 3:23).

Fruits of the Spirit are not only cognitive. When we inquire after them, we should not investigate propositional truth alone. Signs of the kingdom have to do with the transformation of life. Good works do not merit grace, but they may signal a response to grace.[52]

We want to do nothing to detract from the uniqueness of Christ's salvation. Jesus is decisive for the participation of anyone in God's kingdom. He is not simply one prophet among many, one way among many. Nevertheless, the quota of members in his body is not limited, and the church is not identical to the kingdom of God. Jesus tells us that people will stream to the kingdom from every quarter, while many of those who believed themselves chosen will be absent (Mt 8:11-12). But how will it be known that they belong to Christ? Behavior that corresponds to the will of God is one of the factors. On the last day, some who confess Christ will be rejected because they refused to do the charitable deeds of the kingdom (Mt 7:21-23).

When Jesus articulated the beatitudes, he did not qualify his statements as we tend to do. We take him to be saying, for example, "Blessed are the meek who sign on the dotted theological line." Jesus puts no such restrictions on the beatitudes. He says, "Blessed are the poor in spirit"—period.

Wolfhart Pannenberg comments,

Others, . . . without even knowing it and without knowing Jesus, honored Jesus and his teaching by the way they treated the needy and will participate in the kingdom of God. Jesus and his teaching are the criteria of the ultimate judgment concerning human participation in final salvation. The final separation is not along the lines of whether somebody knew Jesus and belonged to his congregation in earthly life. Rather, the point is whether the behaviour of human persons corresponds to the requirements of the kingdom embodied in Jesus' teaching and activity.

Jesus is the criterion of salvation even for those who never knew him or his message. Participation in salvation is not impossible for people outside the church. The factors are behavioral as well as cognitive.[53]

The ways of God are admittedly hard to track, but movements of the Spirit in history can be seen because they are movements of the Spirit of Jesus. Because of him we know what we are looking for, at least in a general way. Jesus, the light of the world, is the criterion for discerning Spirit. The history of the Spirit reaches its climax in him and is therefore identified by him. As I noted earlier, some things about the *filioque* disturb me, but not everything. The truth of it is precisely the point about Christ's being the criterion of Spirit activity.

In pointing to Christ, however, Spirit is not pointing to any worn-out interpretations of Christ or baptizing everything that the church's tradition has said about him. Spirit also convicts the church where it has gone wrong and helps us grasp old truths in new ways. The Spirit helps us recognize signs of the times and position the words of Jesus in changing situations. The criterion cannot be equated with what we have thought so far, because we may not have been true to the gospel in our thinking. We may be standing in need of correction. Restrictivism is a good example of this. Therefore, let us listen to what the Spirit of Jesus is saying to the churches (Rev 2:7). The Jesus criterion keeps us focused, but the Spirit also has to prevent us from falling into ways that do not honor Christ. The criterion and canon have to be negotiated in creative ways.[54]

Spirit and Universality

God's universal salvific will is broad and generous, but how do those who have not heard the gospel in any clear or empowered way gain access to it? Spirit is the key to the universality of our particularity. Grace is always present by the Spirit. Though one is free to accept or refuse the offer, the possibility of salvation exists for everyone, grounded in the generous and reckless love of God. Life is filled with opportunities to say yes or no to God.[55]

It is possible to reject grace, of course. John Paul II in his book about hope insists that hell is a possible outcome of human life, though no one can say who or how many end up there. He is right—hell can be the final outcome for impenitent sinners who persist in faithlessness and lovelessness. The possibility of everlasting ruin exists and attests to the high significance of creaturely freedom.[56]

I want in this chapter to foster hope and diminish the pessimism of salvation that has long afflicted tradition. God is a serious lover who does not allow persons to perish without any opportunity to respond to his love. We do not know how the opportunity presents itself, but we can be sure that it does because of the loving heart of God.

Some may say I am guilty of hoping too much. Am I driven in this direction by wishful thinking? It is proper to ask about the context of a theological position and the motives behind various points of view. I do not think that I am drawn to hope only by wishful thinking, but I take the question seriously.

But since motives can be involved, I also wonder what possible motivations may underlie restrictivism. Why has tradition restricted the scope of divine mercy? After all, this is a strange thing to be doing. Is there something more at work than theological considerations? The Bible suggests one. Why was Jonah displeased by God's generosity to Nineveh, and why were the Pharisees unhappy with Jesus for welcoming sinners? Why did they object so to his generosity? One has the feeling that they lacked a certain sense of the reckless divine generosity that would culminate in the giving of the beloved Son for the world. One gets the sense that they thought those who attend God's party have a greater right to be there than others.

The elder brother sulked when the prodigal was welcomed home. I imagine he said to himself: *I am the one who deserves a party, not this worthless fellow*. There are really two lost sons in that parable, and one remains lost at the end of it. Though the elder brother had lived his whole life with the father, he did not really know him. At least he did not share his father's generosity and experienced no joy at the prodigal's return, only resentment. He was angry and refused to go in to the feast. The story ends with the father appealing to him: "All that is mine is yours—come in!" (see Lk 15:25-32). I wonder if he changed his mind and went in.

It is easy to feel resentful at the universality of grace. We may think to ourselves: Have we not done our duty? Have we not been faithful all our lives? Why should undeserving outsiders get in easily? Would it not be fairer for those outside the church to be outside salvation too? There is a voice in us, isn't there, that says no one ought to gain entry to the kingdom who doesn't really belong and is not wearing the proper badges.

I am glad to see a shift to greater hope in Christian thinking and a growing reluctance to restrict grace. This is a result not of contemporary cultural pressures but of paying closer attention to the nature of God and—I think—to the pervasive presence of the Spirit. As a result, God's universal salvific will registers higher now in the hierarchy of doctrine than formerly. Belief in God as a serious lover who does not readily give up on the lost occupies a more primary position on the list, giving us more freedom to hope and to believe all things (1 Cor 13:7).

Many Christians are becoming optimists of salvation. God's mercies are great—every person is loved by God and touched by the Spirit. Rather than assuming others are hopeless, we regard them as loved by God and not-yet-Christians. Had we met Saul of Tarsus before his conversion, we might well have concluded that this persecutor of the church was beyond the pale. But we would have been wrong. Isn't it wiser to engage in mission with hope, trusting the God who has been at work beforehand? Hope can be an encouragement rather than an impediment to evangelism. It fosters good relationships and encourages points of contact. God does not send us into mission knowing the final destiny of every soul. It is not our job to judge the world or identify the elect. Jesus did not do so, and he warned that there would be surprises for those who tried. He said that the first would be last and the last first.

Let us never give up hope for those who have not yet believed. For one thing, who can say what a no means? What if the gospel was heard from a drunken sailor? What if the message was distorted? What if a zealous restrictivist had portrayed God as particularly niggardly? What would a no mean then? What if the no will turn into a yes by the last day? Do we have any notion how hard it must be for not-yet-Christians to extricate themselves from their own cultural-linguistic communities and become baptized Christians? Have many of us had to make a costly decision like that? Let us be filled with sympathy and not at all judgmental, even toward those who have seemed to say no to Jesus until now.

In our mission we are not motivated out of the fear of hell. God sends us forth to proclaim the coming of his kingdom in the power of the Spirit, to make disciples for the reign of God. We go not because of a mere commandment or because of fear, but because we have been caught up in the mission of God by the Spirit, who makes us witnesses and enables us to speak. Let the whole world know that Jesus Christ has died for it and reconciled it. Let the nations come home and take their place at the table of God.

SEVEN

SPIRIT &
TRUTH

*I*N THIS FINAL CHAPTER we consider issues of truth and revelation, of inspiration and illumination, which are concerns of the Spirit of truth, who guides the community into truth (Jn 16:13). We want to inquire how the Spirit reveals God's identity and brings revelation to fruition.

Here I want to raise an issue of doctrinal fidelity that is often neglected—the imperative of timeliness. Theology must be faithful to revelation but also speak about things that matter in present situations. God wants worship in Spirit and truth—that is, grounded in the truth of Jesus and open to the Spirit who takes us more deeply into it (Jn 4:24-25). A theology that does not inquire after God's will for the present may be orthodox but is not really listening to God. Doctrines are to be timely witnesses, not timeless abstractions. Theologians must wait on God concerning what is crucial. Fidelity and creativity are both called for.[1]

Was not the subject of the last chapter an example? People are eager to know how other religions should be viewed from a Christian point of view. This is only one of many issues on which we need light. We wonder about ministries of women, how to integrate faith with modern science, how to be open to gifts of the Holy Spirit. Theology must read the Bible and also listen to what the Spirit is saying. In this way we grow as hearers of the word of God.

Challenges present themselves, and we seek the mind of Christ. Out of the interaction of challenge and response, fresh insights can come. We have to engage in strenuous theological reflection. We need the mind of Christ on many issues today. It is essential to be able to discern how God is acting and where Christ is in the events of history. More than intellectual training is needed for this. It requires the spiritual formation of the whole person. This book is an attempt to view old truths from fresh angles and in new contexts in order to hear a relevant word from the Lord. Its success will depend on whether this is what happens.[2]

I do not intend God's leading into truth to be a matter of only parochial interest. It should be placed in a global setting, because God's interests are much wider than the church. God is self-revealed in creation and history as well as in the experiences of Israel and the story of Jesus. God does not leave himself without witness among the nations. The Athenians were expected to know God because he was not far from them (Acts 14:17; 17:27). The Spirit is guiding, luring, wooing, influencing, drawing all humanity, not just the church. He wants every person to come to a knowledge of the truth so that through Christ justification and life may be provided for them all (Rom 5:18; 1 Tim 2:4). Not everyone listens, but God speaks to all.

God is not parochial in his interests. He is concerned to gather the nations. His heart aches over the alienation of humankind; his arms are outstretched to the world. He wants the human race to know him, to come higher up and deeper in. If only the world would let itself be gathered into the Father's arms! The nations belong to God, who is at work among them (Jer 18:7). Beyond the revelation to Israel and by Jesus Christ, God reveals and inspires, leads and guides. Amos said that God led the Philistines from Caphtor and the Syrians from Kir as he led Israel out of Egypt (9:7). Redemptive activity is broad and ought to be placed within the framework of a universal outreaching.

At this time in history, peoples of the earth have their own traditions and resources, but God wants to bring them to the heavenly Jerusalem. Isaiah sees Israel in the future as part of an international community of worshipers: "Blessed be Egypt my people, and Assyria the work of my hands" (Is 19:25). The biblical hope is that all nations will one day fear the Lord (Ps 102:15, 22).

> All the ends of the earth shall remember
>> and turn to the LORD;
> and all the families of the nations
>> shall worship before him.
> For dominion belongs to the LORD,
>> and he rules over the nations. (Ps 22:27-28)

Nations now experience revealing activity in their midst and are intended to be incorporated into God's people. The nations of earth will be blessed through faithful Abraham and will become God's peoples (Rev 21:3—note the plural).[3]

It is not just Christians whom God would bring to the unity of faith and knowledge of the Son. He has an interest in the salvation of all nations and is leading them as well as us into truth. Ecumenism has to do with more than just Protestants getting along with each other, Catholics and Protestants reconciling, and Eastern and Western churches exchanging recognition. God wants to bring humanity into unity in Jesus Christ (Eph 2:15). God's leading should be viewed broadly. There is a drawing of nations that leaves them in possession of some insights into God's ways. The form such insights take is never ideal, and the rendition may even be poor, but truth impinges on every people. By means of dialogue, we can hope for development within traditions, leading to more adequate understandings. We approach other faiths as possible sources of truth, however fallible and culturally situated they (and we) are.[4]

Growing as Hearers

My intention is not to make the global aspect of the Spirit's work central, but to focus attention on the need for Christians to grow as hearers of the Word of God. The need for growth in insight is evident. We always need a better accounting of what we believe. Our faith seeks understanding. Who among us does not need to know God and discern his will better? Changing circumstances require timely applications.

I have touched on certain aspects of Spirit in relation to truth; for example, I have noted that the Spirit makes the truth come alive and provides a witness in the hearts of believers (1 Cor 2:4; 1 Jn 2:27). But let us address now the issue of Spirit's guiding the church into truth. For we pilgrims need clarity as we travel toward the heavenly city. We need the Spirit to help us recover and maintain unity in the bond of peace (Eph 4:3). A situation of disunity has been permitted to arise which grieves the Spirit, impedes the church's mission and renders church discipline very difficult. We need the reunion of a divided church *in truth* so that we might walk together and the world might believe.[5]

One aspect of sanctification is maturing as hearers of the Word of God, as we open ourselves to all the dimensions of the biblical witness. Not as isolated individuals but as members of the community, God calls us to listen to other interpretations and experience a deepening of insight. Through the Word of God, the Spirit continues to transform our lives and lead us into a stronger love for God and neighbor. Just as Spirit gradually sanctifies individuals, so he leads the church into a deeper apprehension over time.

The issue is the appropriation of God's Word. On the one hand, as Paul says, the church of the living God is pillar and bulwark of the truth (1 Tim 3:15). It has received a treasure, bears witness to the gospel and passes the message on. On the other hand, the community needs the ongoing leading that God promises: "I will instruct you and teach you the way you should go" (Ps 32:8). We need that gentle luring and persuading that summons from us an increasingly intelligent response. God's leading is normally gentle and noncoercive, of a kind that respects the creativity and even the folly of human beings.

The Spirit cares for truth in the locus of Christ's body and fosters movement toward truth, despite our mistakes and errors. In this matter we should be both hopeful about receiving fresh insight and sober about possibilities of our being mistaken. Because God's leading is experienced in all the churches, we must be open to what can be learned from any quarter.[6]

Growing as hearers is essential because the truth of profound matters is not easily grasped and the implications not quickly apparent. In matters of ultimacy, one discovers treasures without completely possessing them. Improvement in understanding is always possible— and also desirable, because of our limitations and shortcomings. Therefore we ever pursue and seek to penetrate the truth more thoroughly.

Insight into divine matters is like a seed that needs to grow into a mature plant. It requires pondering truth and dwelling on it in mind and heart, as individuals and communities, with respect for what others think. Advances in understanding occur as the church meditates on the mysteries of salvation. "Even if revelation is already complete, it has not been made completely explicit; it remains for Christian faith gradually to grasp its full significance over the course of the centuries" (Catechism par. 66).

Mary, who treasured the things that she experienced and pondered them in her heart (Lk 2:51), is our example. She needed time to meditate on what she had seen and heard, time to consider what it might mean. This is true of the community. The truth once delivered to the saints is sufficient for every age, but we need time to reflect on it in order to gain better comprehension. Mature knowledge does not come quickly or easily, given the limitations of human nature and our fallenness. It takes time to penetrate profound matters and make them our own.

But seeking truth is exciting and promising. God has so much more to tell us than we have grasped thus far. Humility must be the order of the day. This is how we learn and grow. Let us cast aside rigidity and that know-it-all attitude and open ourselves to more light that God can shed on his Word and the human situation.[7]

As an evangelical, I admit to having failed to reflect much on how the Spirit leads into truth or on issues of development of doctrine. The evangelical emphasis on the propositional nature of truth has directed attention almost entirely toward biblical exegesis, to the neglect of other dynamics involved in interpretation. Those who like to call themselves biblical Christians often think of themselves as unaffected by the historical processes that affect others. We suffer from a naive realism, as if our interpretations have sprung without mediation from our reading of the Bible. We sometimes act as if historical elements played no part in them. It is not so.

Another reason I neglected the development of doctrine was a certain anxiety about the possibility that tradition might usurp primacy over Scripture and that the truth might change. For such reasons I took notice of negative but not positive aspects of tradition. If Catholics tend to be overly positive about developments in doctrine throughout the church's history, evangelicals tend to forget how much they have benefited from God's leading in tradition. We need a better balance of hope and realism. Let us be hopeful because the Spirit leads us and realistic because of our fallibility and proneness to error. Both progression and regression occur in the development of our under-standing.[8]

Development is not only concerned with the conservation of past interpretations but is also oriented to the future. It is essential that if the church is to go forward in mission, it be open to the Spirit's leading. Mission is hindered when the church becomes ossified, clinging to its past. Such a posture jeopardizes its effectiveness. Though our tradi-tions are rich and ancient, we must resist the temptation to choose the past and refuse today's issues. We must be faithful to original revelation but also move forward with God, listening to what the Spirit is saying to the churches.

We are a pilgrim community traveling toward the future. Many forms and images of faith have changed over the centuries and continue to change. How we think about doctrines and practices is always subject to reconsideration. There are new models for thinking and acting. Although what we decide about them must grow out of original revelation and be rooted in Scripture, freshness and relevance, aptness and timeliness should also be at work.[9]

Spirit works in the history of salvation to help the church enter divine revelation and make it our own. He secures the church in truth and leads it to further insight. Spirit, power of Jesus' birth and power leading him through life, has been poured out now to bring the community to birth and to lead it forward. Indwelling Christ's body, Spirit opens it up to the truth, to a fuller comprehension of the truth over time. God has promised to guide his people: "The LORD will guide you continually, and satisfy your needs in parched places" (Is 58:11). The psalmist says: "This is God. . . . He will be our guide forever" (Ps 48:14). God says, "I will instruct you and teach you the way you should go; I will counsel you with my eye upon you" (Ps 32:8). And Jesus promises, "When the Spirit of truth comes, he will guide you into all the truth" (Jn 16:13).[10]

Spirit helps us in the development of our understanding. The Paraclete, Spirit of truth, is with us to lead us (Jn 14:16-17). "Where the church is, there is the Spirit of God; where the Spirit of God is, there is the church and every kind of grace—the Spirit is truth" (Irenaeus *Against Heresies* 3.24.1). The church continues in the truth because the Spirit abides with it. Though capable of making mistakes, the church knows that God will not abandon it, come what may. The church persists in the truth by grace through the presence of the Spirit.[11]

This is crucial when it comes to grasping the significance of the Word for today. In mission, the community needs to be able to understand the message in fresh contexts—not in ways that go beyond revelation but in ways that penetrate it, not new revelation apart from the gospel but an understanding of the Word of God in new circumstances. The words of Jesus are quantitatively complete, not needing additions, but they are not qualitatively grasped—they need pondering. They need to become fresh and alive for each generation. Revelation is not a closed system of propositional truths but a divine self-disclosure that continues to open up and challenge. Hans Küng writes, "The Spirit cannot give new revelation but through the preaching of witnesses can cause everything that Jesus said and did to be revealed in a new light."[12]

Spirit sheds light along the pathway of mission, helping the church respond to challenges in timely ways. It is not enough to know what is written; we also need to grasp the *significance* of the Word. It is not enough to recite the text, if we are not saying what is crucial for the present situation. Spirit makes us sensitive to what God wants to be said now. Jesus warned against dwelling on trivialities and neglecting weighty matters (Mt 23:23). Paul sought to be timely and relevant in the cultural situations he entered as an evangelist. He gave thought to how he could be a Jew among Jews and a Greek among Greeks in order to save some (1 Cor 9:19-23). He did not achieve this by staring at Bible texts but by thinking and praying things through.[13]

The church always needs to grow and to experience reform. There are always errors to be overcome and new directions to be taken that would enhance mission. Because it is easy to lose our way, God's promise to lead us and not abandon us is most precious. Pilgrims may take wrong turns and stumble. Like the traveler in Jesus' parable, an entire community can fall among thieves and be left at the side of the road. When that happens, God pours oil on our wounds and provides restoration.

The confession "I believe in one holy catholic and apostolic church" is not a claim to perfection. It is an expression of confidence that whatever happens, we are Christ's church, against which the gates of hell will not prevail. Particular churches may falter and languish, but the church universal will continue (Augsburg Confession 7). We are not abandoned amid earthly struggles but enjoy the grace of perseverance through the Spirit.

Though we possess a faith once delivered, we do not grasp its significance completely—nor will we till the end of time. Revelation itself is only in part—how much more the insights latent in it! We are on the road to truth, not at the end of the journey. God's Word has not been mastered, nor can it be. Growth in the knowledge of truth is always possible. Furthermore, we are never beyond falling into error. Therefore let us not be quick to condemn others but always be open to improved insight. Humility is fundamental for growing as hearers. We must not be too proud to have second thoughts; we need not regard changing one's mind as a weakness. Newman had it right: to live is to change, and to be perfect is to have changed often.[14]

Given God's promise to lead us, progress in understanding should be possible, in spite of mistakes. Theology can always be improved, practice always made more appropriate. Revelation itself does not grow, but our understanding of it may be refined and amplified through action and reflection. Growth can occur in the elucidation of truth. Ideas can unfold without changing, and there can be progress in articulation. Implications can be clearer and a better understanding gained. In contrast to wooden orthodoxy, we confess the faith of Jesus freely and openly in each new present. Our grasp on it is neither complete nor absolute. Though it is the final truth for all time, we also seek the concrete truth of it for this time. It is God's living Word, powerful for the occasion when first spoken and significant for all other times and places as well. It is never surpassed but always richly interpreted.[15]

Development does not only have to do with mental concepts. The truth that unfolds in our understanding does not consist only (or even mainly) of abstract ideas. It concerns life in the community and guidance on issues of discipleship. It concerns the deployment of the Word of God—for example, to help people who are trapped and powerless. It concerns how to signal the victory of Christ over the powers of this age. The Word of Jesus needs to be made effective in concrete situations by the Spirit.[16]

Yet this does not imply an inevitability of progress. Early thoughts may well be superior to recent ones. We may regress rather than progress. Certain aspects of modern theology indeed have that appearance. So the promise of the Spirit's leading into deeper apprehension does not translate into a guarantee of evolutionary progress. Therefore we pray in the words of the collect:

Most gracious God, we humbly beseech thee for thy holy catholic church. Fill it with all truth; in all truth with all peace. Where it is corrupt, purify it; where it is in error, direct it; where anything is amiss, reform it; where it is right, strength and confirm it; where it is in want, furnish it; where it is divided and rent asunder, make it whole again; through Jesus Christ our Lord.

What Is Revelation?

Without revelation there would be no good news to be unfolded. Only because the silence has been broken and God is self-revealed do we have insight into God's triune nature and gracious purposes. Revelation is an act of interpersonal communication. By acting in history to save humanity, God has drawn back the veil of mystery and disclosed a portion of who he is. The knowledge of God arises from his identity as embodied in the narrative of salvation. It is theology's task to reflect on the meaning of this history, drawing out the truth of the story without replacing it. We need to understand the nature of revelation in order to understand how it can be opened up and developed over time. For if revelation had no content or if the content were fixed in timeless propositions, theological development would be either wildly subjectivist or dead in the water.[17]

On the one hand, liberal theology views revelation in relation to human experience rather than as historical and cognitive. In this view revelation is not tied down at all in its content but is viewed as a transforming event that sets people free. For Adolf von Harnack, for example, revelation was an ethical project aimed at moral renewal.[18] Doctrine in that case is viewed sociologically, as what Christians are thinking in any given generation. Doctrine is not really considered to be of the essence of faith. It tends to be fluid and not tied to Scripture or past decisions of tradition. In this way of thinking the essence of faith does not consist in a set of truths deposited in a book or in a creed but is a new way of being in the world, grounded in the life of Jesus. What faith may become doctrinally is anyone's guess. Its development is very open-ended. In a transformist theory of development, continuity is sought more in spirit than in doctrine.[19]

This is not a sound view of revelation or a valid theory of its development. God's self-revelation certainly makes an impact on the soul, but more attention needs to be given to the truth claims inherent in the event of transformation. That which transforms people through the gospel is the self-disclosure of the triune God in history. Liberalism places too much emphasis on experience and too little on cognitivity. In revelation God also causes light to shine out of darkness, giving us true if partial knowledge of triune relationality and salvation.[20]

On the other hand, evangelical theology errs on the other side. It very often views revelation in terms of timeless, propositional content.

This way of thinking has a long history among Protestants and Catholics. It characterized the approach of the First Vatican Council and characterizes some streams of evangelical thinking today. In this model revelation is thought of as the communication of truths otherwise inaccessible. As a result, the task of theology is to assemble these truths, like pieces of a puzzle, and form them into a system. Charles Hodge likened this process to the way a naturalist systematizes species of plants. This is a strong view of revelation as conceptual-verbal, with little room for historical and contextual factors. Theology becomes a kind of summarizing activity. It implies a criticism of the Bible as the grand narrative it actually is. Imagine God giving us a Bible with thousands of unassembled pieces and hundreds of stories far from conceptual.[21]

On this view, possibilities of theological development are limited. They can really only be of a logical or exegetical kind. Theology might grow by tightening its grasp on certain aspects of biblical truth. A better job might be done collecting and synthesizing the facts of revelation. Hodge, for example, thought that the Westminster Confession of Faith was the finest system of doctrine precisely because in his opinion it best synthesized the facts of revelation. The Westminster Confession, essentially a compendium of biblical texts, represented progress because of improvements in gathering, defining and organizing the data. This view leaves little room for revelation to be opened up by the Spirit and little room for timeliness. After someone like Hodge assembled the data, there really wouldn't be much for later theologians to do. Perhaps God permitted the vagaries of canonical and textual criticism to force us to rely on him as revealed through the Bible rather than on the Bible itself.[22]

This is not a sound view of revelation or a satisfactory theory of development. Revelation is not primarily a communication of timeless truths otherwise inaccessible. Revelation is conveyed in the story of the mighty acts of God. There is no box full of pieces for the theological jigsaw puzzle. The Bible offers little if any truth expressed abstractly, in noncontextual ways. Scripture does not provide detailed legislation for every situation. Paul, for example, didn't even like to lay down the law, because he considered Christians to be sons and daughters, not slaves (Gal 4:1-6; 5:1). Furthermore, there is considerable variety in the subject matter of Scripture and in the way topics are handled. There is unity amidst plurality, a running together of the human and the divine, and a historical texturing through the scriptural genres. One does not receive the impression that the writers of Scripture are secretaries having timeless truths dictated to them. The Bible is an inspired but also human witness to revelation. God is heard to speak through historicity and human weakness. Küng writes, "Through all human fragility and the whole historical relativity and limitation of the biblical authors, who are often able to speak only stammeringly and with inadequate conceptual means, it happens that God's call as it is finally sounded out in Jesus is truthfully heard, believed, and realized."[23]

There is a better way to understand both revelation and doctrinal development. Revelation is neither contentless experience (liberalism) nor timeless propositions (conservatism). It is the dynamic self-disclosure of God, who makes his goodness known in the history of salvation, in a process of disclosure culminating in Jesus Christ. Revelation is not primarily existential impact or infallible truths but divine self-revelation that both impacts and instructs. The mode of revelation is self-disclosure and interpersonal communication. As such it is pregnant with significance and possible development.[24]

Revelation comes to us through what has happened in history, and especially in Jesus Christ, in whom God comes into view. Jesus Christ himself is the self-revelation and image of the invisible God (Jn 1:18; Col 1:15). Vatican II states, "Jesus perfected revelation by fulfilling it through his work of making himself present and manifesting himself: through his words and deeds, his signs and wonders, and especially through his death and glorious resurrection from the dead and final sending of the Spirit of truth" (*Dogmatic Constitution on Divine Revelation* par. 4).

Revelation is neither human transformation alone nor a set of propositions on a variety of topics. It is our introduction to a Person. Jesus said, "Whoever has seen me has seen the Father" (Jn 14:9). Revelation is addressed not only to the intellect but to the whole person. There are truths implicit and explicit in it, but they point to the personal center.

Revelation is dynamic, historical and personal, and being faithful means being faithful to God himself in his self-disclosure. It means being faithful to the story of God's saving actions to which the Bible bears witness. Theology is a secondary language that lives off the power of the story and explicates its meaning to God's people on the move. It uses the biblical story in the context of the community to make sense of life and put people into touch with the divine mystery. Revelation is the act of self-disclosure revealing ultimate truth. It cannot be surpassed, but our understanding of its relevance can always be surpassed.[25]

A model of revelation as *self*-revelation allows for possibilities of unfolding and development. Revelation is more than propositional, more than experiential. It informs and shapes us, it transforms and instructs us. We can grow into its truth as we can grow into Christ himself. Because it is so dynamic, Spirit can direct the community through it. As we respond, the meaning of revelation can unfold toward fuller consciousness. Spirit can foster a growing apprehension of divine revelation and (despite mistakes on our part) lead the church into truth. Because the power that generated revelation is at work in the church, the meaning and significance of revelation can be gradually unfolded.[26]

Inspiration and Illumination

Inspiration is the action of the Spirit that secures the Scriptures of and for the church. It is an act of God for the purpose of securing what has been revealed for the salvation of the nations. Inspiration ensures that the truth of the story will abide perpetually in its integrity and be handed down to all generations. For this reason the divine self-disclosure was given a literary attestation. We use the term *inspiration* to refer to a divine activity that secures in written form the portions of revelation that God wanted to have fixed in writing. Vatican II states,

> In composing the sacred books, God chose men and while employed by him they made use of their powers and abilities, so that with him acting in them and through them, they, as true authors, consigned to writing everything and only those things

that he wanted. Therefore, since everything asserted by the inspired authors or sacred writers must be held to be asserted by the Holy Spirit, it follows that the books of scripture must be acknowledged as teaching firmly, faithfully, and without error that truth which God wanted put into the sacred writings for the sake of our salvation. (*Dogmatic Constitution on Divine Revelation* chap. 2)

Inspiration is part of a larger action of the Spirit in forming and sustaining community. Scriptures contribute mightily to the strengthening and vitalizing of a people. The biblical testimonies were recorded to keep the good news alive and to ensure a future for the people of God. Spirit assembled this plurality of witnesses to point to saving reality. Scripture's very richness and variety supplies a standard that is capable of being used to guide the church on every step of its journey. Inspiration is an act that forms and reforms the community. The Spirit's guiding influence works alongside human literary activity in the community to secure a canonical text, which is part and parcel of God's larger work of gathering and shaping his covenant people.[27]

The Bible is prime testimony to God's self-disclosure and keeps the church on track. It bears witness to revelation and secures the knowledge of saving events, together with their interpretation. The Bible is the document of revelation, which makes Jesus accessible to those who have not known him in the flesh. The witness has been placed in a literary form so as to be reliably transmitted.[28]

Inspiration is another aspect of the Spirit's work of bringing God's plans to fruition. Spirit brings writings into existence so that revelation might continue to be effective for succeeding generations. Inspiration secures a classic text through which the Spirit can continue to speak, making texts live and helping us grasp their significance. The Bible is a product of the Spirit's working in the community to sustain it.

The canon of Scripture sustains and liberates. Its many voices preserve rich meaning and describe a field of play for the community. It is original testimony to Jesus Christ, valid for all time, a testimony that cannot be replaced or canceled by later authority. It constitutes the criterion for discerning spirits and evaluating revelations. The church must never cease to reflect on these primary witnesses to ensure its own authenticity. These testimonies keep us rooted in and oriented to original revelation. They indicate the boundaries of our habitation.[29]

Scripture as the Spirit's text enjoys a privileged position. We give it our full consent and pledge ourselves to observe its truth. Every other claim to revelation and development of doctrine is tested by it and must be shown to be included in it. We seek in the Bible both the meaning of the words and the truth toward which they point. The Spirit intends not only what was understood by the inspired authors but also the truth toward which their witness is pointing. Therefore we attend not only to original meanings but also to understandings that arise from subsequent reflection. God is at work in the history of salvation, illuminating as well as inspiring.

The need for guidance is evident in the formation of the canon itself. How was the church led to this collection of texts? One cannot explain the canon on historical grounds alone. There is no list revealed of what books ought to make up the Bible. The canon was not a decision of episcopal authority. It was the result of the Spirit's working within diverse believing communities. It resulted from an interplay of objective and subjective factors. The books were gathered within the experience of the community, and by a process only partly visible, the canon achieved unanimous recognition.

While it is true that Christians are people of the Book, it is also true that the Bible is a book of the people. It was the Spirit's gift to them collectively. The canon was determined by the churches as they listened to the Spirit. If this is so, and if we respect the wisdom of tradition in giving us the canon, ought we not to respect it in other ways too—for example, in matters of interpretation?

The guidance needed to secure the text of the canon is also needed in areas of interpretation, which is never final and which continues within the community in a never-ending conversation. We require *illumination* for ongoing interpretation. As believers interact in the course of their Bible reading, fresh insights and applications arise. God's revelation unfolds as we search for understanding. If inspiration secures Scripture, illumination is meant to enable readers to recognize Scripture's timely meaning. Spirit causes the Word to be heard and opens up the truth, helping readers experience and communicate it.

The Spirit helps us correlate God's Word with the challenges of our day. Spirit takes the Word of Jesus and helps us place it in new situations, not adding to what Christ said but bringing it to remembrance and causing it to be revealed in a new light.[30]

We can speak of an inspiration of text *and* reader. Past inspiration secures Scripture, and present inspiration empowers readers. We need illumination if we are to be transformed by the text. The Scriptures would remain a dead letter apart from the power of God. The goal of interpretation lies beyond exegesis and aims at the existential augmentation of the reader. The text projects a world and clears a space into which we enter and experience transformation. It projects an alternate world and invites us to follow Jesus in it. Spirit puts us into touch with the very subject matter of revelation.[31]

Interpretation is not laying new foundations or establishing new meanings. Any valid interpretation must be congruent with Scripture and must not twist it. If this were not so, the Bible would be not the judge of issues but a lump of wax that could be manipulated. Despite the literary theories of postmodernity, a text does not mean anything whatever but something definite. Our goal is to find out what that is and to ask the Spirit to open up the dimensions of its significance. We need it to point out the sins of our culture, to indicate the direction of our mission and to lead us to the implications of doctrine.

Inspiration and illumination together require a style of interpretation that takes both the ancient text and the modern horizon seriously. We should care about original meanings and about current concerns of discipleship. We want to be led in the direction of the kingdom. As we await its consummation, we look to the Spirit for a better apprehension of what God is calling us to be and do. We need to know what is fitting and right. We need Spirit to help us get a grip on the significance of the Word.[32]

Spirit opens up what is written in a controlled liberty of interpretation. To ignore past inspiration would be to risk heresy by straying outside the field of play. To ignore present inspiration would be to risk dead orthodoxy by neglecting what is crucial and timely. God gives us freedom to operate within biblical boundaries by the Spirit, who inspired the witnesses and also opens the significance of scriptural words.

Heresy often parades itself as liberating, but in fact it usually narrows interpretive options and reduces mystery. Orthodoxy is richer because it keeps more things in play and opens things up to richer possibilities.

A Theory of Development

As an evangelical, I had not considered the unfolding of God's Word much because of an anxiety about how tradition might take primacy over Scripture. I sensed the danger that tradition in the guise of development might engineer a takeover and insert ideas into the faith which are unknown and even contrary to the Bible. Tradition might bring revelation under human control, under the guise of development. Therefore it is important always to observe the principle of *apostolicity*. Any insight being claimed as a valid interpretive development must be tested by revelation. All interpretations must be in harmony with scriptural revelation and at least implicit in it. Revelation must not be increased or changed by subsequent illumination.

At the same time, the negative possibilities must not frighten us so much that we refuse to listen to the Spirit. We enjoy a covenantal relationship into which the Spirit wants us to enter ever more deeply. As we meditate on Scripture, we can advance in understanding and gain fuller elucidations of truth, leading to deeper relationship with God. The community ought always to seek the unfolding of God's Word and development in its understanding. The Lord goes with us even through dark valleys and ever strives to make himself better known. The psalmist pleads, "O that today you would listen to his voice!" (Ps 95:7).

Because the Spirit works to shed light on us, the truth is not something merely external: it is also internal. God is working the mind of Christ into us (1 Cor 2:16). The meaning of the Word of God is being worked on within the entire community, not just among the leaders. We saw that in the way the canon was gathered. In the context of diverse and geographically separated churches, agreement was reached. It happened because God's people were listening, and the scriptural canon was only the first of many treasures. The creeds and liturgies and styles of spirituality are our priceless heritage, and we have the Spirit to thank for them.

Looking to the development of doctrine, think for example of the Holy Trinity. The basis for trinitarian theology was given in the gospel, but clarification was required and took time. The disciples had experienced God in his threefoldness as Father, Son and Spirit, but it all had to be thought through. How is the oneness to be reconciled with the threefoldness? How can we avoid falling into modalism or tritheism? The result was not a rational solution but a statement of the mystery of three Persons in one divine being. We should view it as an achievement of Christian thinking directed by the Spirit.

The same pattern obtained with Christology. The disciples experienced Jesus of Nazareth as the incarnate and risen Son of God. Various interpretations were given in the New Testament concerning his humanity, his deity and his anointing with the Spirit. Only after discussion and prayer did the community grasp the mystery of his sonship, being human yet at the same time fully divine. Christology was not the product of human thought alone but arose from the worship of the community and its liturgy.

Spirit has been guiding Christian understanding toward a sounder grasp of truth. These developments were not corruptions or results only of human processes. They represent a finer comprehension of a revelation that is unsurpassable. Thus our respect for tradition is not the result of blind submission to external norms and authorities. It derives from our confidence in the leading of the Spirit—not of individuals in isolation but of the church as a whole, not in ways chiefly theoretical but in the context of worship and obedience. The Spirit keeps the church in the truth. We depend on God's promise to be with us in our understanding as we walk the pathway of mission.

A mystical approach to matters of development is better than a legal orientation. The truth is tested not by experts but by the people, the mystical body of Christ. Truth is not external to the church but the gift of the indwelling Spirit. Revelation is pregnant, and development arises from the presence of the Spirit in community. There are authoritative sources—Scripture and tradition, ecumenical councils, reason and experience, elders and bishops—but authority is ultimately charismatic. There is no law of development other than dependence on the Spirit, who helps us reach a better articulation of our faith and practice. Development is a historical process that cannot be controlled by ironclad norms. There are no formal criteria of truth, no absolute guarantees that we will not make a mistake.[33]

Authority in matters of development, then, rests not only with leaders but with all the people and their giftedness. The Bible asserts its authority in community. We listen with anticipation for God's voice and respect the expertise of the community in interpretation. The cumulative reflection of the community over centuries has greater authority than one's individual opinions. As in medicine, though the community of doctors can be mistaken, one is inclined to trust it, for we have nothing better. Readers should not consider their interpretations valid without regard for community. We are not autonomous readers, and tradition may save us from making irresponsible judgments.

Let us drop our prejudice against tradition. The wisdom of past generations who have negotiated the canon before us is valuable, not because of a "democracy of the dead" but because the Spirit is interpreting the meaning of Jesus in the community over time. Let us not read the Bible in isolation but in the context of the historical community. Let us read it with the creeds, liturgical practices and teachings of the fathers in mind. This is being attentive to the presence of the Spirit in the church and having a sense of a living continuity.[34]

Development in understanding is an internal process orchestrated by the Spirit who guides the community, speaking through Scripture and tradition. One danger to avoid in this area is a too-controlled objectivity. One can become obsessed with formally defined criteria, as though an institution or a book could guarantee truth. We can be attracted to hyperobjectivity if we are concerned to control outcomes. John Henry Cardinal Newman illustrates this error. Having identified several principles that would help to identify valid developments in doctrinal understanding, he finally fixed on papal infallibility as the decisive criterion. It is attractive to think that we have a final, infallible authority. We devoutly desire such objectivity. But this is a temptation in disguise. It tempts us not to listen to the Spirit because we have an infallible office to clear away doubts. Newman himself admitted to not having believed in the doctrine of transubstantiation before becoming Catholic, but upon accepting papal infallibility, he had no further difficulties believing it. How convenient to be able to give a blank check to an infallible authority, which then becomes the decisive criterion.[35]

With such an office, the Roman Church becomes itself guardian of truth and authoritative teacher among other churches. It can teach by the authority of its office and demand obedience without having to explain. But this situation yields an authoritarian result—people believe they are obeying God by submitting to Rome. The criterion of development becomes the magisterium itself.[36]

Protestants can fall into the juridical posture too. Scripture can be put to such use when it is treated as a book of rules and an authority external to the church. It is much harder to make it work, however, without an authoritarian magisterium to decide between varying interpretations of the Bible.

The papacy is an obstacle to church unity for Orthodox and Protestant. John Paul II is aware of this and asks for forgiveness (as his predecessor had done) for past abuses of the office. In his letter "Christian Unity" (1995) he seems to want to remove this obstacle to unity. It sounds as if he wants to make the papacy an office that would serve the church and not dominate it. Pope John XXIII had viewed his role in that way, as servant of the people, not so much sovereign. A papacy that enshrined the primacy of service rather than dominion would permit closer unity with churches that cannot accept the papacy as the final authority and criterion of truth. John Paul has not yet offered to relinquish the primacy of dominion, but he does present himself as a servant. Were he ever to do so, the impact would be momentous.[37]

Another danger is uncontrolled subjectivity. Westerners today often practice interpretive individualism and forget that the Spirit guides *the community*. The Scriptures are not in every way external to the church but belong in its bosom. It ought to be the exception, not the rule, that a conflict would exist between Scripture and tradition. Of course Scripture enjoys primacy over tradition, where there is a dispute. It is canon—nothing can be added to it. But normally Scripture should be read in the context of the church and its traditions.[38]

Luther created a problem in the way he appealed to the Bible. Though his emphasis on grace and faith were on target and appropriate at the time, the way he made the point could encourage us to place our own interpretations against those of the church. The modern turn to the subject thus began (unintentionally) with Luther. His appeal to Scripture against the church, in a pitting of private judgment against the historic community, laid foundations for subjectivity in theology. A painful controversy set Luther against the institution of the church and led many in the direction of subjectivism. To interpret the Bible not along lines established over centuries but according to one's private judgment leads to chaos.[39]

We trust the Spirit to help us continue in the truth. Our hope lies in the mystery of the Spirit, who is present in the church. Formal criteria and offices can help protect us but do not guarantee anything. They are gifts of God, not substitutes for the Spirit. Let every Christian think and act as a responsible person and seek truth within the communion of saints.

Theology makes progress by penetrating revelation ever more profoundly and also by encountering voices outside the community. Combining the two horizons is fruitful because it brings the Word of God to bear on new situations. It absorbs (as it were) the lesser lights that shine in the world as a result of the Spirit's prevenience and makes them subject to the revelation in Jesus Christ. The result is a Christian message that is faithful to the apostolic witness and able to speak to the present-day world. This contrasts with a theology that pulls up the drawbridges and refuses to interact, as well as with a theology that sacrifices Christian identity in an effort to appear relevant.[40]

Criteria of Development

Are there criteria to help us identify valid theological developments? Do we have anything to go by? Here are seven useful tests proposed by Newman: (1) A genuine development would preserve the original idea of a doctrine. (2) There would be a continuity in the outworking of its development. (3) It would reveal the power of assimilation and absorb what is good from the outside. (4) It would exhibit logical sequence. (5) It would anticipate its own future. (6) It would exert a conserving action on the past. (7) It would manifest chronic vigor and persistence. These principles provide a basis for discernment and give a good start.[41]

Newman's tests are hopeful but may lack realism. They do not take the possibility of corruption very seriously. Developments that a Protestant might consider accretions and additions can be defended as authentic according to these tests. It is understandable that Newman, a convert to Rome, would not be emphasizing corruption and the possible need for reformation in the church. But we do need to place a law of corruption alongside the laws of positive development. Sometimes, it is true, an idea is refined and developed over the years, but sometimes it may be twisted in the wrong direction. There can be a departure from instead of a preservation of the original impulse. Exaggeration, excess, superstition can creep in. There can be both good and bad assimilation, good and bad "chronic vigor."

Not all developments are necessarily positive. Lenin and Mao developed Marxist theories in murderous directions. Welfare-state thinking has addicted governments to overspending without doing much to alleviate the condition of the poor. Development cannot be assumed ipso facto to be a good thing. Elaboration can be imperfect or mistaken. We cannot assume that a modern interpretation is the right one.

Belief in papal infallibility itself does not pass Newman's tests. It was not original. It did not lie within the horizon of biblical or patristic thought. That God might guarantee the truth by means of a magisterium is an attractive idea, but that does not make it true. The history of doctrine is complex, and the doctrine of papal infallibility might be viewed as an attempt at a shortcut. Having such an office diminishes reliance on the Spirit to guide the community.

Consultation among churches is important in regard to development. Such consultation is impeded but not prevented by church divisions. In principle, developments ought to find general acceptance and not be the view of one communion only. A single denomination should not promulgate new dogmas without consulting others. Rome has created problems in this way by promulgating belief, for example, in the immaculate conception and bodily assumption of Mary. Though not required by Scripture, these beliefs are rooted in the devotional life of Catholic churches and have power there. But Rome ought not to have developed them without consultation. It is doubtful that it would do so again after Vatican II, now that consultation has become an important part of Catholic practice. Pope John Paul II desires full communion with all the churches and is unlikely to do anything that would further jeopardize unity.

Protestants, for their part, have to explain why their various schisms continue and appear permanent. The Reformation rightly pointed to some important issues. We needed to hear about grace alone, faith alone, Scripture alone. But now that Rome has heard these things and largely reformed itself, why do we remain separate? Would Luther have gone into schism if he had faced Rome as it is today? I doubt it. When will it be time to call off the schism?[42]

Applying the Criteria

Theology as a discipline pursues truth by clarifying and substantiating biblical claims. It asks what we should believe and why. Theologians are members of the church who interpret the Word of God and speak on the church's behalf. Their role is not to spin out opinions and speculations but put forth proposals for wider deliberation. They propose interpretations, while others ponder and render verdicts on them. It is fair to expect that any insight theologians offer be well founded in the Scriptures and tradition and that it resonate with the hearts of God's people.

What individual theologians think is not identical with the faith of the church. Not every belief of particular theologians will become part of the common faith. Various issues are interacting today in the consciousness of the church. Though there are divisions, the truth as seen by one ecclesial community is often balanced by truth as seen by another, and out of the interaction fruitful insights can often emerge. Profound truths are seldom perfectly expressed in any one formulation, so we seek movement in the direction of the truth by way of relative truth and error.

To make our investigation more specific, I propose to take up issues of development in relation to the moves actually made in this book. Are they private opinions or of broader interest? Are they timely and crucial? Are they in touch with developments in the thinking of the community, or are they products of one person's thinking? Since wisdom resides in the larger community, is the community picking up on them? In a divided church, it is inevitable that some communities will not like what I say at certain points, but how does this work stand generally?

1. The book is committed to being ecumenical, drawing on insights about the Spirit from many traditions. Theology has not always been done this way, but the Spirit is leading us in this direction. We need to be catholic in space and in time, loving the church of every century and every continent—because Spirit desires unity in the body. It is wrong to adopt a sectarian tack and despise insights of others. There is variety in theology to celebrate, and each tradition has its logic and grammar. There are strengths and weaknesses in them, but theology is enriched when matters are considered ecumenically. Spirit is behind current tendencies toward unity—Roman and conciliar, evangelical and charismatic. There are gifts of God scattered over a wide variety of places in the church. They need to be gathered together.[43]

2. A move that I had expected to make but then did not make was to employ the feminine pronoun consistently for Spirit. At first I thought it biblically permissible as well as timely, but later I reconsidered. Spirit imagery in Scripture is often feminine, and recognizing this would not have been a capitulation to feminism. It would have been a response to concerns about the dignity of women and the value of their experience, and it would have allowed feminine imagery into what is otherwise wholly masculine speech about the triune Persons. But I realized that it would not be quite right because, in the case of Spirit, all three pronouns *(he, she, it)* can at times be suitable, and the feminine pronoun would not always be right. As illustrated by my own hesitation, the church is not sure what to do in the area of gender and God language. Only time will tell how our speech about God will be affected by the current discussion.

3. My decision to adopt the model of the social Trinity and to explore the Spirit's identity as a Person within the trinitarian society proved

important. It lets us move away from the quasi-modalism of Western theology toward an ontology of Persons in communion, which seems to hold promise. All theologians, when they speak of Father and Son, sound like social trinitarians, but some fear sounding tritheistic. On this point the book sides with Orthodoxy and also a number of Western theologians, stressing the divine threefoldness and triperson-ality.

4. This relational ontology is dynamic, zeroing in on the interaction within the Godhead and God's openness to relationships outside. The doctrine of the Trinity supplies a way to understand God as truly open and personal. It offers a creedal way of correcting the immobility of classical theism without falling into process philosophy. Trinity presents a picture of interactive change, playful relationship and familial dynamic. It illustrates how light can break forth from ancient symbols and illuminate present-day conditions. It also eases the move away from theological determinism toward seeing God's power in terms of his resourcefulness in dealing with free creatures rather than totally controlling them.[44]

5. The book attempts to recover Spirit's cosmic role, focusing on the creedal designation "Lord and giver of life." This is an ancient truth, and one that bears on contemporary concerns, including evolution and ecology. It helps us transcend the warfare between science and theology around evolution and suggests how we might conceptualize Spirit's presence in ongoing creation more in keeping with today's scientific understanding. Recovering the Spirit's cosmic role also lifts up a continuity of grace in creation and redemption and helps us think of grace working outside the church. This notion is found in Wesley, Vatican II and the Protestant mainline churches, but has encountered resistance among evangelicals of the classic Reformed type.

6. I thought it timely to recover Spirit Christology, given its solid biblical foundations, in a way that would balance Logos Christology without denying it. Even more promising was its implications for atonement in terms of recapitulation. In agreement with the Greek fathers, this reduced somewhat the too-central role that juridical thinking has played in the theology of the cross in the West. I found

myself agreeing with Orthodoxy, in tension with those for whom penal substitution dominates.

7. Lifting up Spirit in the sacraments is not innovation for theology in Catholic traditions, since the roots of such thinking are ancient. Coming from a Baptist it may lift an eyebrow. What influenced me in this direction was not only Scripture and the weight of tradition but also a sense of liturgical barrenness in the churches that have abandoned sacramental mysteries and other ancient practices. My sense is that I am not alone in wanting to enrich the evangelical and charismatic with the liturgical, and that this bodes well for church unity.

8. My openness to the charismatic is not surprising, since I, like so many, have been touched by the renewal. Without becoming charismatic in affiliation, I have long been sure that God is pouring out the Spirit in Pentecostalism. I can think of no more important event in modern church history than the rediscovery of Pentecost. The mind of the wider church appears to be changing and becoming more open to this new (though actually old) form of faith. Cessationist attitudes still impede reform, but they are in retreat. Because theology has not been the strength of the renewal movement, I dare to hope that this book might be of some help in the construction of a theology for it.

9. An attempt was also made in ecclesiology to overcome one-sidedness in the Christian mission. One wants to acknowledge God's concern for the whole creation—for evangelization, justice and healing. This emphasis has been accepted by Catholics and mainline Protestants already in a remarkable consensus.[45]

10. Viewing salvation more as union with God than as right legal standing places me with Orthodoxy over against the juridical orientation of Western theology. It is appropriate to question the way the doctrine of justification has been made so central in Protestantism. The truth of this doctrine is not questioned here, only its relative place in the larger picture. Justification has a goal: an outworking in sanctification and vocation, and ultimately a sharing in the glory of God. As Barth said, the doctrine of justification need not be absolutized or granted a monopoly.[46]

11. An issue of timeliness facing theology is religious pluralism and

accessibility to grace. I have suggested a way to see these issues in the context of the Spirit's work. The universal salvific will of God is implemented by the Spirit, who is at work everywhere in creation. We ought to be saying not that "outside the church" but that "outside grace" is no salvation. Inside the church there is salvation in fullness— but outside the church there is still grace and hope. There has plainly been development in thinking on this matter among Catholics, Orthodox and the Protestant mainline. Again, opposition tends to be limited to evangelicals of the classic Reformed type. Their own position is burdened by difficulties, and the consensus does not seem to be moving in their direction.

12. This chapter suggested a Spirit-oriented model of development that understands Spirit as bearing witness to truth in the bosom of community. Assessing theological developments for validity amounts to sensing the mind of the church and the *sensus fidelium*. The chief obstacle to theological unity in the broader church seems to be the papacy in the present definition. Given the spirit expressed in "Ut Unum Sint," a breakthrough could happen at any time. May God so grant.

Discerning Valid Developments

The test of truth and vitality in theology is, first, fidelity to original revelation and, second, responsiveness to challenges of the day. Theology ought to be true to the Word of God and ought to deliver a timely word. In order to do this, theologians must study the Word and listen to God. We are not lacking in wonderful examples. It was the Spirit who led the church of Antioch to commission and send Paul and Barnabas on the first missionary journey to the Gentiles (Acts 13:1-3). It was the Spirit who convinced the leadership in Jerusalem not to burden Gentile converts with regulations meant for Jews. Similarly, William Carey sensed it was time to take the gospel to the Indian subcontinent, William Wilberforce knew that slavery should be abolished, and Martin Luther King Jr. became convinced that it was time to extend the full rights of citizenship to black Americans.

Spirit is active in development. What happened in these cases was based on the gospel but went further than the biblical text in terms of specific application. So how did these people know what to do? They listened to the Spirit as they read the gospel. They were able to say, "It has seemed good to the Holy Spirit and to us" (Acts 15:28).

As we wait for the coming of the Lord, let us look to the Spirit to enable a speaking of God's Word to new generations. When we allow our minds to be transformed by the Word, we are able to recognize and test the will of God (Rom 12:2). Spirit gives us the ability to make decisions in concrete situations. We can be understanding of the will of the Lord and avoid foolishness (Eph 5:17). Spirit enabled the disciples to see through what the Sanhedrin was planning (Acts 4:8-12). It enabled them to unmask the plans of their persecutors (14:5-6). It gave them something to say at decisive moments (Mk 13:11). Spirit does not add to what Jesus said but causes what he did say to be revealed in a new light. Revelation is not a closed system of timeless truths but can continually prove fruitful and confront new challenges. Spirit makes the Word of Jesus a fresh word for those with ears to hear.[47]

At the same time, discernment is crucial. The criterion cannot be vitality alone, for there is plenty of pagan vitality in the world (1 Cor 12:1-2). John warns us not to believe every spirit (1 Jn 4:1). Spirit is not to be confused with any old form of life. The Nazi and Marxist movements were full of vitality, but they were not from God. Claims to inspiration have to be scrutinized, because wolves dress up in sheep's clothing.

Paul was aware of the dangers implicit in the charismatic structure of the church. Disorder and abuse forced him to raise issues of authority and tradition within the community. In the course of his reflections, he laid down some fundamental principles that serve us still. He says, first, that God has placed apostles in the church. Paul himself, commissioned by the risen Lord, could exercise authority, though he preferred to exhort rather than to command. Today we continue to respect this apostolic authority when we submit to the New Testament. Second, Paul identifies local ministries such as prophets and teachers, elders and deacons. They are servants of the servants of God, charged with seeking the well-being of the people. Third, authority is vested in the community itself (1 Thess 4:19). Paul expects a congregation to discipline itself, to test claims by the gospel and by the evidence of fruit bearing.[48]

On these foundations the church has developed means for evaluating claims to illumination and discernment. First, it holds fast to what it received from the Lord and the apostolic traditions (1 Cor 15:1-5). It respects the truth as it has unfolded within the apostolic mission. Second, it submits to the Scriptures as norm of the truth. A complex and multifaceted witness, the Bible supplies the counsel of God and relevant direction when listened to in community. Third, it takes prayer and worship seriously. If a doctrine "will not preach," it is probably seriously flawed. We are interested in how the community as a whole receives a theological interpretation. Does it hang together, does it bear good fruit?

Fourth, gifts such as distinguishing between spirits (1 Cor 12:10-11) are given to discern the source of prophetic words. They guard the community against prophets who are only speaking visions of their own minds (Jer 23:16). Fifth, the church has offices to help. Paul appeals, "We appeal to you, brothers and sisters, to respect those who labor among you, and have charge of you in the Lord and admonish you" (1 Thess 5:12). The New Testament does not require any one order of church leadership, but in most denominations there is a threefold pattern. There are bishops to oversee the work of churches in a particular area, elders and ministers to lead congregations in Word and sacrament, and deacons to lead in service of the needy. From time to time there are also councils as described in Acts 15.

As I have suggested, even the papacy, were it a servant presence and a voice for articulating the sense of faith of people, might be recognized by the churches separated from Rome. A teaching office of some kind could find a place. The *Constitution on Revelation* puts it well: "This teaching office is not above the word of God, but serves it, teaching only what has been handed on, listening to it devoutly, guarding it scrupulously, and explaining it faithfully by divine commission and with the help of the Holy Spirit" (chap. 2). Even on this topic there is room for Protestants and Catholics to come together.[49]

Sometimes enlightenment occurs as tradition is adapted to new challenges so that it speaks more readily to them. This essentially cautious approach ensures maximum continuity with the past. Other times tradition has to be challenged and a call issued to return to original revelation (as happened at the Reformation) so that God's Word can stand in judgment over corruption. It would be nice if tradition were pure and never required challenging, but often in the history of the church the Bible has had to serve as a correcting, liberating counterauthority.[50]

Such tests have procedural value. They help us recognize truth and unmask deceit. The community must weigh what is being said (1 Cor 14:29). It has to develop sound practices of listening and remembering what it has learned. If hearing and receiving are undisciplined, teaching may come to naught. The church that listens to the Spirit must be a responsible community; otherwise it can fall into confusion and even error. The Spirit wants to teach us, but human responsibility is required if real learning is to occur.[51]

In the midst of division, Spirit wants the church to become a united, loving, open communion. There is one body of Christ; let us seek to manifest our oneness that the world might believe. Let us move closer together in truth. In our day God is calling forth a spirit of remorse for our dividedness and a great longing for unity. Let us promote the restoration of unity among Christians and a continual reformation. As the *Decree on Ecumenism* puts it, "During its pilgrimage on earth, this people, though still in its members liable to sin, is growing in Christ and is being gently guided by God, according to his hidden designs, until it happily arrives at the fullness of eternal glory in the heavenly Jerusalem."

Philip Schaff remarks,

Union is no monotonous uniformity, but implies variety and full development of all the various types of Christian doctrine and discipline as far as they are founded on constitutional differences, made and intended by God himself, and as far as they are supplementary rather than contradictory. True union is essentially inward and spiritual. It does not require an external amalgamation of existing organizations into one, but may exist with their perfect independence in their spheres of labor.[52]

The early church was a group of different communities, united in the confession of one Lord Jesus Christ but not identical with one another. Its unity was unity in diversity, not a unity of sameness or a unity imposed from above. We must remember that unity does not spell uniformity. God's own unity is triune, and he gives existence to a vast diversity of creatures. God also brings into church people from every tribe and gives them a diversity of gifts for a variety of ministries. So God is not against diversity. He does not want lifeless uniformity. He loves a unity that celebrates variety and rejoices in what is different.

There have always been differing forms of church down through history. Such differences do not pose a threat to unity. What threatens unity is hostility and competition. The early churches were different but lived in communion.

May the Spirit take us forward to appropriate the truth of the gospel together for our time. May our desire for unity help the world see and believe, to the end that every fragment of truth and righteousness be gathered up into the storehouse.

Conclusion

My heart cries out, Living flame of love, ever burn on the altar of my heart. Welcome, Holy Spirit! Come and renew creation. Breathe on these dead bones, fill us with hope, lead us into God's embrace. You are at work everywhere, even where unnamed and unnoticed, preparing for new creation and the marriage supper of the Lamb. Therefore we adore you, Lord and giver of life; come to us and set us free. Be no more a stranger or a lost relation, but fill us up with your love.

I began this book with the idea that certain things had been forgotten and even wondered whether even a few corrections might be needed, but I was not thinking that a constructive vision of Spirit would take shape. But it did, and this is my gift to the reader. I invite us to view Spirit as the bond of love in the triune relationality, as the ecstasy of sheer life overflowing into a significant creation, as the power of creation and new creation, as the power of incarnation and atonement, as the power of new community and union with God, and as the power drawing the whole world into the truth of Jesus.

The book reflects my own faith journey. The spiritual vitality so evident in Scripture is rare and thin in the religious circles I inhabit. The atmosphere is restrained and the style highly cognitive; expectations are rather low regarding the presence of the kingdom in power. So I thirst to experience the reality of Spirit in my heart and church. I am tired of spiritless Christianity with only rumors and occasional glimpses of wonder and signs. But I am glad to report that in the course of writing my heart has been blessed. I have caught the fire again.

I hope the book helps people to grow in understanding the Spirit. We have reviewed the basic symbols, conducted searches of tradition and engaged challenges of our time. Risks were taken in interpretation, with the intention of stimulating discussion. Nobody has all the answers—I certainly do not. But one way to make progress is to look at issues in a new way and enter into conversation. Theology does not depend on any single theologian. Truth will yield its secrets to the body of Christ if we will listen to God and to one another humbly, accepting correction.

God bless you, my dear readers. May a gift be imparted to you. May the wind of God blow on you, may the Spirit draw you closer to God's loving heart. May Father, Son and Spirit make their home in you. Let us pray:

> O Thou who camest from above,
> The pure celestial fire to impart,
> Kindle a flame of sacred love
> On the mean altar of my heart.
>
> There let it for Thy glory burn
> With inextinguishable blaze,
> And trembling to its source return
> In humble prayer and fervent praise.
>
> Jesus, confirm my heart's desire
> To work, and speak, and think for Thee;
> Still let me guard the holy fire,
> And still stir up Thy gift in me:
>
> Ready for all Thy perfect will,
> My acts of faith and love repeat,
> Till death Thy endless mercies seal
> And make the sacrifice complete.
> (Charles Wesley)

Notes

Introduction

[1] *The Complete Works of St. John of the Cross,* ed. P. Silverio De Santa Teresa, trans. E. Allison Peers (London: Burns and Oates, 1964), pp. 1-195, and Richard Rolle, *The Fire of Love* (1434; Millwood, N.Y.: Kraus Reprint, 1979). Jean-Jacques Suurmond captures the playful dynamic of Spirit in *Word and Spirit at Play: Towards a Charismatic Theology* (Grand Rapids, Mich.: Eerdmans, 1995), picking up on Jürgen Moltmann's theology of sabbath rest: *God in Creation: A New Theology of Creation and the Spirit of God* (San Francisco: Harper & Row, 1985), chap. 11.

[2] *An Encyclical Letter of the Supreme Pontiff, John Paul II* (Sherbrooke, Quebec: Editions Paulines, 1986), p. 69. Clark H. Pinnock, "The Great Jubilee," in *God and Man,* ed. Michael Bauman (Hillsdale, Mich.: Hillsdale College Press, 1995), pp. 91-101.

[3] References in Philip J. Rosato, *The Spirit as Lord: The Pneumatology of Karl Barth* (Edinburgh: T & T Clark, 1981), pp. 3-5. See "Concluding Unscientific Postscript on Schleiemacher" (1968), in Karl Barth, *The Theology of Schleiermacher,* ed. Dietrich Ritschl (Grand Rapids, Mich.: Eerdmans, 1982), pp. 261-79.

[4] Among late-twentieth-century books on the Holy Spirit, three are of particular value: Yves M. J. Congar, *I Believe in the Holy Spirit,* 3 vols. (New York: Seabury, 1983); Jürgen Moltmann, *The Spirit of Life: A Universal Affirmation* (Minneapolis: Fortress, 1992); Michael Welker, *God the Spirit,* trans. John F. Hoffmeyer (Minneapolis: Fortress, 1994).

[5] Stanley M. Burgess, *The Holy Spirit: Eastern Christian Traditions* (Peabody, Mass.: Hendrickson, 1989), pp. 1-19.

[6] Neglect of the Spirit in systematic theology is even visible (surprisingly) in J. Rodman Williams, a charismatic theologian. He deals with the Spirit primarily in the area of salvation but does little to overcome neglect in the areas of Trinity, creation, Christology, ecclesiology, etc. His title therefore is less than apt: *Renewal Theology: Systematic Theology from a Charismatic Perspective,* 3 vols. (Grand Rapids, Mich.:

Zondervan, 1988-1992). Wayne Grudem introduces a charismatic dimension into soteriology but fails to notice the Spirit's relevance for other aspects of his paleo-Reformed framework: *Systematic Theology: An Introduction to Biblical Doctrine* (Grand Rapids, Mich.: Zondervan, 1994).

[7]Tom Smail, "The Cross and the Spirit: Toward a Theology of Renewal," in *The Love of Power and the Power of Love,* ed. Tom Smail, Andrew Walker and Nigel Wright (Minneapolis: Bethany House, 1994), pp. 15-16.

[8]John Baillie models for me the integration of theology and prayer. A rich devotional life stood at the center of his fine academic work. More than balance, what he achieved was integration. See especially his *A Diary of Private Prayer* (New York: Walker, 1986) and *The Sense of the Presence of God* (New York: Scribner, 1962).

[9]Welker emphasizes that the line of biblical teaching on the Spirit is coherent and should not be thought of as obscure *(God the Spirit)*. It might also be said that Welker omits from his discussion certain elements of what is clear. He lays great emphasis on the liberational aspects.

[10]Regarding the preparation of my own heart, my wife and I spent two months on retreat with the community at Schloss Mittersill, Austria, and nourished our souls. Besides that, and in addition to regular spiritual disciplines, I would be ungrateful not to acknowledge the influence of the Toronto Blessing during this period of writing. The flow of grace and love in this remarkable awakening can only be marveled at: see John Arnott, *The Father's Blessing* (Orlando, Fla.: Creation House, 1995).

In speaking of the heart, I appreciate what Orthodoxy calls the "apophatic." This term is used by St. Basil, for example, to indicate how God surpasses all our thoughts about him and how we know God not by reason alone but by spiritual sensitivity as well. Compare Daniel B. Clendenin, *Eastern Orthodox Christianity: A Western Perspective* (Grand Rapids, Mich.: Baker Book House, 1994), chap. 3. The apophatic does not imply agnosticism concerning the truth of dogmatic formulations. It surpasses but does not negate the truth: Verna E. F. Harrison, "The Relationship Between Apophatic and Kataphatic Theology," *Pro Ecclesia* 4 (1995): 318-32. Win Corduan finds a form of mysticism based in the New Testament: *Mysticism: An Evangelical Option?* (Grand Rapids, Mich.: Zondervan, 1991), chap. 7. Compare Nelson Pike, *Mystic Union: An Essay in the Phenomenology of Mysticism* (Ithaca, N.Y.: Cornell University Press, 1992). In terms of theological method, this means that a theologian is not limited to biblical data alone but also reflects on the experiences generated by it.

[11]Hans Küng, "How Should We Speak Today About the Holy Spirit?" in *Conflicts About the Holy Spirit,* ed. Hans Küng and Jürgen Moltmann (New York: Seabury, 1979), pp. 114-17.

[12]*The Cloud of Unknowing,* trans. Clifton Wolters (New York: Penguin, 1961).

[13]Moltmann, *Spirit of Life,* p. 289. Liberal theology tried to show a continuity between God and the world, the dynamic nature of creation and the nearness of God to every human soul, but did it in theologically revisionist ways. The Spirit of the triune God on the other hand offers aspects of continuity, dynamism and religious accessibility in the classical framework. Therefore Spirit is the bridge between evangelical and liberal theologies: compare Kenneth Cauthen, *The Impact of*

American Religious Liberalism (New York: Harper & Row, 1962).

[14]The Shakers struggled with this issue and may stimulate our own thinking: see Linda A. Mercadante, *Gender, Doctrine and God: The Shakers and Contemporary Theology* (Nashville: Abingdon, 1990).

[15]William H. Shepherd Jr., *The Narrative Function of the Holy Spirit as a Character in Luke-Acts* (Atlanta: Scholars, 1994). Compare Alasdair I. C. Heron's decision to use *it: The Holy Spirit* (Philadelphia: Westminster Press, 1983), pp. 8, 176.

[16]Gordon D. Fee chooses the masculine pronoun: *God's Empowering Presence: The Holy Spirit in the Letters of Paul* (Peabody, Mass.: Hendrickson, 1994), p. xxiii.

[17]The reference to Aphrahat is found in Francis Martin, *The Feminist Question: Feminist Theology in the Light of Christian Tradition* (Grand Rapids, Mich.: Eerdmans, 1994), p. 242. Those who propose thinking of the Spirit in feminine ways include Congar, *I Believe in the Holy Spirit,* 3:155-64; Moltmann, *Spirit of Life,* pp. 157-58; John J. O'Donnell, *The Mystery of the Triune God* (London: Sheed & Ward, 1988), pp. 97-99; F. X. Durrwell, *Holy Spirit of God* (London: Geoffrey Chapman, 1986), pp. 151-57; Donald L. Gelpi, *The Divine Mother: A Trinitarian Theology of the Holy Spirit* (New York: University Press of America, 1984).

[18]Thomas N. Finger, *Christian Theology: An Eschatological Approach* (Scottdale, Penn.: Herald, 1987), 2:486; Pike, "God as Lover and Mother," chap. 4 in *Mystic Union.*

[19]Elizabeth A. Johnson, *She Who Is: The Mystery of God in Feminist Theological Discourse* (New York: Crossroad, 1992), pp. 50-54, 83-87.

[20]Plus there is a political calculation for an evangelical writer: is it worth using the feminine pronoun when the likely result is to lose a host of conservative readers while gaining approval from a handful of feminists, most of whom have their sights set on much larger and less orthodox changes? The answer is no, it is not prudent

[21]Mark A. Noll, *The Scandal of the Evangelical Mind* (Grand Rapids, Mich.: Eerdmans, 1994).

[22]On the deployment of canon in faithful and creative ways, see Delwin Brown, *Boundaries of Our Habitations: Tradition and Theological Construction* (Albany: State University of New York Press, 1994).

[23]I resonate, for example, with John Wesley, who moved close to Orthodoxy. See Randy L. Maddox, "John Wesley and Eastern Orthodoxy: Influences, Convergences and Differences," *Asbury Theological Journal* 45 (1990): 29-53.

[24]I have always been moved by J. Rodman Williams, *The Pentecostal Reality* (Plainfield, N.J.: Logos International, 1972).

[25]Alan J. Roxburgh, *Reaching a Generation: Strategies for Tomorrow's Church* (Downers Grove, Ill: InterVarsity Press, 1993), chap. 8. Our culture is intrigued with mystery: Reginald W. Bibby, *Unknown Gods: The Ongoing Study of Religion in Canada* (Toronto: Stoddart, 1993), pp. 117-37.

Chapter 1: Spirit & Trinity

[1]John D. Zizioulas strikes this note as regards the divine nature: "Personhood and Being," chap. 1 in *Being as Communion: Studies in Personhood and the Church* (Crestwood, N.Y.: St. Vladimir's Seminary Press, 1985).

[2]For a sound introduction to the doctrine of the Trinity, see William J. Hill, *The*

Three-Personed God: The Trinity as a Mystery of Salvation (Washington, D.C.: Catholic University of America, 1982).

[3]Other excellent books on the Trinity include Ted Peters, *God as Trinity: Relationality and Temporality in Divine Life* (Louisville, Ky.: Westminister/John Knox, 1993), and Colin E. Gunton, *The Promise of Trinitarian Theology* (Edinburgh: T & T Clark, 1991).

[4]One can find the aphorism in Millard J. Erickson, *Christian Theology* (Grand Rapids, Mich.: Baker Book House, 1983), 1:342. The skeptical response to it is in John Hick, *God Has Many Names* (Philadelphia: Westminster Press, 1982), p. 124.

[5]On the meaningfulness of the doctrine of the Trinity understood as loving relationality, see Catherine M. LaCugna, *God for Us: The Trinity and Christian Life* (San Francisco: HarperSanFrancisco, 1991).

[6]For background to this usage, see Walter Eichrodt, *Theology of the Old Testament* (London: SCM Press, 1961), 1:210-20.

[7]On divine spirituality see Wolfhart Pannenberg, *Systematic Theology* (Grand Rapids, Mich.: Eerdmans, 1991), 1:370-84.

[8]This is the error of Geoffrey W. H. Lampe, who refuses to accept evidence for the distinct personhood of Son and Spirit alongside the Father: *God as Spirit* (Oxford: Clarendon, 1977).

[9]Leonard Hodgson, *The Doctrine of the Trinity* (London: James Nisbet, 1943), p. 140.

[10]John J. O'Donnell, *The Mystery of the Triune God* (New York: Paulist, 1989), chap. 3, and Pannenberg, *Systematic Theology,* vol. 2, chap. 5.

[11]I am indebted here to Cornelius Plantinga for his Ph.D. thesis, "The Hodgson-Welch Debate and the Social Analogy of the Trinity" (Princeton University, 1982), chap. 3, which is summarized in "Social Trinity and Tritheism," in *Trinity, Incarnation and Atonement,* ed. Ronald J. Feenstra and Cornelius Plantinga (Notre Dame, Ind: University of Notre Dame Press, 1989), pp. 21-47.

[12]For data supporting the personhood of the Spirit, see Gordon D. Fee, *God's Empowering Presence: The Holy Spirit in the Letters of Paul* (Peabody, Mass.: Hendrickson, 1994), pp. 829-42.

[13]Stephen T. Davis, *Risen Indeed: Making Sense of the Resurrection* (Grand Rapids, Mich.: Eerdmans, 1993).

[14]Leonard Hodgson, *The Doctrine of the Trinity* (London: James Nisbet, 1943), pp. 89-96.

[15]Pannenberg, *Systematic Theology,* 1:395-96, 422-23, 428-32.

[16]On the mystery of the Trinity and the Spirit within the trinity, see George A. Maloney, *The Spirit Broods over the World* (New York: Alba House, 1993), chaps. 2-3.

[17]LaCugna, *God for Us,* chap. 8.

[18]Johnson, *She Who Is,* 220; John L. Gresham, "The Social Model of the Trinity and Its Critics," *Scottish Journal of Theology* 46 (1993): 325-43; Robert L. Wilkin, "Not a Solitary God: The Triune God of the Bible," *Pro Ecclesia* 3 (1994): 36-55; Donald G. Bloesch, "The Mystery of the Trinity," chap. 7 in *God the Almighty: Power, Wisdom, Holiness, Love* (Downers Grove, Ill.: InterVarsity Press, 1995).

[19]Johnson, *She Who Is,* chap. 11. John Sanders traces the influence of Hellenistic assumptions about the divine nature on the Christian doctrine of God in Clark H. Pinnock et al., *The Openness of God: A Biblical Challenge to the Traditional*

Understanding of God (Downers Grove, Ill.: InterVarsity Press, 1994), pp. 59-100.

[20]Pannenberg, *Systematic Theology,* 1:370-84; A. Okechukwu Ogbonnaya, *On Communitarian Deity: An African Interpretation of the Trinity* (New York: Paragon House, 1994).

[21]Karl Rahner equates the immanent and the economic Trinity: *Foundations of Christian Faith* (New York: Seabury, 1978), p. 136.

[22]Francis Martin, *The Feminist Question: Feminist Theology in the Light of Christian Tradition* (Grand Rapids, Mich.: Eerdmans, 1994), pp. 284-89.

[23]Edmund J. Fortman, *The Triune God: A Historical Study of the Doctrine of the Trinity* (Philadelphia: Westminister Press, 1972), chap. 5, and Hill, *Three-Personed God,* pp. 78-79, 225-32.

[24]William Hasker, "Tri-unity," *Journal of Religion* 50 (1970): 6-11; Hill, *Three-Personed God,* pp. 59-62; Hodgson, *Doctrine of the Trinity,* pp. 144-57.

[25]Karl Barth, *Church Dogmatics* 1/1, trans. G. T. Thompson (Edinburgh: T & T Clark, 1936), p. 400. Robert Jensen asks tellingly, "You Wonder Where the Spirit Went?" *Pro Ecclesia* 2 (1993): 296-304. Hendrikus Berkhof sounds like a unitarian in *The Doctrine of the Holy Spirit* (Atlanta: John Knox Press, 1964), chap. 6.

[26]Hill discusses them under the heading "Neo-modal Trinitarianism: The Uni-personal God of Three Eternal Modes of Being," chap. 5 in *Three-Personed God.*

[27]Hans Küng, *Credo: The Apostles' Creed Explained for Today* (New York: Doubleday, 1993), pp. 150-56.

[28]Blair Reynolds, *Toward a Process Pneumatology* (London: Associated University Presses, 1990).

[29]William C. Placher, "The Triune God: The Perichoresis of Particular Persons," chap. 3 in *Narratives of a Vulnerable God* (Louisville, Ky.: Westminister John Knox, 1994).

[30]Jürgen Moltmann, *The Trinity and the Kingdom* (San Francisco: Harper & Row, 1991), p. 16.

[31]Johnson, *She Who Is,* p. 228.

[32]LaCugna warns against doing what I am doing here but also provides help with doing it: *God for Us,* pp. 296-300.

[33]Peters, *God as Trinity,* pp. 34-37; LaCugna, *God for Us,* pp. 288-92; Vincent Brummer, *The Model of Love: A Study in Philosophical Theology* (Cambridge: Cambridge University Press, 1993).

[34]O'Donnell, *Mystery of the Triune God,* pp. 77-80.

[35]Iconography uses the dove to represent the Spirit. *Catechism of the Catholic Church,* par. 701. Walter Kasper, *The God of Jesus Christ* (New York: Crossroad, 1986), p. 226.

[36]Peter J. Cullen, "Euphoria, Praise and Thanksgiving: Rejoicing in the Spirit in Luke-Acts," *Journal of Pentecostal Theology* 6 (1995): 13-24.

[37]Kasper, *God of Jesus Christ,* p. 226; O'Donnell, *Mystery of the Triune God,* p. 79. The theme is central to Gregory A. Boyd's interaction with process theology in *Trinity and Process: A Critical Evaluation and Reconstruction of Hartshorne's Di-polar Theism Towards a Trinitarian Metaphysics* (New York: Peter Lang, 1992).

[38]Augustine *On the Holy Trinity* 15.17-19.

[39]On this matter see Congar, *I Believe in the Holy Spirit,* 1:85-92; David Coffey, "Holy Spirit as the Mutual Bond Between the Father and the Son," *Theological Studies* 51

(1990): 193-229; Peters, *God as Trinity*, pp. 67-70; and LaCugna, *God for Us*, pp. 296-300.

[40]Heribert Muhlen, *Der Heilige Geist als Person: Ich-Du-Wir*, 2nd edition (Münster, Germany: Verlag Aschendorff, 1966); Maloney, "Holy Spirit Within the Trinity," chap. 3 in *Spirit Broods over the World*.

[41]Michael Welker, *God the Spirit*, trans. John F. Hoffmeyer (Minneaplis: Fortress, 1994), pp. 50-51, 184.

[42]Gunton, *Promise of Trinitarian Theology*, pp. 48-55; Pannenberg, *Systematic Theology*, 1:315-19.

[43]Joseph A. Bracken, *The Triune Symbol: Persons, Process and Community* (New York: University Press of America, 1985); Hill, *Three-Personed God*, pp. 218-25.

[44]John Breck, "The Face of the Spirit," *Pro Ecclesia* 3 (1994): 165-78; replied to by Robert Dotzel in *Pro Ecclesia* 4 (1995): 5-10.

[45]Anthony C. Thiselton notes the value of the social Trinity for issues of theological intelligibility today: *Interpreting God and the Postmodern Self* (Grand Rapids, Mich.: Eerdmans, 1995), p. 158.

[46]Vincent Brummer, *What Are We Doing When We Pray? A Philosophical Inquiry* (London: SCM Press, 1984); John J. O'Donnell, *Trinity and Temporality: The Christian Doctrine of God in the Light of Process Theology and the Theology of Hope* (Oxford: Oxford University Press, 1983), and Pinnock et al., *Openness of God*.

[47]Karl Barth, *Church Dogmatics* 2/1, trans. T. H. L. Parker (Edinburgh: T & T Clark, 1957), p. 656. Barth risks calling theology a science, despite the connotation of science as a collection of facts. Hodge's view of theology as a science fostered neglect of Spirit. In Barth theology is really more of an art than a science.

[48]LaCugna, *God for Us*, pp. 300-304.

[49]Placher, "The Vulnerable God," chap. 1 in *Narratives of a Vulnerable God*.

[50]A recurring theme in Boyd, *Trinity and Process*, pp. 377, 384, 391, 392.

[51]O'Donnell, *Trinity and Temporality*, pp. 23-25, 198-200.

[52]On creation as sabbath play, see Jürgen Moltmann, *God in Creation: A New Theology of Creation and the Spirit of God* (San Francisco: Harper & Row, 1985), pp. 276-96. On charismatic theology as picking up on this theme, see Jean-Jacques Suurmond, *Word and Spirit at Play: Towards a Charismatic Theology* (Grand Rapids, Mich.: Eerdmans, 1995).

[53]Karl Barth, *Church Dogmatics* 3/1, trans. G. W. Bromiley (Edinburgh: T & T Clark, 1958), p. 95.

[54]Frank G. Kirkpatrick, *Together Bound: God, History and the Religious Community* (New York: Oxford University Press, 1994), pp. 175, 177, 179.

[55]Developed in Barth, *Church Dogmatics* 3/1, and considered central to American theology by Herbert W. Richardson, *Toward an American Theology* (New York: Harper & Row, 1967), chap. 5.

[56]Consider the "theo-dramatics" of Hans Urs von Balthasar: John J. O'Donnell, *Hans Urs von Balthasar* (Collegeville, Minn.: Liturgical, 1992), pp. 16-17, 66, 74-75, 108, 142.

[57]Martin Smith, *The Word Is Very Near You: A Guide to Praying with Scripture* (Cambridge, Mass: Cowley, 1989), pt. 1.

[58]On meaning in music see Edward Rothstein, *Emblems of the Mind* (New York: Times Books, 1994).

Chapter 2: Spirit in Creation

[1]Pope John Paul II, *On the Holy Spirit*, p. 95.

[2]H. I. Lederle, *Treasures Old and New: Interpretations of Spirit-Baptism in the Charismatic Renewal Movement* (Peabody, Mass.: Hendrickson, 1988), p. 338.

[3]Samuel Rayan, *Breath of Life: The Holy Spirit, Heart of the Gospel* (London: Geoffrey Chapman, 1979), p. 65.

[4]This creative function, though largely absent in Western dogmatics, is prominent in Wolfhart Pannenberg, *Systematic Theology* (Grand Rapids, Mich.: Eerdmans, 1991), 2:76-115, and Jürgen Moltmann, *The Spirit of Life: A Universal Affirmation* (Minneapolis: Fortress, 1992), and *God in Creation: A New Theology of Creation and the Spirit of God* (San Francisco: Harper & Row, 1985). See also T. F. Torrance, *Theology in Reconstruction* (London: SCM Press, 1965), p. 227. One could overemphasize it, I suppose, but neglect seems a more pressing danger, despite Gerald F. Hawthorne, *The Presence and the Power: The Significance of the Holy Spirit in the Life and Ministry of Jesus* (Dallas: Word, 1991), p. 20.

[5]Larry Christenson, "The Spirit in Creation and Redemption," in *Welcome, Holy Spirit: A Study of Charismatic Renewal in the Church*, ed. Larry Christenson (Minneapolis: Augsburg, 1987), chap. 8; Elizabeth A. Johnson, *She Who Is: The Mystery of God in Feminist Theological Discourse* (New York: Crossroad, 1992), pp. 125-28.

[6]Cornelius A. Buller, *The Unity of Nature and History in Pannenberg's Theology* (Lanham, Md.: Littlefield Adams, 1996), pp. 199-203.

[7]On Spirit as God's creative power in the New Testament, see Eduard Schweizer, *The Holy Spirit* (London: SCM Press, 1980), pp. 15-19.

[8]Alasdair I. C. Heron, *The Holy Spirit* (Philadelphia: Westminster Press, 1983), pp. 31-38.

[9]W. H. Griffith Thomas, *The Holy Spirit of God* (Grand Rapids, Mich.: Eerdmans, 1964), pp. 187, 196, 201.

[10]Abraham Kuyper, *The Work of the Holy Spirit* (Grand Rapids, Mich.: Eerdmans, 1973), pp. 22-42.

[11]Catherine M. LaCugna, *God for Us: The Trinity and Christian Life* (San Francisco: HarperSanFrancisco, 1991), pp. 353-56.

[12]Daniel J. Migliore, *Faith Seeking Understanding: An Introduction to Christian Theology* (Grand Rapids, Mich.: Eerdmans, 1991), pp. 85-86.

[13]Gregory A. Boyd, *Trinity and Process: A Critical Evaluation and Reconstruction of Hartshorne's Di-polar Theism Towards a Trinitarian Metaphysics* (New York: Peter Lang, 1992), pp. 391-92.

[14]Pannenberg, "The Creation of the World," chap. 7 in *Systematic Theology*, vol. 2.

[15]Suurmond links the sabbath delight of creation with the charismatic celebration of Easter and Pentecost, bringing creation and redemption together: *Word and Spirit at Play*.

[16]On creation as benefit to God and humankind: William J. Hill, *The Three-Personed God: The Trinity as a Mystery of Salvation* (Washington, D.C.: Catholic University of America, 1982), pp. 275-78.

[17]In relation to theodicy, see Pannenberg, *Systematic Theology*, 2:161-74.

[18]Stanley J. Grenz, *Theology for the Community of God* (Nashville: Broadman & Holman, 1994), pp. 133-39.

[19]Pannenberg, *Systematic Theology,* 2:21-32, 61-76.

[20]John J. O'Donnell, *Hans Urs von Balthasar* (Collegeville, Minn.: Liturgical, 1992), pp. 66-67.

[21]Pannenberg, *Systematic Theology,* 2:32-35, 76-79.

[22]Ibid., 2:109-15.

[23]Doctrine Commission of the Church of England, "Holy Spirit and the Future," in *We Believe in the Holy Spirit* (London: Church House, 1991), pp. 170-86.

[24]Johnson, *She Who Is,* p. 213.

[25]For Wesley's theme of prevenient, restoring grace, see Randy L. Maddox, *Responsible Grace: John Wesley's Practical Theology* (Nashville: Kingswood, 1994), pp. 83-93.

[26]Basil *On the Holy Spirit* 38.

[27]In opposition to this idea, see Bruce C. Demarest, *General Revelation* (Grand Rapids, Mich.: Zondervan, 1982), pp. 44, 54, 56, 69, 183, 246, 251, and Jack W. Cottrell, *What the Bible Says About God the Creator* (Joplin, Mo.: College Press, 1983), pp. 340, 342, 346.

[28]Demarest *(General Revelation)* sees a degree of continuity when he says that God is known as a loving God by general revelation (p. 250) and admits that it might happen that a sinner could cast himself on God for mercy and be forgiven (p. 260) as happened in Old Testament times (p. 261). He leaves the door only narrowly open, but progress is occurring in the work of evangelicals in this area. R. Douglas Geivett and W. Gary Phillips also grant that God is known to be benevolent via general revelation in *More Than One Way? Four Views on Salvation in a Pluralistic World,* ed. Dennis L. Okholm and Timothy R. Phillips (Grand Rapids, Mich.: Zondervan, 1995), p. 217.

[29]Wolfhart Pannenberg, *An Introduction to Systematic Theology* (Grand Rapids, Mich.: Eerdmans, 1991), pp. 37-52.

[30]Ian G. Barbour, *Religion in an Age of Science* (San Francisco: Harper & Row, 1990), chap. 1; John Polkinghorne, *Serious Talk: Science and Religion in Dialogue* (Valley Forge, Penn.: Trinity Press International, 1995); and Clark H. Pinnock, "Scripture and Science: An Interactive Theory," *McMaster Journal of Theology* 3 (1993): 82-93. John M. Templeton is leading a movement to integrate the new fruits of science with religious insight: *The Humble Approach: Scientists Discover God* (New York: Continuum, 1995).

[31]Leading the charge against naturalism posing as unvarnished truth is Phillip E. Johnson, *Reason in the Balance: The Case Against Naturalism in Science, Law and Education* (Downers Grove, Ill.: InterVarsity Press, 1995).

[32]Howard J. Van Till, Davis A. Young and Clarence Menninga, *Science Held Hostage: What's Wrong with Creation Science and Evolutionism* (Downers Grove, Ill.: InterVarsity Press, 1992).

[33]Pannenberg, *Systematic Theology,* 2:115-36. The "creationomic" perspective was named by Howard J. Van Till in *The Fourth Day* (Grand Rapids, Mich.: Eerdmans, 1986), chap. 12. See also R. J. Berry, *God and Evolution* (London: Hodder & Stoughton, 1988); Charles Hummel, *The Galileo Connection: Resolving Conflicts Between Science and the Bible* (Downers Grove, Ill.: InterVarsity Press, 1986); Bernard Ramm, *The Christian View of Science and Scripture* (London: Paternoster, 1955), pp. 73-79, 155-56. The discussion continues in a theme issue, "Creation,

Evolution and Christian Faith," *Christian Scholar's Review* 24 (1995): 380-493.

[34]On the dialogue of theology and science, see Stanley J. Grenz, *Reason for Hope: The Systematic Theology of Wolfart Pannenberg* (New York: Oxford University Press, 1990), pp. 102-3; Wolfhart Pannenberg, *Toward a Theology of Theology of Nature: Essays on Science and Faith* (Louisville, Ky.: Westminster John Knox, 1993).

[35]Doctrine Commission of the Church of England, "Spirit and Creativity," chap. 9 in *We Believe in the Holy Spirit* (London: Church House, 1991).

[36]Ted Peters, "God and the Continuing Creation," chap. 4 in *God—the World's Future* (Minneapolis: Fortress, 1992).

[37]Langdon Gilkey, *Nature, Reality and the Sacred: The Nexus of Science and Religion* (Minneapolis: Fortress, 1993); David R. Griffin, ed., *The Reenchantment of Science: Postmodern Proposals* (Albany: State University of New York Press, 1988); Lindon Eaves and Lora Gross, "Exploring the Concept of Spirit as a Model for the God-World Relationship in the Age of Genetics," *Zygon* 27 (1992): 261-85; K. Helmut Reich, "The Doctrine of the Trinity as a Model for Structuring the Relations Between Science and Theology," *Zygon* 30 (1995): 383-405.

[38]On the interpretation of creation texts, see Gerhard F. Hasel, "The Polemic Nature of the Genesis Cosmology," *Evangelical Quarterly* 46 (1974): 81-102; Bruce K. Waltke, "The Literary Genre of Genesis Chapter One," *Crux* 27 (1991): 2-10; Clark H. Pinnock, "Climbing out of the Swamp: The Evangelical Struggle to Understand the Creation Texts," *Interpretation* 43 (1989): 143-55.

[39]Philip J. Rosato, *The Spirit as Lord: The Pneumatology of Karl Barth* (Edinburgh: T & T Clark, 1981), pp. 148-55.

[40]On the debate about the significance of the big bang, see William L. Craig and Quentin Smith, *Theism, Atheism and Big Bang Cosmology* (Oxford: Clarendon, 1993).

[41]Doctrine Commission of the Church of England, "The Spirit and Creation," chap. 8 in *We Believe in the Holy Spirit* (London: Church House, 1991).

[42]We need more theologians with backgrounds in science like Ted Peters: see *God—the World's Future,* pp. 122-39.

[43]Gordon D. Kaufman, *In Face of Mystery: A Constructive Theology* (Cambridge, Mass.: Harvard University Press, 1993), chaps. 19-20.

[44]Pannenberg, *Systematic Theology,* 2:76-136.

[45]Moltmann, *God in Creation,* p. 100. Interestingly, this idea does not make its appearance in his book on the Spirit, *Spirit of Life.*

[46]M. A. Corey, *God and the New Cosmology: The Anthropic Design Argument* (Lanham, Md.: Rowman & Littlefield, 1993); Hugh Montefiore, *The Probability of God* (London: SCM Press, 1985). On the design parameters, see J. P. Moreland, ed., *The Creation Hypothesis: Scientific Evidence for an Intelligent Designer* (Downers Grove, Ill.: InterVarsity Press, 1994), pp. 160-72; Hugh Ross, *The Creator and the Cosmos* (Colorado Springs, Colo.: NavPress, 1993).

[47]Percival Davis and Dean H. Kenyon, *Of Pandas and People: The Central Question of Biological Origins,* 2nd ed. (Dallas: Haughton, 1993).

[48]So Arthur R. Peacocke, *Theology for a Scientific Age* (Oxford: Basil Blackwell, 1990), pp. 113-14, 157-59, 175-76; Robert C. Neville, *Eternity and Time's Flow* (Albany: State University of New York Press, 1993); Alan G. Padgett, *God, Eternity and the*

Nature of Time (New York: St. Martin's, 1992).

[49]On the work of the Spirit in continuing creation, see Moltmann, *God in Creation,* chap. 8. A parallel reflection in the process framework is Sallie McFague, "God and the World," chap. 5 in *The Body of God: An Ecological Theology* (Minneapolis: Fortress, 1993). For the proleptic concept of creation see Peters, *God—the World's Future,* pp. 134-39.

[50]Peter C. Hodgson, *Winds of the Spirit: A Constructive Christian Theology* (Louisville, Ky.: Westminster John Knox, 1994), pp. 179-82; John Hick, *An Interpretation of Religion* (New Haven, Conn.: Yale University Press, 1989), pp. 91-95.

[51]Richard Swinburne, *The Evolution of the Soul* (Oxford: Clarendon, 1986), and *The Existence of God* (Oxford: Clarendon, 1979), chap. 9; Mortimer J. Adler, *The Difference of Man and the Difference It Makes* (New York: Holt, Rinehart and Winston, 1967). On language, see John W. Oller Jr. and John L. Omdahl, "Origin of the Human Language Capacity: In Whose Image?" in *The Creation Hypothesis: Scientific Evidence for an Intelligent Designer,* ed. J. P. Moreland (Downers Grove, Ill.: InterVarsity Press, 1994), pp. 235-69.

[52]Paul Davies, *The Mind of God: The Scientific Basis for a Rational World* (New York: Simon & Schuster, 1992), p. 232; Barbour, *Religion in an Age of Science,* pp. 135-36; Ross, *The Creator and the Cosmos,* pp. 86, 114-17, 120; Pannenberg, *Systematic Theology,* 2:74, 115.

[53]Karl Rahner, *On the Theology of Death* (New York: Herder and Herder, 1972), pt. 2. David H. Lane resists rethinking issues in this manner: "Theological Problems with Theistic Evolution," *Bibliotheca Sacra* 150 (1994): 155-74.

[54]Rosato, *Spirit as Lord,* pp. 141-48.

[55]Heron, *Holy Spirit,* chap. 9; Hodgson, *Winds of the Spirit,* pp. 179-80, 279-80, 284-87; Pannenberg, *Systematic Theology,* 2:1-2.

[56]Johnson, *She Who Is,* p. 125.

[57]On chaos and order in the Hebrew Bible see Jon D. Levenson, *Creation and the Persistence of Evil: The Jewish Drama of Divine Omnipotence* (San Francisco: Harper & Row, 1985).

[58]Correlating insights of anthropology and theology, see Pannenberg, *Systematic Theology,* 2:202-31, and Grenz, *Theology for the Community of God,* pp. 169-73. On the yes God longs to hear, see Henri J. M. Nouwen, *Life of the Beloved* (New York: Crossroad, 1995), pp. 106-7.

[59]Pannenberg, *Systematic Theology,* 2:166-67.

[60]Peters, *God—the World's Future,* pp. 155-68. His reflections on sin's dynamics are more fully developed in *Sin: Radical Evil in Soul and Society* (Grand Rapids, Mich.: Eerdmans, 1994).

[61]E. Frank Tupper, *A Scandalous Providence: The Jesus Story of the Compassion of God* (Macon, Ga.: Mercer University Press, 1995), pp. 330-31; Douglas J. Hall, *God and Human Suffering: An Exercise in the Theology of the Cross* (Minneapolis: Augsburg, 1986); Pannenberg, *Systematic Theology,* 2:161-74.

[62]H. Paul Santmire, *The Travail of Nature: The Ambiguous Ecological Promise of Christian Theology* (Philadelphia: Fortress, 1985); Roger E. Olson, "Resurrection, Cosmic Liberation and Christian Earth Keeping," *Ex Auditu* 9 (1993): 123-32; Michael Cromartie, ed., *Creation at Risk? Religion, Science and Environmentalism* (Grand

Rapids, Mich.: Eerdmans, 1995).

[63]Henri Boulad, *All Is Grace: God and the Mystery of Time* (New York: Crossroad, 1991), pp. 114-18. Yves Congar has admitted neglect of the Creator Spirit in his work: "The Holy Spirit and the Cosmos," chap. 8 in *The Word and the Spirit* (London: Geoffrey Chapman, 1986).

Chapter 3: Spirit & Christology

[1]On "Messiah" as a title see Richard N. Longenecker, *The Christology of Early Jewish Christianity* (London: SCM Press, 1970), pp. 63-82. The only book given over to a study of the Spirit in the ministry of Jesus is Gerald F. Hawthorne, *The Presence and the Power: The Significance of the Holy Spirit in the Life and Ministry of Jesus* (Dallas: Word, 1991). James D. G. Dunn, *Jesus and the Spirit* (London: SCM Press, 1975), does not in fact make Spirit Christology the sole focus, despite its title.

[2]Roger Haight, "The Case for Spirit Christology," *Theological Studies* 53 (1992): 257-87; Ralph Del Colle, "Spirit Christology: Dogmatic Foundations for Pentecostal-Charismatic Spirituality," *Journal of Pentecostal Theology* 3 (1993): 91-112. Edward Irving focused on the work of the Spirit in the humanity of Jesus; see Gordon Strachan, *The Pentecostal Theology of Edward Irving* (Peabody, Mass.: Hendrickson, 1988).

[3]Jean-Jacques Suurmond, *Word and Spirit at Play: Towards a Charismatic Theology* (Grand Rapids, Mich.: Eerdmans, 1995), pp. 46-47.

[4]Yves Congar, "The Place of the Holy Spirit in Christology," chap. 6 in *The Word and the Spirit* (London: Geoffrey Chapman, 1986); Aloys Grillmeier, *Christ in Christian Tradition,* 2nd ed. (Atlanta: John Knox, 1975), 1:106-49.

[5]Lewis B. Smedes, *Union with Christ: A Biblical View of the New Life in Jesus Christ,* rev. ed.(Grand Rapids, Mich.: Eerdmans, 1983); Trevor A. Hart, "Irenaeus, Recapitulation and Physical Redemption," in *Christ in Our Place,* ed. Trevor A. Hart and Daniel P. Thimell (Exeter, U.K.: Paternoster, 1989), pp. 152-81.

[6]On salvation through union with Christ see Robert Letham, *The Work of Christ* (Downers Grove, Ill.: InterVarsity Press, 1993), pp. 75-87.

[7]"The Joint Mission of the Son and the Spirit," in *Catechism of the Catholic Church,* pp. 181-82. The addition of the *filioque* to the Nicene Creed seems to subordinate the Spirit to the Son, and for this reason I do not favor it. Jürgen Moltmann, *The Spirit of Life: A Universal Affirmation* (Minneapolis: Fortress, 1992), pp. 71-73, 306-9.

[8]Greek church father Irenaeus in *Against Heresies* stresses the continuity of creation and redemption against the Gnostics, who saw the world as inherently evil and refused to identify the God of creation with the God of Jesus Christ. Against them, he emphasizes that God is both Creator and Redeemer and that the Spirit is active in both realms. Alasdair I. C. Heron, *The Holy Spirit* (Philadelphia: Westminster Press, 1983), pp. 64-67.

[9]Stuart C. Hackett, *The Reconstruction of the Christian Truth Claim: A Philosophical and Critical Apologetic* (Grand Rapids, Mich.: Baker Book House, 1984), pp. 166-76.

[10]Wolfhart Pannenberg, "The Reality of God and the Gods in the Experience of the Religions," chap. 3 in *Systematic Theology,* vol. 1 (Grand Rapids, Mich.: Eerdmans, 1991).

[11]Discussion of the *filioque* awaits chapter six, but it is evident already that I regard

it as an impediment to a recognition of Spirit operations apart from and prior to Christ.

[12]A fine exposition of Rembrandt's painting and the parable is found in Henri J. M. Nouwen, *The Return of the Prodigal Son* (New York: Doubleday, 1994), pp. 44, 78.

[13]Michael Welker, *God the Spirit,* trans. John F. Hoffmeyer (Minneapolis: Fortress, 1994), chap. 2.

[14]David Ewert, *The Holy Spirit in the New Testament* (Scottdale, Penn.: Herald, 1983), pp. 27-32; Welker, *God the Spirit,* chap. 3; Moltmann, *Spirit of Life,* pp. 51-57.

[15]Joachim Jeremias, *New Testament Theology: The Proclamation of Jesus* (New York: Charles Scribner's Sons, 1971), pp. 76-85; Hawthorne, "The Spirit in the Conception and Birth of Jesus," chap. 2 in *The Presence and the Power;* Pannenberg, *Systematic Theology,* 2:168-74.

[16]I will assume the reliability of the Gospel records. As a theologian, I think with assent—that is, as a believer in Jesus Christ, I think in the context of God's revelation. However, this is not an unwarranted leap but a reasonably well-founded assumption. On the current debate about Jesus, see Michael J. Wilkins and J. P. Moreland, eds., *Jesus Under Fire* (Grand Rapids, Mich.: Zondervan, 1995), and Gregory A. Boyd, *Cynic, Sage or Son of God?* (Wheaton, Ill: Victor, 1995).

[17]James D. G. Dunn, "The Spirit of Jesus" and "The Spirit and the Body of Christ," in *The Holy Spirit: Renewing and Empowering Presence,* ed. George Vandervelde (Winfield, B.C.: Wood Lake Books, 1988), pp. 11-12, 17-18; Heribert Muhlen, *A Charismatic Theology: Initiation in the Spirit* (London: Burns and Oates, 1978), pp. 105-9.

[18]James B. Shelton, *Mighty in Word and Deed* (Peabody, Mass.: Hendrickson, 1991), pp. 119-20. On the self-emptying of the Son see Walter Kasper, *The God of Jesus Christ* (New York: Crossroad, 1986), pp. 189-97.

[19]On his reticence to speak about the Spirit, see Eduard Schweizer, *The Holy Spirit* (London: SCM Press, 1980), pp. 47-50.

[20]C. K. Barrett, *The Holy Spirit and the Gospel Tradition* (London: SPCK, 1947), pp. 5-24; Jürgen Moltmann, *The Way of Jesus Christ: Christology in Messianic Dimensions* (San Francisco: Harper & Row, 1990), pp. 78-87; Shelton, "Holy Spirit and the Infancy Witnesses," chap. 2 in *Mighty in Word and Deed.*

[21]Hawthorne, "The Spirit in the Boyhood and Youth of Jesus," chap. 3 in *The Presence and the Power.*

[22]Dunn, "Jesus' Experience of God—Sonship," chap. 2 in *Jesus and the Spirit;* John J. O'Donnell, *The Mystery of the Triune God* (New York: Paulist, 1989), chap. 3; Moltmann, *Way of Jesus Christ,* pp. 87-94.

[23]James D. G. Dunn drives a wedge between water baptism and Spirit baptism, making water unimportant: *Baptism in the Holy Spirit* (London: SCM Press, 1970), pp. 32-37. This move is typical of free church Protestants but strains the text. See Shelton, *Mighty in Word and Deed,* chap. 4; Moltmann, *Way of Jesus Christ,* pp. 87-94.

[24]Hawthorne, "The Spirit at the Baptism and Temptation of Jesus," chap. 4 in *The Presence and the Power;* Thomas A. Smail, *Reflected Glory: The Spirit in Christ and Christians* (Grand Rapids, Mich.: Eerdmans, 1975), pp. 90-103.

[25]On the human nature of Christ in the thought of Edward Irving, see Strachan,

Pentecostal Theology of Edward Irving.

[26]Shelton, "The Holy Spirit and Jesus' Temptation," chap. 5 in *Mighty in Word and Deed;* Ewert, *Holy Spirit in the New Testament,* pp. 54-57.

[27]Hawthorne, "The Spirit as the Key to the Kenosis," chap. 7 in *The Presence and the Power.*

[28]Welker, God the Spirit, pp. 195-203; Hawthorne, "The Spirit in the Ministry of Jesus," chap. 5 in *The Presence and the Power;* Shelton, *Mighty in Word and Deed,* chap. 6; Roger Stronstad, *The Charismatic Theology of St. Luke* (Peabody, Mass.: Hendrickson, 1984), pp. 42-46; Moltmann, *Way of Jesus Christ,* pp. 94-136.

[29]Welker, *God the Spirit,* pp. 211-19. The text identifies the truly impenitent who will be excluded from the kingdom. Such people know the truth and stand against it. About no one else should we be certain that they are outside.

[30]Rene Latourelle, *The Miracles of Jesus and the Theology of Miracles* (New York: Paulist, 1988), pp. 257-62; Shelton, *Mighty in Word and Deed,* chap. 7.

[31]O'Donnell, "Trinity and the Paschal Mystery," chap. 4 in *Mystery of the Triune God;* Moltmann, *Spirit of Life,* pp. 62-65; Hawthorne, "The Spirit in the Death and Resurrection of Jesus," chap. 6 in *The Presence and the Power;* Richard Foster, "The Prayer of Relinquishment," chap. 5 in *Prayer: Finding the Heart's True Home* (San Francisco: HarperSanFrancisco, 1992).

[32]Moltmann, *Spirit of Life,* pp. 65-66; Hendrikus Berkhof, *The Doctrine of the Holy Spirit* (Atlanta: John Knox Press, 1964), pp. 104-8; Richard B. Gaffin, *Resurrection and Redemption: A Study in Paul's Soteriology* (Grand Rapids, Mich.: Baker Book House, 1978), pp. 66-70; Stephen T. Davis, *Risen Indeed: Making Sense of the Resurrection* (Grand Rapids, Mich.: Eerdmans, 1993), chap. 9.

[33]Del Colle, "Spirit Christology," p. 97; Berkhof, *Doctrine of the Holy Spirit,* pp. 20-21. Kasper, *God of Jesus Chirst,* pp. 184-89; Grillmeier, *Christ in Christian Tradition,* 1:108-9, 167-69. In Barth, Logos Christology also marginalizes Spirit-oriented understanding; see Philip J. Rosato, "Christology in a Pneumatic Framework," chap. 8 in *The Spirit as Lord: The Pneumatology of Karl Barth* (Edinburgh: T & T Clark, 1981).

[34]O'Donnell, *Mystery of the Triune God,* pp. 80-84.

[35]Paul W. Newman, *A Spirit Christology: Recovering the Biblical Paradigm of Christian Faith* (Lanham, Md.: University Press of America, 1987); John Hick, *The Metaphor of God Incarnate: Christology in a Pluralistic Age* (Louisville, Ky.: Westminster John Knox, 1993).

[36]Ralph Del Colle, "Pneumatological Christology in the Orthodox Tradition," chap. 1 in *Christ and the Spirit: Spirit Christology in Trinitarian Perspective* (New York: Oxford University Press, 1994); Yves Congar, *I Believe in the Holy Spirit,* 3 vols. (New York: Seabury, 1983), 3:165-73.

[37]This idea, which goes back to Irenaeus, understands the incarnation as God himself recapitulating the human journey. Christ, the representative of humanity, sums up, transforms, consummates and restores all aspects of our condition. For exposition see Jean Danielou, *Gospel Message and Hellenistic Culture* (London: Darton, Longman & Todd, 1973), pp. 166-83; Aidan Nicholls, *The Art of God Incarnate: Theology and Image in Christian Tradition* (London: Darton, Longman & Todd, 1980).

[38]T. F. Torrance, *Theology in Reconstruction* (London: SCM Press, 1965), p. 248.

[39]Few authors give attention to the meaning of Christ's representation. Dorothee Solle is an exception: *Christ Our Representative* (Philadelphia: Fortress, 1967).

[40]E. P. Sanders, *Paul and Palestinian Judaism: A Comparison of Patterns of Religion* (Minneapolis: Fortress, 1977), pp. 467-68, 549.

[41]Douglas Farrow, "St. Irenaeus of Lyons," *Pro Ecclesia* 4 (1995): 333-55. On the subjective genitive see Richard N. Longenecker, *Galatians* (Dallas: Word, 1990), p. 87.

[42]*Catechism of the Catholic Church,* par. 518.

[43]Gustaf Aulen, *Christus Victor: An Historical Study of the Three Main Types of the Idea of Atonement* (London: SPCK, 1953), chap. 2; Pannenberg, *Systematic Theology,* 2:403-4.

[44]Donald G. Bloesch, *Jesus Is Victor: Karl Barth's Doctrine of Salvation* (Nashville: Abingdon, 1976), chaps. 3-4. Morna Hooker finds the motif of salvation through the representative journey of Jesus throughout the New Testament: *Not Ashamed of the Gospel: New Testament Interpretations of the Death of Christ* (Grand Rapids, Mich.: Eerdmans, 1994). Kenneth Grayston also finds participatory atonement in the New Testament: *Dying We Love: A New Enquiry into the Death of Christ in the New Testament* (New York: Oxford University Press, 1990).

[45]Gaffin, *Resurrection and Redemption,* pp. 114-27; Christian D. Kettler, *The Vicarious Humanity of Christ and the Reality of Salvation* (New York: University Press of America, 1991).

[46]Pannenberg, *Systematic Theology,* 2:429-37.

[47]On the rationality of solidarity see Walter Kasper, *Jesus the Christ,* trans. V. Green (New York: Paulist, 1976), pp. 204-5, 215-25; Pannenberg, *Systematic Theology,* 2:419-21, 429-30.

[48]Karl Rahner, *Foundations of Christian Faith* (New York: Seabury, 1978), p. 200.

[49]On Christ as last Adam see James D. G. Dunn, *Christology in the Making: A New Testament Inquiry into the Origins of the Doctrine of the Incarnation* (Philadelphia: Westminster Press, 1980), chap. 4; Russell P. Shedd, *Man in Community: A Study of Paul's Application of Old Testament and Early Jewish Conceptions of Human Solidarity* (London: Epworth, 1958); C. Marvin Pate, *Adam Christology as the Exegetical and Theological Substructure of 2 Corinthians 4:7—5:21* (New York: University Press of America, 1991), pp. 97-98, 144-47.

[50]Hendrikus Berkhof, *Christian Faith: An Introduction to the Study of the Faith,* trans. Sierd Woudstra (Grand Rapids, Mich.: Eerdmans, 1986), pp. 319-20.

[51]Clark H. Pinnock, "Salvation by Resurrection," *Ex Auditu* 9 (1993): 1-11; Anthony J. Tambasco, *A Theology of Atonement and Paul's Vision of Christianity* (Collegeville, Minn.: Liturgical, 1991), pp. 76-81.

[52]Smail, "His Life-Giving Body," chap. 9 in *Reflected Glory;* Keith Ward, *Religion and Revelation* (Oxford: Clarendon, 1994), pp. 299-302; Stephen T. Davis, "Resurrection and Meaning," chap. 10 in *Risen Indeed: Making Sense of the Resurrection* (Grand Rapids, Mich.: Eerdmans, 1993).

[53]Tambasco, *Theology of Atonement,* pp. 85-93.

[54]Rahner, *Foundations of Christian Faith,* pp. 297-98.

[55]Pannenberg, *Systematic Theology,* 2:136, 389-96.

[56]Karl Barth, *Church Dogmatics* 4/1, trans. G. W. Bromiley (Edinburgh: T & T Clark, 1956), pp. 157-210.

[57]The image of the father giving up the beloved son roots in Abraham's binding of Isaac: Jon D. Levenson, *The Death and Resurrection of the Beloved Son: The Transformation of Child Sacrifice in Judaism and Christianity* (New Haven, Conn.: Yale University Press, 1993).

[58]John V. Dahm, "Dying with Christ," *Journal of the Evangelical Society* 36 (1993): 15-23. Colin E. Gunton, "Christ the Sacrifice: A Dead Metaphor?" chap. 5 in *The Actuality of Atonement* (Grand Rapids, Mich.: Eerdmans, 1989). Compare Leon Morris, *The Atonement: Its Meaning and Significance* (Downers Grove, Ill.: InterVarsity Press, 1983); Hooker, *Not Ashamed of the Gospel,* pp. 43-44.

[59]Pannenberg, *Systematic Theology,* 2:449-54.

[60]C. S. Lewis, *Mere Christianity* (London: Collins, 1952), pp. 53-58, 153, and *The Lion, the Witch and the Wardrobe* (London: Penguin, 1959), p. 148; Richard L. Purtill, *C. S. Lewis' Case for the Christian Faith* (San Francisco: Harper & Row, 1981), pp. 49-52; Richard B. Cunningham, *C. S. Lewis: Defender of the Faith* (Philadelphia: Westminister Press, 1967), pp. 115-16.

[61]Millard J. Erickson, *Christian Theology* (Grand Rapids, Mich.: Baker Book House, 1983), pp. 815-16; Wayne Grudem, *Systematic Theology: An Introduction to Biblical Doctrine* (Grand Rapids, Mich.: Zondervan, 1994), pp. 574-79; James I. Packer, "What Did the Cross Achieve? The Logic of Penal Substitution," *Tyndale Bulletin* 25 (1974): 3-45.

[62]John R. W. Stott, *The Cross of Christ* (Downers Grove, Ill.: InterVarsity Press, 1986), pp. 7-12.

[63]Ernst Benz, *The Eastern Orthodox Church, Its Thought and Life* (New York: Doubleday, 1963), pp. 43-47; Daniel B. Clendenin, *Eastern Orthodox Christianity: A Western Perspective* (Grand Rapids, Mich.: Baker Book House, 1994), pp. 120-25; Timothy Ware, *The Orthodox Church* (London: Penguin, 1963), p. 234.

[64]Pannenberg, *Systematic Theology,* 2:403-16.

[65]Karl Barth, *Church Dogmatics* 2/1, trans. T. H. L. Parker (Edinburgh: T & T Clark, 1957), pp. 351-406, and 4/1, pp. 211-83. Donald G. Bloesch, "Re-interpreting the Atonement," chap. 4 in *Jesus Is Victor.*

[66]Barth, *Church Dogmatics* 4/1, pp. 253-54.

[67]Jürgen Moltmann, *The Crucified God* (London: SCM Press, 1974), pp. 292, 145-53, 178-96; E. Frank Tupper, *A Scandalous Providence: The Jesus Story of the Compassion of God* (Macon, Ga.: Mercer University Press, 1995), pp. 371-89.

[68]On atonement as a participatory journey see Tambasco, *Theology of Atonement.*

[69]Clark H. Pinnock and Robert C. Brow, *Unbounded Love: A Good News Theology for the 21st Century* (Downers Grove, Ill.: InterVarsity Press, 1994), chap. 9. On interpreting Paul in noncommercial terms see Douglas Campbell, "The Atonement in Paul," *Anvil* 11 (1994): 237-50; Pannenberg, *Systematic Theology,* 2:425-29.

[70]On the Trinity in the paschal mystery, see O'Donnell, *Mystery of the Triune God,* chap. 4.

[71]Barth, *Church Dogmatics* 4/1, p. 253, from "The Judge Judged in Our Place" (pp. 211-83).

Chapter 4: Spirit & Church

[1]Paul S. Minear, *Images of the Church in the New Testament* (Philadelphia: Westminster Press, 1960); Avery Dulles, *Models of the Church* (New York: Doubleday, 1974).
[2]Hans Küng, *The Church* (New York: Sheed and Ward, 1967), pp. 150-203; William R. Barr and Rena M. Yocum, eds., *The Church in the Movement of the Spirit* (Grand Rapids, Mich.: Eerdmans, 1994). Unfortunately Spirit ecclesiology is not one of the five models in Dulles, *Models of the Church*.
[3]John J. O'Donnell, *The Mystery of the Triune God* (New York: Paulist, 1989), pp. 84-88.
[4]Tom Smail, Andrew Walker and Nigel Wright, *The Love of Power or the Power of Love* (Minneapolis: Bethany House, 1994), pp. 23-24.
[5]Yves Congar, "The Spirit Animates the Church," chap. 1 in *I Believe in the Holy Spirit*, vol. 2 (New York: Seabury, 1983). On the ecclesial nature of Christianity see Karl Rahner, *Foundations of Christian Faith* (New York: Seabury, 1978), chap. 7.
[6]Stanley J. Grenz, *Theology for the Community of God* (Nashville: Broadman & Holman, 1994), p. 636.
[7]Jürgen Moltmann, "The Fellowship of the Spirit," chap. 11 in *The Spirit of Life: A Universal Affirmation* (Minneapolis: Fortress, 1992).
[8]Ted Peters, *God—the World's Future* (Minneapolis: Fortress, 1992), pp. 261-63; Stanley Hauerwas and William H. Willimon, *Resident Aliens: Life in the Christian Colony* (Nashville: Abingdon, 1989).
[9]Heribert Muhlen, *A Charismatic Theology: Initiation in the Spirit* (London: Burnes & Oates, 1978), pp. 117-18.
[10]Michael Welker, *God the Spirit,* trans. John F. Hoffmeyer (Minneapolis: Fortress, 1994), p. 235.
[11]Sally Morgenthaler, *Worship Evangelism: Inviting Unbelievers into the Presence of God* (Grand Rapids, Mich.: Zondervan, 1995).
[12]Charles H. Kraft explains why churches are powerless due to the modern worldview in *Christianity with Power* (Ann Arbor, Mich: Servant, 1989). Brian J. Walsh and J. Richard Middleton focus on this dualism in *The Transforming Vision* (Downers Grove, Ill.: InterVarsity Press, 1984), pt. 3. Also see Peter E. Gillquist, *The Physical Side of Being Spiritual* (Grand Rapids, Mich.: Zondervan, 1979).
[13]On the early church as sacramental and charismatic, see Kilian McDonnell and George T. Montague, *Christian Initiation and Baptism in the Holy Spirit: Evidence from the First Eight Centuries* (Collegeville, Minn.: Liturgical, 1991). On the importance of fire burning in the fireplaces of historic churches, see Charles E. Hummel, *Fire in the Fireplace: Charismatic Renewal in the Nineties* (Downers Grove, Ill.: InterVarsity Press, 1993). Robert Webber also looks for the confluence of sacramental and charismatic in *Signs of Wonder* (Nashville: Abbott Martyn, 1992).
[14]Barr and Yocum, "The Spirit in the Worship and Liturgy of the Church," chap. 3 in *Church in the Movement of the Spirit*. On the nature of the sacred liturgy and its importance in the church's life, see *Constitution on the Sacred Liturgy*, pars. 5-13.
[15]Neville Clark, *An Approach to the Theology of the Sacraments* (London: SCM Press, 1956).
[16]On Jesus as the primordial sacrament see Herbert Vorgrimler, *Sacramental Theology*

(Collegeville, Minn.: Liturgical, 1992), pp. 30-32.

[17]Dulles, "The Church as Sacrament," chap. 4 in *Models of the Church*. At the end of this chapter Dulles remarks that this notion of the church has found little by way of response from Protestant thought. Perhaps so, but it finds a positive response from me.

[18]For the larger sense of sacrament see Hendrikus Berkhof, *Christian Faith: An Introduction to the Study of the Faith,* trans. Sierd Woudstra (Grand Rapids, Mich.: Eerdmans, 1986), pp. 345-92. On sacraments as means of growing into union with Christ, see Georgios I. Mantzaridis, *The Deification of Man: St. Gregory Palamas and the Orthodox Tradition* (Crestwood, N.Y.: St. Vladimir's Seminary Press, 1984), chap. 2.

[19]Calling for a recovery of richness in worship is Barry Liesch, *People in the Presence of God: Models and Directions for Worship* (Grand Rapids, Mich.: Zondervan, 1988), chap. 8.

[20]On the importance of ritual see Delwin Brown, *Boundaries of Our Habitations: Tradition and Theological Construction* (Albany: State University of New York Press, 1994), pp. 91-109.

[21]G. R. Beasley-Murray, *Baptism in the New Testament* (London: Macmillan, 1963), pp. 275-79; McDonnell and Montague, *Christian Initiation and Baptism in the Holy Spirit,* pp. 76-80, 316-42.

[22]Dunn grants that water baptism is an occasion for the coming of the Spirit but balks at calling it a sacrament. This is odd, since acknowledging the former sounds like granting the latter. The explanation may be that he defines sacrament as an *ex opere operato* action apart from faith, while I do not. James D. G. Dunn, *Baptism in the Holy Spirit* (London: SCM Press, 1970), pp. 224-29.

[23]One sees the dualism in Dunn, *Baptism,* pp. 219, 227-28, and in Gordon D. Fee, *God's Empowering Presence: The Holy Spirit in the Letters of Paul* (Peabody, Mass.: Hendrickson, 1994), pp. 860-63. For a more integrative interpretation see H. I. Lederle, *Treasures Old and New: Interpretations of Spirit-Baptism in the Charismatic Renewal Movement* (Peabody, Mass.: Hendrickson, 1988), pp. 66-73, 104-43; Frederick D. Bruner and William Hordern, "Of Water and the Spirit," chap. 2 in *The Holy Spirit—Shy Member of the Trinity* (Minneapolis: Augsburg, 1984); Karl Barth, *Church Dogmatics* 4/4, trans. G. W. Bromiley (Edinburgh: T & T Clark, 1969).

[24]On baptism in the Reformers and the role of Zwingli, see Jack W. Cottrell, "Baptism According to the Reformed Tradition," in *Baptism and the Remission of Sins,* ed. David W. Fletcher (Joplin, Mo: College, 1990), pp. 39-80.

[25]Muhlen understands the sacrament as an expression of the charismatic self-surrender of Jesus: *Charismatic Theology,* pp. 124-25.

[26]Stanley M. Burgess, *The Holy Spirit: Eastern Christian Traditions* (Peabody, Mass.: Hendrickson, 1989), p. 167; Congar, *I Believe in the Holy Spirit,* 3:250-74.

[27]Peters, *God—the World's Future,* pp. 275-92; F. X. Durrwell, *Holy Spirit of God* (London: Geoffrey Chapman, 1986), pp. 91-107.

[28]Ernst Benz, *The Eastern Orthodox Church, Its Thought and Life* (New York: Doubleday, 1963), pp. 36-38.

[29]On the relation of faith to sacrament see Vorgrimler, *Sacramental Theology,* pp.

82-86.

[30]Kraft exposes the modern bias against belief in the miraculous in *Christianity with Power,* and Langdon Gilkey exposes the bias against it in the area of sacraments in *Catholicism Confronts Modernity: A Protestant View* (New York: Seabury, 1975), chaps. 1-2.

[31]Robert E. Webber, *Evangelicals on the Canterbury Trail: Why Evangelicals Are Attracted to the Liturgical Church* (Wilton, Conn.: Morehouse-Barlow, 1985).

[32]Grenz sees a greater willingness to accept the sacramental principle in the free churches: *Theology for the Community of God,* pp. 67-172.

[33]Ronald A. N. Kydd, *Charismatic Gifts in the Early Church* (Peabody, Mass.: Hendrickson, 1984).

[34]Siegfried Schatzmann, *A Pauline Theology of Charismata* (Peabody, Mass.: Hendrickson, 1987).

[35]Philip J. Rosato, *The Spirit as Lord: The Pneumatology of Karl Barth* (Edinburgh: T & T Clark, 1981), pp. 160-66.

[36]The need of wise oversight is regularly tested where the "Toronto Blessing" is active: Dave Roberts, *The Toronto Blessing* (Eastbourne, U.K.: Kingsway, 1994), chap. 10.

[37]Küng, *The Church,* pp. 173-79.

[38]Ibid., pp. 179-91.

[39]Welker, *God the Spirit,* chaps. 2-3.

[40]Rene Latourelle, *The Miracles of Jesus and the Theology of Miracles* (New York: Paulist, 1988), pp. 258-62; Jon Ruthven, *On the Cessation of the Charismata: The Protestant Polemic on Postbiblical Miracles* (Sheffield, U.K.: Sheffield Academic Press, 1993), pp. 195-97, 202-5.

[41]Ruthven, *On the Cessation of the Charismata,* chaps. 2-3. Jack Deere believes that a deficit in experience best explains the cessationist position: *Surprised by the Power of the Spirit* (Grand Rapids, Mich.: Zondervan, 1993), chap. 5. Also see Gary S. Greig and Kevin N. Springer, eds., *The Kingdom and the Power* (Ventura, Calif.: Regal, 1993).

[42]Moltmann, "The Charismatic Powers of Life," chap. 9 in *Spirit of Life.*

[43]On the meaning of Pentecost see Harry R. Boer, *Pentecost and Missions* (Grand Rapids, Mich.: Eerdmans, 1961), chap. 5; Dunn, *Baptism in the Holy Spirit,* chap. 4. On the transference of power see Roger Stronstad, *The Charismatic Theology of St. Luke* (Peabody, Mass.: Hendrickson, 1984), chap. 4; James B. Shelton, *Mighty in Word and Deed* (Peabody, Mass.: Hendrickson, 1991), chap. 11.

[44]Opposed to this openness is Richard B. Gaffin, *Perspectives on Pentecost: New Testament Teaching on the Gifts of the Holy Spirit* (Phillipsburg, N.J.: Presbyterian & Reformed, 1979), p. 117. Welcoming it was A. B. Simpson, founder of the Christian and Missionary Alliance, a forerunner of charismatic renewal; see Charles W. Nienkirchen, *A. B. Simpson and the Pentecostal Movement: A Study in Continuity, Crisis and Change* (Peabody, Mass.: Hendrickson, 1992).

[45]George T. Montague, *The Spirit and His Gifts* (New York: Paulist, 1974), chap. 3.

[46]The case of the Kansas City prophets should give us pause; see James A. Beverley, *Holy Laughter and the Toronto Blessing* (Grand Rapids, Mich.: Zondervan, 1995), chap. 8. Jim is now researching the career of Paul Cain in regard to testing prophecy.

[47]Tom Harpur calls on churches to recover ministries of healing: *The Uncommon Touch: An Investigation of Spiritual Healing* (Toronto: McClelland & Stewart, 1994).

[48]On healing as anticipatory of the coming kingdom, see Oscar Cullmann, "The Proleptic Deliverance of the Body According to the New Testament," chap. 7 in *The Early Church* (London: SCM Press, 1956); Richard L. Swinburne, *The Existence of God* (Oxford: Clarendon, 1979), pp. 237-39. The desire for miracles can lead to dishonesty in claims: Beverley, *Holy Laughter and the Toronto Blessing,* chap. 7.

[49]Jan Veenhof, "Charismata—Supernatural or Natural?" in *The Holy Spirit: Renewing and Empowering Presence,* ed. George Vandervelde (Winfield, B.C.: Wood Lake Books, 1988), pp. 73-91; Hummel, *Fire in the Fireplace,* pp. 280-82. James D. G. Dunn takes the opposite point of view, though even he admits a gift may "chime in with an individual disposition and temperament": *Jesus and the Spirit* (London: SCM Press, 1975), pp. 255-56.

[50]Friedrich Nietzsche, *Thus Spoke Zarathustra* (New York: Viking, 1966), p. 92; John White, *When the Spirit Comes in Power* (Downers Grove, Ill.: InterVarsity Press, 1985), on what happens in revivals.

[51]On the effects of the Western worldview on openness, see Kraft, *Christianity with Power.* What is needed is a spirituality of openness to God: Joyce Huggett, *Open to God* (London: Hodder & Stoughton, 1989).

[52]Moltmann, *Spirit of Life,* p. 188.

[53]*The Malines Document* (1974): "Theological and Pastoral Orientations on the Catholic Charismatic Renewal," pp. 17-18.

[54]There are dangers inherent in charismatic religion and many warnings about them: Doctrine Commission of the Church of England, "The Spirit and Power," chap. 6 in *We Believe in the Holy Spirit* (London: Church House, 1991); Peter Hocken, "Addressing the Shame," chap. 24 in *The Glory and the Shame* (Guildford, Surrey, U.K.: Eagle, 1994); Smail, Walker and Wright, *Love of Power;* Edward D. O'Connor, *The Pentecostal Movement in the Catholic Church* (Notre Dame, Ind.: Ave Maria Press, 1971), chap. 8. It is remarkable how Pentecostalism can be a truly great movement of revival and be so awash with abuses at the same time.

[55]The image is used by Hummel in *Fire in the Fireplace,* pp. 20-21.

[56]On charism and office see Dunn, *Jesus and the Spirit,* pp. 298-99, and on diaconal structure, Küng, *The Church,* pp. 393-444.

[57]Karl Rahner, *The Dynamic Element in the Church* (New York: Herder and Herder, 1964); "The Church—an Ordered Body," in *Welcome, Holy Spirit: A Study of Charismatic Renewal in the Church,* ed. Larry Christenson (Minneapolis: Augsburg, 1987), chap. 47; Yves Congar, *The Word and the Spirit* (London: Geoffrey Chapman, 1986), pp. 58-62, 78-83.

[58]Lederle, *Treasures Old and New,* p. 234.

[59]Theology has neglected the mission of the church. An exception is Karl Barth: "Holy Spirit and the Sending of the Christian Community," in *Church Dogmatics* 4/3 (2) trans. G. W. Bromiley (Edinburgh: T & T Clark, 1962), as noted by Hendrikus Berkhof, *The Doctrine of the Holy Spirit* (Atlanta: John Knox Press, 1964), chap. 2.

[60]John Fuellenbach, "The Kingdom and the Holy Spirit," in *The Kingdom of God: The Message of Jesus Today* (Maryknoll, N.Y.: Orbis, 1995), pp. 236-47.

[61]Hauerwas and Willimon, *Resident Aliens,* p. 171.

[62]In addition to Barth and Berkhof, see Boer, *Pentecost and Missions,* chaps. 5-7.

[63]Nicholas Lash, *His Presence in the World: A Study of Eucharistic Worship and*

Theology (London: Sheed and Ward, 1968), pp. 155-63; Ronald J. Sider, *One-Sided Christianity? Uniting the Church to Heal a Lost and Broken World* (Grand Rapids, Mich.: Zondervan, 1993).

[64]William J. Abraham, *The Logic of Evangelism* (Grand Rapids, Mich.: Eerdmans, 1989); David J. Bosch, *Transforming Mission: Paradigm Shifts in Theology of Mission* (Maryknoll, N.Y.: Orbis, 1991).

[65]Peters, "Proleptic Ethics," chap. 12 in *God—the World's Future.*

[66]Welker relates intimacy with God to costly discipleship: *God the Spirit,* pp. 331-41.

[67]Richard J. Mouw, "Life in the Spirit in an Unjust World," in *The Holy Spirit: Renewing and Empowering Presence,* ed. George Vandervelde (Winfield, B.C.: Wood Lake Books, 1988), pp. 119-40.

[68]Cardinal Suenens and Dom Helder Camara, *Charismatic Renewal and Social Action: A Dialogue,* Malines Document III (Ann Arbor, Mich.: Servant, 1979). On Luke's mission paradigm see Bosch, *Transforming Mission,* chap. 3.

[69]Larry Christenson, *A Charismatic Approach to Social Action* (Minneapolis: Bethany House, 1974).

[70]Walter Wink, *Engaging the Powers* (Minneapolis: Fortress, 1992), chap. 16; Richard J. Foster, *Prayer: Finding the Heart's True Home* (San Francisco: HarperSanFrancisco, 1992), chap. 21.

[71]Beverly R. Gaventa, *From Darkness to Light: Aspects of Conversion in the New Testament* (Philadelphia: Fortress, 1986); Berkhof, *Doctrine of the Holy Spirit,* pp. 100-104, and *Christian Faith,* pp. 507-12. Pannenberg on church and society: Stanley J. Grenz, *Reason for Hope: The Systematic Theology of Wolfart Pannenberg* (New York: Oxford University Press, 1990), pp. 178-82.

[72]Welker, *God the Spirit,* pp. 124-34; John Howard Yoder, *The Original Revolution* (Scottdale, Penn.: Herald, 1972), chap. 1.

Chapter 5: Spirit & Union
[1]Bernard of Clairvaux *On the Song of Songs* 1 (Kalamazoo, Mich.: Cistercian Publications, 1976), pp. 45-52. There is a plurality of salvations, not just one model in Christianity and in world religions: S. Mark Heim, *Salvations: Truth and Difference in Religion* (Maryknoll, N.Y.: Orbis, 1995); J. A. DiNoia, *The Diversity of Religions: A Christian Perspective* (Washington, D.C.: Catholic University of America Press, 1992); Harold A. Netland, *Dissonant Voices: Religious Pluralism and the Question of Truth* (Grand Rapids, Mich.: Eerdmans, 1991).

[2]Gordon D. Fee, *God's Empowering Presence: The Holy Spirit in the Letters of Paul* (Peabody, Mass.: Hendrickson, 1994), pp. 362-65, 693-97.

[3]T. F. Torrance pleads for a recovery of the notion of theosis in *Theology in Reconstruction* (London: SCM Press, 1965), p. 243.

[4]A. M. Allchin, *Participation in God: A Forgotten Strand in Anglican Tradition* (Wilton, Conn.: Morehouse-Barlow, 1988); Robert V. Rakestraw, "Becoming like God: An Evangelical Doctrine of Theosis," *Journal of the Evangelical Theological Society,* forthcoming; Philip E. Hughes, "The Deification of Man in Christ," chap. 24 in *The True Image: The Origin and Destiny of Man in Christ* (Grand Rapids, Mich.: Eerdmans, 1989); Daniel B. Clendenin, "The Deification of Humanity: Theosis," chap. 6 in *Eastern Orthodox Christianity: A Western Perspective* (Grand Rapids,

NOTES ————————————————————————— *269*

Mich.: Baker Book House, 1994). It is not absent from the Reformation: Tuomo Mannermaa, "Theosis as a Subject of Finnish Luther Research," *Pro Ecclesia* 4 (1995): 37-48. It is found to be central in Calvin by Leanne Van Dyk, who cites many scholars in support: *The Desire of Divine Love: John McLeod Campbell's Doctrine of the Atonement* (New York: Peter Lang, 1995), p. 151.

[5]Al Wolters, "Partners of the Deity: A Covenantal Reading of 2 Peter 1:4," *Calvin Theological Journal* 25 (1990): 28-44.

[6]Neil Q. Hamilton, *The Holy Spirit and Eschatology in Paul* (Edinburgh: Oliver and Boyd, 1957); Paul's category of "in Christ" supports the idea of salvation as union and communion, according to Richard N. Longenecker, *Paul, Apostle of Liberty* (New York: Harper & Row, 1964), pp. 160-70. Hans Urs von Balthasar, *The Glory of the Lord*, vol. 1 (Edinburgh: T & T Clark, 1982); Francis K. Nemick and Marie T. Coombs, *The Way of Spiritual Direction* (Collegeville, Minn.: Liturgical, 1985).

[7]Pope John Paul II, *The Gospel of Life* (New York: Random House, 1995), p. 4; John J. O'Donnell, *The Mystery of the Triune God* (New York: Paulist, 1989), pp. 163-67.

[8]Fee, in a book on Paul's theology of Spirit, acknowledges that the apostle places the community before the individual in his thinking (p. 846) but still arranges his chapters in the opposite order: see *God's Empowering Presence,* chaps. 14-15.

[9]On this theme in Orthodoxy see Christoforos Stavropoulos, *Partakers of Divine Nature* (Minneapolis: Light and Life, 1976).

[10]Ernst Benz, "Liturgy and Sacraments," chap. 2 in *The Eastern Orthodox Church, Its Thought and Life* (New York: Doubleday, 1963).

[11]Vladimir Lossky, "Redemption and Deification," chap. 5 in *In the Image and Likeness of God* (London: Mowbrays, 1975).

[12]Timothy Ware, *The Orthodox Church* (London: Penguin, 1963), pp. 236-42. In opposition to Stace, Nelson Pike claims that no Christian mystics ever meant to erase the Creator-creature distinction in their discussion of union: Pike, *Mystic Union: An Essay on the Phenomenology of Mysticism* (Ithaca, N.Y.: Cornell University Press, 1992), pp. 208-13.

[13]Keith Ward, *Religion and Revelation: A Theology of Revelation in the World's Religions* (Oxford: Clarendon, 1994), pp. 134-56.

[14]C. S. Lewis, *Mere Christianity* (London: Collins, 1952), p. 138; Georgios I. Mantzaridis, "The Mystical Experience of Deification," chap. 4 in *The Deification of Man: St. Gregory Palamas and the Orthodox Tradition* (Crestwood, N.Y.: St. Vladimir's Seminary Press, 1984).

[15]This is the theme of H. Paul Santmire, *The Travail of Nature: The Ambiguous Ecological Promise of Christian Theology* (Philadelphia: Fortress, 1985), pp. 217-18.

[16]Millard J. Erickson makes it the primary dimension of salvation: *Christian Theology* (Grand Rapids, Mich.: Baker Book House, 1983), pp. 904-5.

[17]Thomas N. Finger rethinks justification in *Christian Theology: An Eschatological Approach,* vol. 2 (Scottdale, Penn.: Herald, 1987), chap. 7. Ronald J. Sider protests exaggeration in the way evangelicals speak of it in *One-Sided Christianity? Uniting the Church to Heal a Lost and Broken World* (Grand Rapids, Mich.: Zondervan, 1993), p. 222. Alister McGrath complains that the Catechism of the Catholic Church does not deal with the sixteenth-century disputes over justification, but I think this was wise; see *First Things* 51 (March 1995): 68-69.

[18]Krister Stendahl, *Paul Among Jews and Gentiles* (Philadelphia: Fortress, 1976).

[19]James D. G. Dunn and Alan M. Suggate, *The Justice of God: A Fresh Look at the Old Doctrine of Justification by Faith* (Grand Rapids, Mich.: Eerdmans, 1993), pt. 1. On justification in Orthodoxy see Clendenin, *Eastern Orthodox Christianity,* pp. 120-25. Donald G. Bloesch balances justification and deification too: *God the Almighty: Power, Wisdom, Holiness, Love* (Downers Grove, Ill.: InterVarsity Press, 1995), pp. 234-36. Justification is just not the dividing issue it used to be between Catholics and Protestants; see Charles Colson and Richard J. Neuhaus, *Evangelicals and Catholics Together: Toward a Common Mission* (Dallas: Word, 1995), pp. 168-69, 199-200.

[20]Protestants can be remarkably self-righteous on this point, in asking whether Rome has finally gotten its doctrine of justification right. We need to ask, Have *we* gotten it right yet? Rome has acknowledged Luther's strengths; when will we acknowledge his weaknesses? A sad book is R. C. Sproul, *Faith Alone: The Evangelical Doctrine of Justification* (Grand Rapids, Mich.: Baker Book House, 1995)—sad because it refuses to credit Catholic and Protestant developments since the Reformation or to offer any hope of Christian unity.

[21]Stanley J. Grenz, "The Dynamic of Conversion," chap. 15 in *Theology for the Community of God* (Nashville: Broadman & Holman, 1994).

[22]John Paul II, *Gospel of Life,* p. 15.

[23]On Wesley's doctrine of prevenient and restoring grace, see Randy L. Maddox, *Responsible Grace: John Wesley's Practical Theology* (Nashville: Kingswood, 1994), pp. 83-93. Hans Urs von Balthasar views the relationship of finite and infinite freedom in the context of a "theo-drama": Edward T. Oakes, *Pattern of Redemption: The Theology of Hans Urs von Balthasar* (New York: Continuum, 1995), chap. 8.

[24]On the mode of God's activity in the world, see E. Frank Tupper, *A Scandalous Providence: The Jesus Story of the Compassion of God* (Macon, Ga.: Mercer University Press, 1995), pp. 30-38.

[25]Rene Latourelle, *The Miracles of Jesus and the Theology of Miracles* (New York: Paulist, 1988), pp. 316-18.

[26]Leon Joseph Suenens, "The Holy Spirit and Mary," chap. 11 in *A New Pentecost?* (London: Darton, Longman & Todd, 1975).

[27]John Murray, *Redemption Accomplished and Applied* (Grand Rapids, Mich.: Eerdmans, 1955), pp. 109-29; Michael Norton, *Putting Amazing Back into Grace* (Grand Rapids, Mich.: Baker Book House, 1994); Wayne Grudem, *Systematic Theology: An Introduction to Biblical Doctrine* (Grand Rapids, Mich.: Zondervan, 1994), chaps. 32-35.

[28]Fee appears to fudge in *God's Empowering Presence,* p. 853.

[29]Harry R. Boer, "The Responding Imago," chap. 5 in *An Ember Still Glowing* (Grand Rapids, Mich.: Eerdmans, 1990); Ware, *Orthodox Church,* pp. 226-30.

[30]Harry J. McSorley, *Luther Right or Wrong: An Ecumenical-Theological Study of Luther's Major Work* (New York: Newman, 1969), pp. 359-66.

[31]Vincent Brummer, "Can We Resist the Grace of God?" chap. 3 in *Speaking of a Personal God* (Cambridge: Cambridge University Press, 1992); H. Orton Wiley, *Christian Theology* (Kansas City, Mo.: Beacon Hill, 1952), 2:356-57.

[32]C. Stephen Evans, "Salvation, Sin and Human Freedom in Kierkegaard," in *The Grace of God, the Will of Man,* ed. Clark H. Pinnock (Grand Rapids, Mich.:

Zondervan, 1989), pp. 181-89; Wolfhart Pannenberg, *Systematic Theology* (Grand Rapids, Mich.: Eerdmans, 1991), 2:48, 52.

[33]*Catechism of the Catholic Church,* pp. 41-42.

[34]This and other sayings like it from the fathers are found in Ware, *Orthodox Church,* pp. 234-36.

[35]Fee, "The Spirit as Eschatological Fulfillment," chap. 12 in *God's Empowering Presence.*

[36]Receiving the Spirit is a topic in Grudem's soteriololgy but not Erickson's: Grudem, *Systematic Theology,* chap. 39; Erickson, *Christian Theology,* pt. 10.

[37]Jonathan Edwards discusses how God impacts us in *Religious Affections,* ed. John E. Smith (New Haven, Conn.: Yale University Press, 1959), pp. 91-124.

[38]Jürgen Moltmann, "Rebirth to Life," chap. 7 in *The Spirit of Life: A Universal Affirmation* (Minneapolis: Fortress, 1992); Beverly R. Gaventa, "Imagery of New Birth and New Life," chap. 4 in *From Darkness to Light: Aspects of Conversion in the New Testament* (Philadlphia: Fortress, 1986).

[39]Michael Welker, *God the Spirit,* trans. John F. Hoffmeyer (Minneapolis: Fortress, 1994), pp. 331-41; James D. G. Dunn, *Baptism in the Holy Spirit* (London: SCM Press, 1970), pp. 225-26; Fee, "The Soteriological Spirit," chap. 14 in *God's Empowering Presence;* Steven J. Land, *Pentecostal Spirituality: A Passion for the Kingdom* (Sheffield, U.K.: Sheffield Academic Press, 1993).

[40]Jon Ruthven, *On the Cessation of the Charismata: The Protestant Polemic on Postbiblical Miracles* (Sheffield, U.K.: Sheffield Academic Press, 1993), pp. 195-205.

[41]Frederick D. Bruner and William Hordern, "Of Water and the Spirit," chap. 2 in *The Holy Spirit—Shy Member of the Trinity* (Minneapolis: Augsburg, 1984); Jack W. Cottrell, *Baptism: A Biblical Study* (Joplin, Mo.: College, 1989); George T. Montague, *The Spirit and His Gifts* (New York: Paulist, 1974), pp. 10-14. Dunn's statement that baptism is not "a channel of grace" is puzzling, since he has also said it is "the expression of faith to which God gives the Spirit" (*Baptism in the Holy Spirit,* pp. 227-28). Fee also loosens the connection between water and Spirit baptism (*God's Empowering Presence,* pp. 860-64).

[42]On the early church as sacramental and charismatic, see Kilian McDonnell and George T. Montague, *Christian Initiation and Baptism in the Holy Spirit: Evidence from the First Eight Centuries* (Collegeville, Minn.: Liturgical, 1991), pp. 76-80, 308-10, 316-42.

[43]Stanley M. Burgess, *The Holy Spirit: Eastern Christian Traditions* (Peabody, Mass.: Hendrickson, 1989), pp. 58-61, 197. Roger Stronstad notes Luke's emphasis on power for vocation as distinct from Paul's emphasis, and concludes that receiving power may well appear to be a second blessing both in Acts and today: *The Charismatic Theology of St. Luke* (Peabody, Mass.: Hendrickson, 1984). Frederick D. Bruner is insensitive to pastoral realities and attacks Pentecostals rather than crediting them for being aware of pastoral concerns: *A Theology of the Holy Spirit: The Pentecostal Experience and the New Testament Witness* (Grand Rapids, Mich.: Eerdmans, 1970).

[44]No one makes this point better than Charles H. Kraft, *Christianity with Power* (Ann Arbor, Mich: Servant, 1989).

[45]H. I. Lederle, *Treasures Old and New: Interpretations of Spirit-Baptism in the*

Charismatic Renewal Movement (Peabody, Mass.: Hendrickson, 1988), pp. 66-73, 238-39; Gordon D. Fee, "Baptism in the Holy Spirit: The Issue of Separability and Subsequence," chap. 7 in *Gospel and Spirit: Issues in New Testament Hermeneutics* (Peabody, Mass.: Hendrickson, 1991). Fee, though he criticizes the Pentecostal doctrine of subsequence, credits the movement for calling the church back to the experience of Pentecost.

[46]Gordon D. Fee, "Toward a Pauline Theology of Glossolalia," *Crux* 31 (1995): 22-31.

[47]Larry W. Hurtado, "Normal but Not a Norm: Initial Evidence and the New Testament," in *Initial Evidence: Historical and Biblical Perspectives on the Pentecostal Doctrine of Spirit Baptism,* ed. Gary B. McGee (Peabody, Mass.: Hendrickson, 1991), pp. 189-201. In agreement is Thomas A. Smail, *Reflected Glory: The Spirit in Christ and Christians* (Grand Rapids, Mich.: Eerdmans, 1975), p. 43.

[48]Montague, *The Spirit and His Gifts,* chap. 2.

[49]Frank D. Macchia, "Tongues as a Sign: Towards a Sacramental Understanding of Pentecostal Experience," *Pneuma* 15 (1993): 61-76.

[50]J. I. Packer, *Keep in Step with the Spirit* (Old Tappan, N.J.: Revell, 1984).

[51]Vladimir Lossky, *Orthodox Theology: An Introduction* (Crestwood, N.Y.: St. Vladimir's Seminary Press, 1978), pp. 119-37, and *In the Image and Likeness of God* (London: Mowbrays, 1975); Jürgen Moltmann, "God's Image in Creation," chap. 9 in *God in Creation: A New Theology of Creation and the Spirit of God* (San Francisco: Harper & Row, 1985).

[52]Smail, "Into His Likeness," chap. 2 in *Reflected Glory.*

[53]Richard Swinburne, *The Existence of God* (Oxford: Clarendon, 1979), chap. 11; John Hick, *Evil and the God of Love* (New York: Harper & Row, 1966), pts. 3-4.

[54]Few authors surpass Henri J. M. Nowen in writing about the nature of Christian living; see *Life of the Beloved* (New York: Crossroad, 1995).

[55]Clendenin, *Eastern Orthodox Christianity,* pp. 133-34.

[56]Pope John Paul II's encyclical "On the Holy Spirit" puts strong emphasis on the sanctifying work of the Spirit, which frees us from sin's domination. Growth, not perfection, was Wesley's emphasis: Maddox, *Responsible Grace,* pp. 177-90.

[57]The likeness of Christ consists of his placing God's cause and humankind's cause first in his life by the Spirit: Hans Küng, *On Being a Christian* (London: Collins, 1974), pp. 214-77.

[58]On Wesley see Maddox, *Responsible Grace,* p. 191. For this view see Hendrikus Berkhof, *Christian Faith: An Introduction to the Study of the Faith,* trans. Sierd Woudstra (Grand Rapids, Mich.: Eerdmans, 1986), pp. 482-90; C. S. Lewis, *Letters to Malcolm: Chiefly on Prayer* (San Diego, Calif.: Harcourt Brace Jovanovich, 1973), pp. 108-9; Clark H. Pinnock, "The Conditional View," in *Four Views of Hell,* ed. William Crockett (Grand Rapids, Mich.: Zondervan, 1992), pp. 129-31; Hick, *Evil and the God of Love,* pp. 381-85.

[59]Moltmann, *Spirit of Life,* pp. 73-77.

[60]On the intractability of sin see Cornelius Plantinga Jr., *Not the Way It's Supposed to Be: A Breviary of Sin* (Grand Rapids, Mich.: Eerdmans, 1995), and Ted Peters, *Sin: Radical Evil in Soul and Society* (Grand Rapids, Mich.: Eerdmans, 1994). Pentecostal experience, because of its liquid ecstasy, can sometimes be a partially trodden mystical way: Jean-Jacques Suurmond, *Word and Spirit at Play: Towards a Charis-*

matic Theology (Grand Rapids, Mich.: Eerdmans, 1995), pp. 151-60; Donald L. Gelpi, "The Theological Challenge of Charismatic Spirituality," *Pneuma* 14 (1992): 185-97.
[61]John Paul II, *Crossing the Threshold of Hope* (New York: Alfred A. Knopf, 1994), p. 194; John Hick, *An Interpretation of Religion* (New Haven, Conn.: Yale University Press, 1989), pt. 5 (I wish Hick did not make it the only criterion).
[62]Berkhof, *Christian Faith,* p. 540.
[63]Nouwen, *Life of the Beloved,* p. 92.
[64]John J. O'Donnell, "Faith as an Aesthetic Act," chap. 3 in *Hans Urs von Balthasar* (Collegeville, Minn.: Liturgical, 1992).
[65]Thomas R. Kelly, *A Testament of Devotion* (San Franscisco: HarperCollins, 1992), p. 9.

Chapter 6: Spirit & Universality
[1]Richard H. Drummond traces the movement of opinion toward greater universality of outlook in *Toward a New Age in Christian Theology* (Maryknoll, N.Y.: Orbis, 1985). One of the most remarkable things about the Second Vatican Council was its broad vision of a world renewed: George A. Lindbeck, *The Future of Roman Catholic Theology* (London: SPCK, 1970), chap. 1.
[2]Quoted phrases are taken from Elizabeth A. Johnson, *She Who Is: The Mystery of God in Feminist Theological Discourse* (New York: Crossroad, 1992), p. 128; Barbara Newman, *Sister of Wisdom: St. Hildegaard's Theology of the Feminine* (Berkeley: University of California Press, 1987).
[3]A theme of this book is to recognize a unity in all God's works. Grace did not begin as a result of the fall into sin. Creation itself was a gift. Every good and perfect gift comes from God (Jas 1:17).
[4]It was formulated at the Council of Florence (1438-1445) but can be found in the writings of Ignatius of Antioch, Irenaeus, Clement of Alexandria, Origen, Cyprian and Augustine. It was given radical expression by Fulgentius, a disciple of Augustine, who said, "Of this you can be certain and convinced beyond any doubt: not only all pagans but all Jews, all heretics and schismatics, who die outside the present Catholic church, will go into the everlasting fire which has been prepared for the devil and his angels." The sources are listed Hans Küng, *The Church* (New York: Sheed and Ward, 1967), pp. 313-14. Its development and interpretation are examined in Francis A. Sullivan, *Salvation Outside the Church? Tracing the History of the Catholic Response* (New York: Paulist, 1992).
[5]The literature on this set of issues continues to grow; see Dennis L. Okholm and Timothy R. Phillips, eds., *More Than One Way? Four Views on Salvation in a Pluralistic World* (Grand Rapids, Mich.: Zondervan, 1995).
[6]It is remarkable how John's Revelation is so often read as a document of gloom and doom, when it ends on such a note of hope and universality. Compare G. B. Caird's hopeful reading, "The Theology of the Book of Revelation," in *A Commentary on the Revelation of St. John the Divine* (London: Adam & Charles Black, 1966).
[7]Neal Punt, *Unconditional Good News* (Grand Rapids, Mich.: Eerdmans, 1980), p. 5; similarly Clark H. Pinnock, "Optimism of Salvation," chap. 1 in *A Wideness in God's Mercy* (Grand Rapids, Mich.: Zondervan, 1992).
[8]William G. T. Shedd, *Dogmatic Theology* (1899; reprint Grand Rapids, Mich.:

Zondervan, 1969), 2:712.

[9]E. P. Sanders speaks of the fatal objection to universalism in Paul—his mentioning of those who will perish and be destoyed on the day of the Lord: *Paul and Palestinian Judaism: A Comparison of Patterns of Religion* (Minneapolis: Fortress, 1977), p. 473.

[10]Karl Barth, *Church Dogmatics* 2/2, trans. G. W. Bromiley (Edinburgh: T & T Clark, 1957), pp. 417-18. On universalism see John Sanders, *No Other Name? An Investigation into the Destiny of the Unevangelized* (Grand Rapids, Mich.: Eerdmans, 1992), pp. 81-115. Attempts to defend universal salvation biblically can be found in W. Sibley Towner, *How God Deals with Evil* (Philadelphia: Westminister Press, 1976), and Thomas Talbott, "The New Testament and Universal Reconciliation," *Christian Scholar's Review* 21 (1992): 376-94. I. Howard Marshall says no to the question "Does the New Testament Teach Universal Salvation?" in *Christ in Our Place,* ed. Trevor A. Hart and Daniel P. Thimell (Exeter, U.K.: Paternoster, 1989), pp. 313-28.

[11]Eastern Orthodoxy, to its credit, has not been as preoccupied with damnation as the Western church: Ernst Benz, *The Eastern Orthodox Church, Its Thought and Life* (New York: Doubleday, 1963), pp. 43-53.

[12]For a discussion of restrictivism see Sanders, *No Other Name?* pp. 37-79. This is the best discussion of it, even though the author is in opposition. It seems as if the proponents are reluctant to spell out their own view and its consequences.

[13]Wayne Grudem, *Systematic Theology: An Introduction to Biblical Doctrine* (Grand Rapids, Mich.: Zondervan, 1994), pp. 684-85. William W. Klein contests this way of thinking in *The New Chosen People: A Corporate View of Election* (Grand Rapids, Mich.: Zondervan, 1990).

[14]For this trinitarian solution see Gavin D'Costa, ed., *Christian Uniqueness Reconsidered* (Maryknoll, N.Y.: Orbis, 1990), chap. 2; similarly Raimundo Panikkar, "The Jordan, the Tiber and the Ganges," in *The Myth of Christian Uniqueness,* ed. John Hick and Paul F. Knitter (Maryknoll, N.Y.: Orbis, 1987), pp. 109-10. Panikkar does not seem to belong to the company of religious pluralists, though he is associated with them in the volume.

[15]John V. Taylor, "The Universal Spirit and the Meeting of Faiths," chap. 9 in *The Go-Between God: The Holy Spirit and the Christian Mission* (London: SCM Press, 1972). On gifts to those outside the church see Abraham Kuyper, *The Work of the Holy Spirit* (Grand Rapids, Mich.: Eerdmans, 1973), pp. 38-42.

[16]One might expect the Pentecostals to develop a Spirit-oriented theology of mission and world religions, because of their openness to religious experience, their sensitivity to the oppressed of the Third World where they have experienced much of their growth, and their awareness of the ways of the Spirit as well as dogma.

[17]This generous approach to non-Christian peoples is found in *The Mystery of Salvation: The Story of God's Gift,* an official report of the Doctrine Commission of the Church of England, chaired by Alec Graham (London: Church House, 1995).

[18]On the double mission of Spirit and Son, see Walter Kasper, *The God of Jesus Christ* (New York: Crossroad, 1986), pp. 198-229, and *Jesus the Christ,* trans. V. Green (New York: Paulist, 1976), pp. 266-68.

[19]Yves Congar, "Christomonism and the *Filioque,"* chap. 7 in *The Word and the Spirit*

(London: Geoffrey Chapman, 1986).

[20]Timothy Ware, *The Orthodox Church* (London: Penguin, 1963), p. 222.

[21]Jürgen Moltmann finds the *filioque* superfluous (*The Spirit of Life: A Universal Affirmation* [Minneapolis: Fortress, 1992], pp. 306-9), and so did John Wesley, according to Randy L. Maddox (*Responsible Grace: John Wesley's Practical Theology* [Nashville: Kingswood, 1994], p. 137).

[22]Yves Congar, *I Believe in the Holy Spirit* (New York: Seabury, 1983), 3:214.

[23]Jack W. Cottrell, *What the Bible Says About God the Creator* (Joplin, Mo.: College Press, 1983), pp. 340-47; Bruce C. Demarest, *General Revelation* (Grand Rapids, Mich.: Zondervan, 1982), pp. 44, 54, 56, 69.

[24]Demarest grants *(General Revelation)* that God's love is disclosed in general revelation (p. 250) and that some pagan might cast himself on God's mercy (p. 260), as happened in the Old Testament (p. 261), and be saved—though, he adds, "in exceptional circumstances" (p. 260). He opens the door of opportunity a crack, but it would be opened wider if it were recognized that unevangelized people are all in exceptional circumstances as regards salvation. Compare John Sanders, *No Other Name?* pp. 224-36.

[25]The text is in *Zwingli and Bullinger,* trans. Geoffrey W. Bromiley (Philadelphia: Westminster Press, 1953), pp. 275-76.

[26]H. Ray Dunning, *Grace, Faith and Holiness: A Wesleyan Systematic Theology* (Kansas City, Mo.: Beacon Hill, 1988), pp. 158, 338, 431-36.

[27]On the possibility of the salvation of non-Christians in Wesley, see Maddox, *Responsible Grace,* pp. 32-34, and Randy L. Maddox, "Wesley and the Question of Truth or Salvation Through Other Religions," *Wesleyan Theological Journal* 27 (1992): 7-29.

[28]Karl Rahner, *Foundations of Christian Faith* (New York: Seabury, 1978), pp. 126-37, 147, 176.

[29]On total depravity and the rise of the category of common grace, see Harry R. Boer, *An Ember Still Glowing* (Grand Rapids, Mich.: Eerdmans, 1990), chaps. 3-4.

[30]Critics of this position agree that God's grace might be inclusive in this way but deny that the Bible supports so hopeful an understanding: see R. Douglas Geivett and W. Gary Phillips in *More Than One Way? Four Views on Salvation in a Pluralistic World,* ed. Dennis L. Okholm and Timothy R. Phillips (Grand Rapids, Mich.: Zondervan, 1995), pp. 133-40. I beg to differ.

[31]Consider the positive spirit that characterizes the "Declaration on the Relationship of the Church to Non-Christian Religions" at the Second Vatican Council.

[32]Dunn goes too far when he writes, "Romans 8:9 rules out the possibility of a non-Christian possessing the Spirit" (*Baptism in the Holy Spirit* [London: SCM Press, 1970], p. 95). We have to assume that the Spirit was at work in Cornelius preparatory to conversion.

[33]Wolfhart Pannenberg, "The Religions from the Perspective of Christian Theology and the Self-Interpretation of Christianity in Relation to the Non-Christian Religions," *Modern Theology* 11 (1995): 285-97. George Lindbeck would accept, I think, that Christians could be stimulated by encountering all sorts of people, but his emphasis would be more on maintaining one's own identity. I focus more on the benefits that can arise from an open and mutually transformative dialogue. See George

Lindbeck, *The Nature of Doctrine: Religion and Theology in a Postliberal Age* (Philadelphia: Westminster Press, 1984), chap. 3.

[34]This is Keith Ward's theme in *Religion and Revelation: A Theology of Revelation in the World's Religions* (Oxford: Clarendon, 1994).

[35]In the light of Romans 5:17 and 11:32, I am not ready to concede that Romans actually is pessimistic. See John Sanders, "Mercy to All: Romans 1-3 and the Destiny of the Unevangelized," in *The Challenge of Religious Pluralism: An Evangelical Analysis and Response* (Wheaton, Ill.: Wheaton Theology Conference, 1992), pp. 216-28.

[36]For documentation see Francis A. Sullivan, *Salvation Outside the Church: Tracing the History of the Catholic Response* (New York: Paulist, 1992). On the mainline Protestant model see Paul F. Knitter, *No Other Name? A Critical Survey of Christian Attitudes Toward the World Religions* (Maryknoll, N.Y.: Orbis, 1985), pp. 97-119.

[37]Karl Barth voices such fears in "The Revelation of God as the Abolition of Religion," in *Church Dogmatics* 1/2, trans. G. T. Thompson (Edinburgh: T & T Clark, 1956), pp. 280-361. Later comments about "lesser lights" outside the church do not change his negative attitude to other religions (*Church Dogmatics* 4/3, trans. G. W. Bromiley [Edinburgh: T & T Clark, 1961], pp. 3-367).

[38]For more along this line see Pinnock, *Wideness in God's Mercy,* chap. 3, and Kenneth Cracknell, *Towards a New Relationship: Christians and People of Other Faith* (London: Epworth, 1986), chaps. 2-3, 5.

[39]Thomas F. O'Meara, "A History of Grace," in *A World of Grace: An Introduction to the Themes and Foundations of Karl Rahner's Theology,* ed. Leo J. O'Donovan (New York: Seabury, 1980). Regarding redemptive bridges see Don Richardson, *Eternity in Their Hearts* (Ventura, Calif.: Regal, 1984).

[40]Taylor, *Go-Between God,* p. 191.

[41]"On the Holy Spirit," p. 76. On such papal teachings after Vatican II see Sullivan, *Salvation Outside the Church,* chap. 11. Pneumatological inclusivism is the path taken by Jacques Dupuis in *Jesus Christ at the Encounter of World Religions* (Maryknoll, N.Y.: Orbis, 1991), chap. 7.

[42]C. S. Lewis, *The Last Battle* (London: Penguin, 1956), p. 149.

[43]On the baptism of desire see *Sacramentum Mundi: An Encyclopedia of Theology* (New York: Herder and Herder, 1968), 1:144-46.

[44]Jacques Dupuis, *Jesus Christ at the Encounter of World Religions* (Maryknoll, N.Y.: Orbis, 1991), especially chap. 7, "Economy of the Spirit" (pp. 152-77).

[45]Lucas Lamadrid, "Anonymous or Analogous Christians? Rahner and von Balthasar on Naming the Non-Christian," *Modern Theology* 11 (1995): 363-84.

[46]Pope John Paul II, *Crossing the Threshold of Hope* (New York: Alfred A. Knopf, 1994), pp. 77-117.

[47]J. A. DiNoia, *The Diversity of Religions: A Christian Perspective* (Washington, D.C.: Catholic University of America Press, 1992); Mark S. Heim, *Salvations: Truth and Difference in Religion* (Maryknoll, N.Y.: Orbis, 1995).

[48]Stuart C. Hackett, *The Reconstruction of the Christian Truth Claim: A Philosophical and Critical Apologetic* (Grand Rapids, Mich.: Baker Book House, 1984), pp. 249-53.

[49]Paul J. Griffiths, "Modalizing the Theology of Religions," *Journal of Religion* 73 (1993): 382-89. For my discussion of modal inclusivism, see Clark H. Pinnock, "An

Inclusivist View," in *More Than One Way: Four Views on Salvation in a Pluralistic World,* ed. Dennis L. Okholm and Timothy R. Phillips (Grand Rapids, Mich.: Zondervan, 1995). In his odyssey Paul F. Knitter has taken many moves beyond this: *One Earth, Many Religions: Multifaith Dialogue and Global Responsibility* (Maryknoll, N.Y.: Orbis, 1995), chap. 1.

[50]Gavin D'Costa, "Revelation and Revelations: Discerning God in Other Religions—Beyond a Static Valuation," *Modern Theology* 10 (1994): 165-83.

[51]Charismatics are often more sensitive to these realities because they take gifting and spiritual warfare seriously: see H. I. Lederle, "Life in the Spirit and World View," in *Spirit and Renewal: Essays in Honor of J. Rodman Williams,* ed. Mark W. Wilson (Sheffield, U.K.: Sheffield Academic Press, 1994), pp. 22-33.

[52]T. J. Gorringe, "The Criterion," chap. 3 in *Discerning Spirit: A Theology of Revelation* (London: SCM Press, 1990); Christopher Morse, *Not Every Spirit: A Dogmatics of Christian Disbelief* (Valley Forge, Penn.: Trinity Press International, 1994), pp. 179-80, 196.

[53]Pannenberg, "Religions from the Perspective of Christian Theology," p. 293. Beginning with dogma does not get us very far in dialogue, but beginning with God's presence in other modes can be fruitful. Let us be sensitive to the presence and goodness of God and only afterward move to conceptual issues. There is merit in the appeal of Buddhist Thich Nhat Hanh, *Living Buddha, Living Christ* (New York: Riverhead, 1995).

[54]Küng, *The Church,* pp. 191-209.

[55]The note of reckless grace is sounded in Robert F. Capon, *The Parables of Grace* (Grand Rapids, Mich.: Eerdmans, 1988).

[56]John Paul II, *Crossing the Threshold of Hope,* pp. 185-87; Clark H. Pinnock, "The Destruction of the Finally Impenitent Wicked," *Criswell Theological Review* 4 (1990): 243-59.

Chapter 7: Spirit & Truth

[1]This is discussed in Clark H. Pinnnock, "Word and Spirit," chap. 7 in *The Scripture Principle* (San Francisco: Harper & Row, 1984).

[2]On theological reflection see Henri J. M. Nouwen, *In the Name of Jesus* (New York: Crossroad, 1993), pp. 65-70. On cruciality in theology see Christopher Morse, *Not Every Spirit: A Dogmatics of Christian Disbelief* (Valley Forge, Penn.: Trinity Press International, 1994), pp. 65-66.

[3]Kenneth Cracknell, "God and the Nations," chap. 3 in *Toward a New Relationship: Christians the People of Other Faith* (London: Epworth, 1986); Joachim Jeremias, *Jesus' Promise to the Nations* (London: SCM Press, 1958).

[4]Keith Ward, *Religion and Revelation: A Theology of Revelation in the World's Religions* (Oxford: Clarendon, 1994), p. 191.

[5]Doctrine Commission of the Church of England, "Spirit of Truth," chap. 7 in *We Believe in the Holy Spirit* (London: Church House, 1991). See John Frame, *Evangelical Reunion: Denominations and the One Body of Christ* (Grand Rapids, Mich.: Baker Book House, 1991), and Rex A. Koivisto, *One Lord, One Faith: A Theology for Cross-Denomination Renewal* (Wheaton, Ill.: Victor, 1993).

[6]This is evident in Clendenin's loving interpretation of Eastern Orthodoxy: Daniel

B. Clendenin, *Eastern Orthodox Christianity: A Western Perspective* (Grand Rapids, Mich.: Baker Book House, 1994), chap. 7. The same spirit is noticeable in John Paul II's encyclical "Christian Unity" (Rome: Vatican Library, 1995). Its fruitfulness is explained by Langdon Gilkey, *Catholicism Confronts Modernity: A Protestant View* (New York: Seabury, 1975), pp. 80-83.

[7]I appreciate John M. Templeton's insistence on this theme in *The Humble Approach: Scientists Discover God* (New York: Continuum, 1995).

[8]An exception to this neglect among evangelicals is Peter Toon, *The Development of Doctrine in the Church* (Grand Rapids, Mich.: Eerdmans, 1979). Toon is Anglican and therefore less prone to ignore the topic than, say, a Baptist.

[9]On the church as a pilgrim people see "Dogmatic Constitution on the Church," par. 48, and Avery Dulles, *Models of the Church* (New York: Doubleday, 1974), chap. 7.

[10]Consider the developmental hermeneutic found in Richard N. Longenecker, *New Testament Social Ethics for Today* (Grand Rapids, Mich.: Eerdmans, 1984), pp. 16-28.

[11]Helpful is Hans Küng's distinction between infallibility and indefectability in *Infallible? An Inquiry* (New York: Doubleday, 1971), pp. 173-240.

[12]Regarding the challenge of "enthusiasm," see Hans Küng, *The Church* (New York: Sheed and Ward, 1967), pp. 191-203.

[13]On the place of cruciality in theological method see Morse, *Not Every Spirit,* pp. 65-66.

[14]Küng, *Infallible?* pp. 178-81.

[15]For a debate concerning progress in history and in understanding, see Patrick Glynn and Glenn Tinder, "Time for Utopia? An Exchange," *First Things* 51 (March 1995): 27-35.

[16]Michael Welker, *God the Spirit,* trans. John F. Hoffmeyer (Minneapolis: Fortress, 1994), pp. 219-27.

[17]On theology as second-order language reflecting on the narrative of salvation, see Clark H. Pinnock, *Tracking the Maze: Finding our Way Through Modern Theology from an Evangelical Perspective* (San Francisco: Harper & Row, 1990), chaps. 10-15.

[18]Adolf von Harnack, *What Is Christianity?* trans. Thomas Bailey Saunders (New York: Putnam, 1904); Toon, *Development of Doctrine,* pp. 55-62; Jan Walgrave, *Unfolding Revelation* (Philadelphia: Westminster Press, 1972), pp. 232-35. On revelation as inner experience amd new awareness, see Avery Dulles, *Models of Revelation* (New York: Doubleday, 1983), chaps. 5, 7.

[19]Compare Sallie McFague, "An Epilogue: The Christian Paradigm," in *Christian Theology: An Introduction to Its Traditions and Tasks,* ed. Peter C. Hodgson and Robert H. King (Philadelphia: Fortress, 1982), pp. 323-36. On transformist theory of the development of doctrine see Walgrave, *Unfolding Revelation,* chap. 8.

[20]On revelation and the Trinity see John J. O'Donnell, *The Mystery of the Triune God* (New York: Paulist, 1989), chap. 2.

[21]Stanley J. Grenz, *Revisioning Evangelical Theology: A Fresh Agenda for the 21st Century* (Downers Grove, Ill.: InterVarsity Press, 1993), pp. 65-72; Dulles, *Models of Revelation,* chap. 3. An early book of mine adopts this approach: *Biblical Revelation: The Foundation of Christian Theology* (Chicago: Moody Press, 1971).

[22]Charles Hodge, *Systematic Theology* (London: James Clarke, 1960), 1:116-18.

[23]Küng, *Infallible?* pp. 215-16; John Goldingay, *Models for Scripture* (Grand Rapids,

Mich.: Eerdmans, 1994), and *Models for Interpretation of Scripture* (Grand Rapids, Mich.: Eerdmans, 1995).

[24]Daniel J. Migliore, "The Meaning of Revelation," chap. 2 in *Faith Seeking Understanding: A Introduction to Christian Theology* (Grand Rapids, Mich.: Eerdmans, 1991).

[25]Stanley J. Grenz, *Theology for the Community of God* (Nashville: Broadman & Holman, 1994), pp. 510-16.

[26]Walgrave, *Unfolding Revelation,* chap. 9.

[27]Welker, *God the Spirit,* pp. 272-78. Although inspiration is of central importance for evangelicals, there is no agreed-upon definition. The difficulty is how to avoid the dictation required for inerrancy; see Louis I. Hodges, "Evangelical Definitions of Inspiration: Critiques and a Suggested Definition," *Journal of the Evangelical Theological Society* 37 (1994): 99-114; Clark H. Pinnock, *The Scripture Principle* (San Francisco: Harper & Row, 1984); Donald G. Bloesch, *Holy Scripture: Revelation, Inspiration and Interpretation* (Downers Grove, Ill.: InterVarsity Press, 1994), chap. 4.

[28]Ward, *Religion and Revelation,* pp. 212-17; James D. G. Dunn, "The Authority of Scripture According to Scripture," chap. 5 in *The Living Word* (London: SCM Press, 1987); Dulles, *Models of Revelation,* chap. 12.

[29]Delwin Brown, *Boundaries of Our Habitations: Tradition and Theological Construction* (Albany: State University of New York Press, 1994), pp. 75-83.

[30]Gordon D. Fee, "Exegesis and Spirituality: Reflections on Completing the Exegetical Circle," *Crux* 31 (1995): 29-35.

[31]Clark H. Pinnock, "The Work of the Holy Spirit in Hermeneutics," *Journal of Pentecostal Theology* 2 (1993): 3-23, and "The Work of the Spirit in Interpretation," *Journal of the Evangelical Theological Society* 36 (1993): 491-97.

[32]Scripture itself illustrates how texts are opened up to fresh significance: Pinnock, *Scripture Principle,* chap. 8. Also Dunn, "The Authority of Scripture According to Scripture," chap. 5 in *Living Word.*

[33]Orthodoxy takes a mystical approach toward the subject: Ernst Benz, *The Eastern Orthodox Church, Its Thought and Life* (New York: Doubleday, 1963), chap. 3; Nicolas Berdyaev, *Freedom and the Spirit* (London: Geoffrey Bles, 1935), p. 143; John Meyendorff, "Light from the East: Doing Theology in an Eastern Orthodox Perspective," in *Doing Theology in Today's World,* ed. John D. Woodbridge and Thomas E. McComiskey (Grand Rapids, Mich.: Zondervan, 1991), pp. 339-58; Clendenin, "The Witness of the Spirit: Scripture and Tradition," chap. 5 in *Eastern Orthodox Christianity.*

[34]Toon, *Development of Doctrine,* pp. 120-24.

[35]John Henry Newman, *Apologia Pro Vita Sua* (London: Longman, Green, 1864), on the magisterium and in a letter to the Duke of Norfolk concerning papal infallibility; Ian Ker, *Newman the Theologian: A Reader* (Notre Dame, Ind.: University of Notre Dame Press, 1990), chaps. 6-7.

[36]Dulles, "The church and Revelation," chap. 11 in *Models of the Church.*

[37]John Paul II, "Christian Unity," p. 98; Küng, *The Church,* pp. 444-80; Clendenin, *Eastern Orthodox Christianity,* pp. 99-102; Benz, *Eastern Orthodox Church,* pp. 43-53.

[38]Clendenin, *Eastern Orthodox Christianity,* pp. 102-6, 109-16.

[39]Walgrave, *Unfolding Revelation,* pp. 179-89.

[40]Hans Küng speaks of method in this way in *Theology for the Third Millennium: An Ecumenical View* (New York: Doubleday, 1988), pp. 164-69.

[41]John Henry Cardinal Newman, *An Essay on the Development of Christian Doctrine,* 6th ed. (Notre Dame, Ind.: University of Notre Dame Press, 1989). Of comparable scholarship today is Jaroslav Pelikan, *The Christian Tradition: A History of the Development of Doctrine,* 5 vols. (Chicago: University of Chicago Press, 1971-1989).

[42]Karl Rahner, *Foundations of Christian Faith* (New York: Seabury, 1978), pp. 359-69; Charles Colson and Richard J. Neuhaus, *Evangelicals and Catholics Together: Toward a Common Mission* (Dallas: Word, 1995).

[43]O'Donnell, *Mystery of the Triune God,* pp. 94-97. The reader may have noticed that I found relatively fewer gifts of insight in high Calvinist orthodoxy. For a defense of this rendering see Thomas R. Schreiner and Bruce A. Ware, *The Grace of God, the Bondage of the Will,* 2 vols. (Grand Rapids, Mich.: Baker Book House, 1995).

[44]David A. S. Fergusson, "Predestination: A Scottish Perspective," *Scottish Journal of Theology* 46 (1993): 457-78. This article shows that not all Reformed theology today espouses what I call high Calvinist orthodoxy. Because of the influence of Barth in particular, Reformed theologians like Migliore, Brummer, Berkhof, Konig, Boer, Moltmann, Torrance et al. sound more like what would have formerly been called Arminian.

[45]Ronald J. Sider, *One-Sided Christianity? Uniting the Church to Heal a Lost and Broken World* (Grand Rapids, Mich.: Zondervan, 1993). On the convergance see Robert E. Webber, *The Church in the World: Opposition, Tension or Opposition* (Grand Rapids, Mich.: Zondervan, 1986).

[46]Karl Barth, *Church Dogmatics* 4/1, trans. G. W. Bromiley (Edinburgh: T & T Clark, 1956), p. 528.

[47]Küng, *The Church,* pp. 201-2; and Jean-Jacques Suurmond, *Word and Spirit at Play: Towards a Charismatic Theology* (Grand Rapids, Mich.: Eerdmans, 1995), pp. 194-98.

[48]James D. G. Dunn, *Jesus and the Spirit* (London: SCM Press, 1975), pp. 271-97.

[49]Küng, *The Church,* pp. 444-80.

[50]Hendrikus Berkhof, *Christian Faith: An Introduction to the Study of the Faith,* trans. Sierd Woudstra (Grand Rapids, Mich.: Eerdmans, 1986), p. 96.

[51]Reinhard Hutter, "The Church as Public: Dogma, Practice and the Holy Spirit," *Pro Ecclesia* 3 (1994): 357-61; Cecil M. Robeck, "Discerning the Spirit in the Life of the Church," in *The Church in the Movement of the Spirit,* ed. William R. Barr and Rena M. Yocum (Grand Rapids, Mich.: Eerdmans, 1994), pp. 29-49.

[52]Philip Schaff, *Christ and Christianity* (New York: Scribner, 1885), p. 16.

Names Index

Subject Index

Scripture Index

Old Testament